The Architecture
of Knowledge

George Towner

121
T7452

Library of Congress Catalog Card Number: 80-5127

82-54

Acknowledgments

My earliest ideas toward this work germinated during conversations with philosophers. For their guidance and patient inspiration, I am grateful to Stephen C. Pepper, William R. Dennes, Bertram Jessup, John Myhill, and Michael Jayne. Later, when I joined the Kaiser Foundation Research Institute, my contacts were largely with scientists. Among the many insights contributed by my colleagues there, those of the late Ellsworth C. Dougherty were most helpful in crystallizing my thoughts.

I am indebted to John Cantwell Kiley, who read the next-to-final draft and provided many useful and penetrating suggestions, as well as a generous measure of encouragement.

Finally, I particularly wish to thank Shirley Walker for her professional advice, her unstinting help with all phases of manuscript preparation, and her warm support during the whole process of creating this book.

What is man in nature? Nothing in relation to the infinite, everything in relation to nothing, a mean between nothing and everything.

PASCAL

Contents

Introduction

> All the world over and at all times there have been
> practical men, absorbed in irreducible and stubborn
> facts; all the world over and at all times there have been
> men of philosophic temperament, who have been ab-
> sorbed in the weaving of general principles.
>
> WHITEHEAD

Much of our knowledge is generated by specialists. The most successful scientists—physicists, biologists, sociologists, mathematicians—are those who concentrate on small regions of their subjects and produce highly detailed accounts of what they find. Their successes have tended to establish an "approved" route to knowledge: make new pronouncements only when they can be supported by an overwhelming mass of minutiae. Obviously such a program can be pursued only in limited areas, by people who are therefore "specialists."

Specialization gets a further boost whenever we examine critically the works of some famous past generalists. Aristotle, for instance, wrote treatises about every subject under the sun. He combined most of the known facts of his day into systems and hierarchies, classifications with headings and subheadings into which every object or event in his world could be sorted. Unfortunately much of what he wrote is now considered wrong. In some cases he was inaccurate because he worked from incomplete data; in other cases he simply blundered, as when he assumed (without experimenting) that heavier bodies must fall faster than lighter ones. Similarly Kant, another generalist, overturned the philosophy of his day by proposing an entirely new way of understanding reality, one in which knowledge examines its own categories. Yet his speculations also wandered off into areas such as astronomy and cosmology, where his pronouncements are today considered naive. From instances such as these, generalizing has gotten a bad name.

But criticizing Aristotle for his physics or Kant for his astronomy presupposes a specialist's point of view. It assumes that the important part of what these people were doing (or should have been doing) was to make accurate

1

and detailed accounts of the nature of reality. Yet that is not in fact the enduring result of their work. Aristotle's enduring contribution to knowledge was the basic idea of classification and systematization, of arranging and docketing facts so others may know where to look for them. In a sense, he invented natural science itself. Kant's enduring contribution was the idea that at least some of the content of our world has been put there by the categorical ways we look at it. He turned our attention to "systems of observation." Without this concept it is unlikely that such essential modern theories as relativity and quantum mechanics would ever have got off the ground. These basic ideas, then—ones such as the technique of classifying known facts, or the concept of examining systems of observation—are the sort of contributions that generalists have left behind.

Examples could be cited indefinitely. In fact any book on the history of philosophy is a compendium of generalists' ideas, many of which have filtered into the background of modern thought. But in an age of specialization these contributions tend to be overlooked. They are often so diffuse, and so deeply implanted in the very way we look at things, that it is easy to imagine they were never new ideas, or that they were always so obvious that no one needed to think of them. Asked to describe what such generalists have done for present knowledge, most specialists will claim that they have left hardly a single description of reality which scientists do not today possess in far superior form. Yet, as I say, that is a narrow view. From the opposite direction, it can be argued that without generalists in the past there would be no such thing as science at all today.

Another argument is sometimes heard in support of specialization. Granted that many techniques of knowledge today are based on the former work of generalists (it runs) nevertheless the time for such work is now past. The basic concepts of science and scientific method have been permanently established; the overwhelming success of the result makes it impossible for us to envision any kind of new foundation. Problems in knowledge today are only symptoms of badly fitting details, not evidence that anything is wrong with the design as a whole. Therefore, claim the specialists, generalists are no longer needed.

On the face of it, this argument can at least be faulted for gross presumption. An instinct tells us to be particularly cautious whenever we are tempted to assert that something we have just done has at last achieved perfection. It is instructive to consider some embarassing prior claims of the same sort. Toward the end of the nineteenth century, just before the discovery of the electron, many physicists were celebrating science's success in creating an ultimate world-view around the concept of indivisible atoms. Earlier, much of the medieval Christian system of thought (such as embodied in the *Summa*

Theologica of Aquinas) was at the time believed to represent an unquestionable permanent structure of knowledge. Today we laugh at such claims; but not at our own.

Yet there are even deeper reasons for being suspicious of any claim that today we possess the ultimate route to knowledge. As Kuhn points out in his important book *The Structure of Scientific Revolutions*,[1] established routines of knowledge tend to become self-protecting and uncritical of themselves. They cook our whole outlook so that we find them more and more satisfying, while making us increasingly blind to other routines. For this reason they seldom initiate radical changes within themselves, as a result of the discovery of incompatible data; instead they endure by patchwork and institutionalization until somehow, somewhere, an entirely new route to knowledge opens up. When that happens our world-view often alters dramatically, and what formerly seemed to us to be ultimate knowledge begins to look ill-conceived and trivial. By this process our search for perfect knowledge undergoes occasional ''revolutions''—not because a theory has been refuted by the facts, but because it has been destroyed by another theory. From this viewpoint our claim to have discovered the ultimate routine in theorizing seems more of a self-serving product of the theory itself than a judgment about reality.

The fact is that revolutions in knowledge are most often instituted by generalists, not specialists. This is the generalist's principal function: to bring us face-to-face with the whole design of knowledge, with its foundations and its presuppositions, and force us to consider whether there is not a different—and hence possibly better—way. The specialist cannot grasp the whole picture in this fashion because he is too much ''in'' the picture.

This book is written from a generalist's standpoint. It is about the total possibilities of knowledge, not about any particular knowledge. In it I mention and discuss a wide variety of theories, attitudes, viewpoints and speculations, all part of what one or another portion of the human race considers to be ''knowledge.'' I cite all these notions not to create an encyclopedia of human belief, but just to illustrate certain threads that I have found running through them. These threads embody several important insights about knowledge—yet they can be appreciated only from a generalist's viewpoint. They cannot be reduced to specific objects or events in reality, nor do they constitute any specific description of the world. My purpose in uncovering them is to open new doors for understanding, in the same way that Aristotle's conception of classification and Kant's emphasis on systems of observation opened new doors for understanding in their times. The patterns I will delineate in this book do not by themselves comprise any hitherto unknown facts; instead, they lead to a general analysis of the *architecture* of knowledge, its construction and its possibilities, from which (by other processes of exploration) it then becomes possible to discover new facts. As I will show, the possibilities of knowledge are enormously greater than our present grasp of them. This is because most thinkers prefer to be specialists: it seems easier and more productive to dig very carefully in a small plot of knowledge, rather than plow whole fields and run the risk of making crooked furrows or stepping into a hole.

To balance this preference, specialists need to hear periodically from the generalists. While specialization may generate the detailed mass we normally call "knowledge," it is generalization that gives this mass shape, direction, and meaning.

1. Maxima and Minima

Most men take least notice of what is plain, as if that were of no use; but puzzle their thoughts, and lose themselves in those vast depths and abysses which no human understanding can fathom.

THOMAS SHERLOCK

Human beings use two opposite approaches in their attempts to understand reality. Their first attempt at knowledge discovers what I call *maxima*. They start with relatively large unanalyzed facts, connecting them to more and more unanalyzed facts and pulling an ever increasing mass of reality into a total understanding. This is the approach of curiosity, of exploration, and of unfettered common sense. It contemplates reality whole in all its aspects—large or small, fundamental or trivial—without refinement or discrimination.

At more sophisticated moments, however, human beings also seek another kind of knowledge: they dissect reality, experimentally and intellectually, to get at its "basic elements." They try to dig below mere surface effects to discover the ultimate units of which reality is built. This is the approach of science and analysis. It is a radically different process from commonsense understanding, and when it succeeds it usually comes up with a totally new picture of reality. This picture is typically composed of new objects of knowledge, which I call *minima*.

For example, we are all familiar with solid objects. They come in all sizes, shapes and weights; some hard, some soft, some brittle, some strong. They are things we can feel with our hands and which resist when we push them. They interact in ways we understand. We can determine whether something is a solid object or not by poking it with a known solid object and seeing what happens. They are typical maxima. But physics offers us a radically different description of these things, a description in terms of minima. It says that solid objects are mostly empty space in which particles—electrons, protons, neutrons, etc.—whirl in unimaginably tiny orbits at incredibly great speeds. Physicists assert that the appearance of solidity derives from the fact that

5

these particles are held in regular arrays by very strong "forces," effects that apply only to such tiny bits of matter. Our felt sensation of hardness results from other forces, which cause the arrays of particles to resist penetration by other arrays of particles, such as those in our fingers. Through all of this, particles of each type are said to be identical. The quatrillions of electrons in a wooden match are all precisely the same; when we burn the match to a cinder they remain the same, even though some of them may now appear to us as smoke and vapor. There is no difference, in other words, between the electrons in wood and the electrons in charcoal or smoke—or for that matter between them and the electrons in a gold ring or a summer breeze. Physicists tell us all these things because they believe they have carefully stripped away the "inessential" features of reality to reveal its ultimate parts, and these parts have turned out to be whirling particles.

On the other hand, none of the physicist's reality is evident to me as I sit at this desk. The pencil functions in my hand not because it is an array of particles but because it is made of wood and graphite. My teacup holds tea because it is glazed porcelain, and the tea is palatable not because it is a collection of molecules banging into each other with a certain average velocity but simply because it is hot. In these terms I could get along very well if theoretical physics had never been thought up. We must remember that its depiction of reality is unknown to more than half of mankind. They and I can lead successful lives without understanding concepts of particles; but no one can survive without knowing what wood, hot water, and other common things are like.

When we first examine the history of science, it seems as if it has always been trying to go in two different directions. On the one hand is an ancient tradition of gathering facts together, of putting "data" at our fingertips in readily appreciable form. Aristotle started assembling known facts, indexing and classifying them without subjecting them to radical re-interpretation. Two thousand years later Francis Bacon was doing much the same thing, and today the bulk of published "scientific research" is of this type. In between, the fathers of medieval Catholicism and the French Encyclopedists undertook similar tasks for what they understood to be facts. On the other hand, every once in a while a thinker appears who takes some part of this body of data and turns it upside-down in our minds. He takes what we thought we understood and processes it in such a way that we now see it entirely differently. Such people—Dalton, Newton, Maxwell, Darwin, Mendeleev, Freud, Einstein, for instance—see the task of knowledge quite differently. They are "theoreticians," and they produce "theoretical knowledge." At first the picture they draw is disbelieved—partly because it seems so odd, partly because we have been getting along very well without it. But eventually we are won over, and science "progresses to a new level of refinement." Nevertheless the new knowledge always seems somewhat unnecessary; it is something we can take or leave alone in a sense not applicable to the conceptions of everyday life.

But doesn't theoretical knowledge prove its own worth? Can't we justify it solely by its successes? The electric light by which I work glows because a filament of tungsten has been connected by copper wires to a coil through which an iron core carries "magnetism." Changes in strength of the magnetism cause a "flow of electrons" in the wires, which heats the filament. No one guided just by a naive commonsense picture of reality would ever have stumbled across the particular configuration of materials called an electric system. For that it is necessary to treat electrons and magnetic forces as real things. The electric system in fact works, and it seems to work by virtue of our having theoretical knowledge. Shouldn't that prove theoretical physicists are right? Shouldn't it establish their view of reality as the "correct" one and ordinary knowledge, natural and convenient as it may seem, as "incorrect"?

Under different circumstances it might be easy to answer these questions affirmatively. If it had turned out that the views of science and common sense blended together—for instance if we could say that a world of particles whirling through empty space is only a clarification of the world of pencils and teacups, a sharpening and redefinition of concepts already implicit— then there would be no conflict, and this book would never have been written. We would simply trace the conceptual steps from one picture to the other. But the whirling particle picture of solid objects was not reached through simple clarification of our natural concepts; it had a long, difficult gestation, filled with sidetracks and abandoned notions. It seems to depend as much on our understanding mathematics as on our visualizing matter. Its very newness suggests it may not be the ultimate view, and in fact modern field theorizing has proposed even odder descriptions to supplant it. Just because certain concepts of physics "work" does not mean other concepts wouldn't also "work," perhaps even better.

As soon as we contemplate both science and common sense from a neutral standpoint, our minds are presented with a challenge: how can we reconcile, or even compare, two views of the same reality that are utterly different, each of which is satisfying and useful in its own sphere? Answering that question, in all its generality, is the first subject to be treated here.

My discussion will not be confined to physics, although this offers one of the clearest examples of the departure of refined theorizing from common sense. The conflict is universal in science. Biologists tell us our sensations occur because electrical currents jump across nerve endings, and emotions result when complex molecules are transported from cell to cell. Logicians analyze our thoughts into propositions, functions, and variables. Sociologists explain our friendships in terms of peer groupings and class values. Throughout, there is a duality of viewpoint: to those versed in scientific categories, everyday appearances seem confused because they are jumbled collections of underlying mechanisms; while to laymen, scientific explanations seem forced, abstracted, unreal. Yet scientists and laymen are supposedly talking about the same reality. Why do they describe it so differently?

Earlier I mentioned a basic difference in method. In one direction the search for knowledge takes us into ever-larger areas of reality, building up an understanding from "maxima." In the other direction it requires us to limit our perceptions, to isolate and purify reality until we expose its most basic bits, which I call "minima." The approach to maxima is typical of everyday laymen's understanding; the approach to minima is typical of science. Both approaches are successful, both are widely practiced, both have their supporters and detractors. Neither can be dismissed outright. Yet wherever they are carried out consistently the results are two non-comparable descriptions—in effect, two realities. The scientific proponent of minima will argue that he has finally, after much work, isolated and exposed some of the fundamental single threads of reality, unconfused by extraneous events. He will say that maxima are merely complicated weavings of such threads, so overlaid with outside factors that they may appear to be a different kind of reality: but they are actually just the complex sum of the units he is describing. The common-sense proponent of maxima, on the other hand, will say that minima are theoretical inventions: useful ideas, perhaps, but still no more than artifacts of thought. They cannot be all that reality is, because there is no way to add them up to the reality we normally see, feel, and understand.

To illustrate this difference, let us return to the physicist's description of solid objects. Working as a minimalist, he has refined and limited his observations to the point where he believes that his instruments show him characteristics of the smallest possible bits of matter, the subatomic particles. Every time he breaks up a solid object—wood, metal or whatever—he observes the same bits. Moreover he seems to be successful in extracting and isolating these bits; he can even rip them from one solid object and implant them in another, using a "particle accelerator." When he does this he is able to predict changes in the solid objects attributable to changes in their particle compositions. As early as 1919 Rutherford transmuted nitrogen into oxygen by bombarding it with "alpha particles." Finally, the physicist can record movements of particles through films and cloud chambers, showing graphi-

8

cally how they enter and leave solid objects and interact in empty space. All this he accomplishes with assurance and regularity, handling these tiny particles almost as easily as laymen handle pencils and teacups. Surely his picture of reality is correct!

But let us now leave the physicist's laboratory, where particles are cleanly isolated in evacuated chambers, and try to apply his picture of reality to ordinary events. I pick up a pencil and it feels hard and smooth: how can I translate this observation into a statement about particles? The physicist will assert that such a statement might be very long and complicated, but "in principle" it can always be made. We start with the surface of the pencil in which quatrillions of electrically charged particles lie, each moving in a small orbit but tightly bound by electrostatic forces to particles farther inside the pencil. The surface of my finger is similarly composed of charged particles. As the two surfaces meet, the charges repel (being of the same "sign"); because the particles in the pencil are more favorably distributed by its cellular structure than are those in my finger, the pencil remains rigid while my finger deforms. The deformation causes certain nerve endings in my finger to release electrically charged particles. These attach themselves to nearby atomic structures, causing further charged particles to be released farther away, so that a chain of charged particle releasing events travels along a nerve to my brain. There I have learned to interpret the occurrence of such events as a message that my finger has encountered something hard. Consequently the pencil feels hard to me.

How good is this explanation? Suppose I have just been holding an ice cube before picking up the pencil, so that my finger is numb and does not feel hardness. The physicist will probably say that certain particles in my finger have decreased their motions enough to interrupt the passage of charges into my nerves. Suppose I have just been hypnotized to believe the pencil is a worm, and so feel that it is soft instead of hard. Here the physicist's explanation may be less clear: perhaps some charged particles have migrated in my brain in such a way as to block those coming up the nerve from my finger. Suppose now I recall a dream in which I felt the hardness of a pencil, when none was actually present. "Now we are getting into psychology," the physicist will say; "that's not my department." But these are just the sorts of knowledge that are useful to me: under what conditions the pencil feels hard, when the hardness is an illusion, and how it relates to my handling of the pencil. The particle explanation has some interest, but by the time I expand it to apply to these questions it has become exceedingly cumbersome and vague. Its applicability "in principle" has turned out to be largely an empty promise.

In general, we find that any explanation in terms of minima works best and is most illuminating when applied under those controlled conditions where the minima are observed directly. As we move toward larger parts of reality—toward maxima—while trying to understand them simply as collections of minima, the whole explanatory system becomes less and less satisfactory.

Can we substitute an explanation purely in terms of maxima? The physicist will immediately object that this is not practical. We cannot populate our description of reality with such things as pencils and teacups, treating them as basic explanatory elements, because such a procedure yields no comprehensible system. Gross objects are too various, too changeable. We must find their common constituents—their elements, units, or building blocks—and reduce our knowledge to permutations of these parts. Thus would a physicist (or indeed any scientist) argue. Yet in fact most of the world's people think in terms of maxima; their "theories" *are* about gross objects. If we made a survey of the human population, asking of what physical reality consists, only a miniscule fraction would give the physicist's answer—electrons, protons, etc. The great majority would have never heard of these objects and wouldn't believe us if we described them. Of those that had heard of particles, a great majority would then say that they were special things studied by scientists (in the same class with galaxies, germs, and sea monsters) but not that they comprised the reality of all ordinary objects. Only a tiny portion of humanity would identify the scientifically "correct" constituents of the physical world; the overwhelming opinion would fill it with various largish things—rocks, clouds, people, etc. And quite a few would further populate it with entities, such as spirits or magical objects, which physics does not recognize even in its own terms. It is perhaps fortunate for scientists that their explication of reality is not subject to world-wide democratic vote.

It is easy to attribute this situation to ignorance. Word of the discoveries of science simply has not spread. The very existence of a scientific community presupposes that anyone of normal mentality, properly introduced to these concepts and exposed to the evidence in their favor, will embrace the scientists' picture of reality. To a limited extent this is true. It is true, for instance, that a person so trained will use physicists' concepts when dealing with certain portions of reality, such as particle interactions. But not even a professional physicist, devoting his career to the exploration of these ideas, uses them in his everyday behavior. He does not treat the pencil in his hand as a mass of whirling particles. Life would be impossible if we had to translate everything into scientifically "correct" terms. The scientists' description of reality, even to themselves, is something one uses in the laboratory but hardly outside it. Thus it is a good question to ask which body of knowledge embodies more ignorance: that of the mass of humanity, who would be unable to cope with the instruments in a laboratory, or that of the scientist, whose special picture of reality is virtually useless in the everyday world.

Of course it is no accident that conditions in the scientific laboratory differ from those in everyday life. A central tenet of "scientific method" is that phenomena must be isolated and purified before they can be understood. For the minimalist, the only way to reach basic reality is to disassemble the flow of life and study its parts one by one, a procedure most conveniently followed in laboratories. But in the long history of human thought, scientific method is so new and so specialized that it is perfectly proper to question its underlying justification. What guarantee have we that theoretical concepts arising from this highly ritualized disassembly procedure represent reality more accurately than the non-scientific understandings held by most of mankind?

The fundamental weakness of theoretical science is that its concepts of minima are superfluous to all but a tiny portion of human activities. They are not generally applicable, in any practical way, to ordinary life. Moreover, the mere fact that they find application in one limited area—primarily, scientific research itself—does not guarantee that they are the best or most correct concepts even there. Thus the argument that concepts of minima "work" (and therefore must truly represent reality) unravels when we examine the conditions which must be satisfied before such working is observed. These conditions turn out to be so remote from ordinary life that we are justified in asking if the postulated minima are not equally remote from common reality. The physicists' assertion that solid objects *really are* collections of particles, for example, should be as significant on a street corner as it is in a laboratory. Before adopting this idea as an amendment to our naive world-view, we should make sure that it illuminates our grasp of reality under all conditions. But in fact we find that it contributes to our understanding only under highly artificial circumstances. Citing its success under these circumstances—under "laboratory conditions"—to support its general validity asks us, in effect, to regard laboratory conditions as "more real" than those in the rest of the world.

In summary, there are good reasons to question the worth of any methodology that generates only theories about minima. But what alternatives do we have? Scientists may argue that in fact no one has ever put forth a lasting theory using maxima, that all the insights of modern knowledge have been achieved by dividing and refining our ideas about reality. As explanatory tools, they will say, concepts of maxima have always given way to concepts of minima. I believe this is largely an illusion, one which I will expose in the pages that follow. We *do* have theories using maxima, but we usually don't recognize them as such; and it is only through neglect that no one has yet pulled them together into an intellectual discipline in the way science has assembled theories of minima. Let us therefore ask what kinds of knowledge maxima can yield directly. To answer this question we reverse the usual procedure of science: instead of dividing objects into basic elements, we put them together into larger and more comprehensive totalities. The result is a description of whole reality rather than elemental reality. This reversal of method, when carried out in a thorough and disciplined manner, yields some remarkable conclusions.

1.1 Orders of Reality

> Every natural science always involves three things:
> the sequence of phenomena on which the science is
> based; the abstract concepts which call these
> phenomena to mind; and the words in which the con-
> cepts are expressed... All three mirror one and the
> same reality.
>
> LAVOISIER

One might at first suppose that any attempt to organize our knowledge of maxima would lead directly to the concept of a single total universe. If we start from the objects of everyday understanding, grouping them in ever larger wholes, do we not finally arrive at the idea of the largest possible whole, containing everything? *The remarkable fact is that we do not.*

Consider a simple illustration. On my desk is an ordinary book, which will serve as well as any other object as a starting point for exploring reality. The minimalist tradition would choose to divide this object into ever smaller parts until it was reduced to its basic individual constituents, then formulate a picture of reality in those terms. It would say the book is made of matter and energy, particles and forces. This approach would conform to the customs of traditional science; however, I propose to explore in the opposite direction. This book before me is part of the physical cosmos. If I move it about on my desk the resulting changes in gravitation will spread throughout the universe, making tiny but measurable changes everywhere. The mathematician Borel calculated that the displacement of just one gram of mass a distance of just one centimeter on the star Sirius would substantially alter the configuration of gases on Earth. In at least this way, then, the book is objectively linked to other physical objects—to the earth and its atmosphere, to my body, to the other planets, and to the distant stars. But even if this were not the case, the book would still be linked to the physical cosmos "as I understand it." By this I mean that I *expect* the book will react upon other physical things. I can drive a nail with it; it will make a bruise if it falls on me; it will burn in air. My natural understanding of reality places this book in a class with many other things, all of which react on one another in familiar ways and all of which add up to the physical cosmos. Thus a first approach to organizing maxima will be to aggregate this book with other objects with which it interacts physically—rocks and radios, comets and clouds—building an ever larger picture. When I need to decide whether or not a proposed object belongs to this picture, I simply ask whether or not it *could* interact physically with this book, even though it may not be interacting at the moment. Answering this question locates the object within my knowledge of maxima. Thus by starting from this book before me, I can define a "physical reality" containing all objects with which it could react.

Once it is located in this reality, I can provide as detailed a physical characterization of the book as I wish. It weighs such-and-such because it interacts with my scales in a certain way. It is hard, rectangular, and so forth, because it interacts in certain ways with the appropriate instruments. I can further determine that it is flammable, does not float, and so on, by bringing it into contact with other physical objects. By such procedures I could eventually determine all the physical "properties" of the book in terms of its practical effects upon other physical things. Such an approach to defining an object is similar to the concept of "positivism" introduced by Comte, and has also been applied to modern physics by P. W. Bridgman under the rubric of "operationalism."[2] By following it we can appreciate directly the difference in orientation toward knowledge discussed earlier, for it contains no reference to elements or ultimate constituents. We do not look inside the object, toward its smallest parts, but outside the object, toward the reality of which it is a part. We contemplate maxima, not minima.

By defining the book in this way, do we eventually exhaust all our possible knowledge about it? There seems to be no natural limit to the detail with which its interactions with other physical objects could be cataloged. But I know that this book also happens to be a copy of Plato's *Dialogues*. Surely such information has a place in human knowledge about this book; but where does it appear in our physical description?

At first it is tempting to say that the fact the book is Plato's *Dialogues* (and not, for instance, Scott's *Ivanhoe*) is a subtle physical property. It is related to the distribution of ink on the pages. By reflecting light from the pages into the eyes of human beings we can elicit the same sorts of reactions as those by which we determined it was hard, rectangular, and so on. They would characterize the book as Plato's and not Scott's. But now several complications ensue. The book on my desk happens to be translated into English; but suppose it were printed in the original Greek? Having been educated in this century I never learned Greek, and hence would probably fail to recognize it or be able to distinguish it from a Greek translation of *Ivanhoe*. I would be "blind" to this property of the book, even though my eyes were receiving the proper light patterns reflected from its pages. To make this distinction about the book, then, we would have to show it to a man who reads Greek. As a physical property, the subject of the book would thus have to be treated as something tested by special human "instruments": namely an English-reader for certain books, a Greek-reader for other books, and so on. But then how are we to distinguish these "instruments"? There is no physical characteristic by which we could group them except that they identify certain classes of books. Thus we are led to the circularity that certain physical properties of Greek books, i.e. their subjects, are only determinable by Greek readers, who are distinguished from other readers solely by the property that they recognize such properties in such books; and the same for English books, Arabic books, etc. By assuming that the subject of a book is a physical property of it we are forced to fragment our concept of physical reality (with respect to this property) into arbitrarily many separate realities.

For a more intense example, suppose my copy of Plato's *Dialogues* has been enciphered into a book-long cryptogram. Only one person knows the key. Then we would have to say that whether the ink on its pages is distributed in the manner of the *Dialogues* or in the manner of *Ivanhoe* can be decided by only one observer in the world. If he dies, then it cannot be determined at all. If he decides to hoax us, we cannot confirm or deny his assertions. In such a situation we would be forced to exclude the *subject* of the book from our range of physical knowledge. We can include in our physical knowledge all kinds of detail about light patterns reflected from the book's pages—how the ink marks are shaped, what variety of marks there are, whether they occur in repeated sequences, and so on; but as soon as we try to extend our knowledge to connect these marks with such concepts as "subject," "meaning," "language," and the like, our knowledge sinks in a quicksand of arbitrary distinctions. Taken physically, these properties of the book become functions of the properties of other objects—the observers who distinguish them—who themselves cannot be distinguished physically.

Does this mean we must abandon any effort to know the subject of a book? Obviously not. Such efforts are impossible *only when confined to our understanding of physical reality*. Let us assume that its subject *is* a property of the book, but call it a "behavioral" property. By a procedure cognate to our locating the book in the physical cosmos we can now locate its contents in a "behavioral cosmos." To do this we bring it into contact with other behavioral objects and observe the reactions. Just as we measured its weight on a scale, we now characterize its subject in the thought processes of human beings. Using the content of the book as a starting point we can explore a new area of reality, *behavioral* reality, by understanding the ever larger totalities of which it is a part.

15

A wealth of new characteristics of the book now emerges. Beside the facts that it is in English and is a collection of dialogues, we find that it is philosophical rather than descriptive; more argumentative than narrative; and so forth. We can analyze its use of language, both in Greek and in English, its style of expression, and all such factors that literary critics discuss. None of these characteristics, so important to us, can be naturally included in any description of a purely physical book located in a physical cosmos. Moreover the "behavioral book"—what we may roughly call the content of the physical book—is found to be part of a very large interconnected reality, just as the physical book was found to be part of a very large physical universe. The statements in the book are products of the thought processes of Socrates and Plato, which were in turn embedded in Greek culture of the fourth century B.C. Behind them lay a tradition of Mediterranean and Middle Eastern cultures; afterwards the writings of Plato were a persistent influence in Roman and European cultures. They helped shape institutions, establish moral values, and determine knowledge. We might compare the intellectual influence of Plato's *Dialogues* moving through time to the gravitational influence of a physical object moving through space. Beyond the cultural effects just mentioned lies the whole of human behavior—drives, values, instincts, skills, and so on. These are further connected to living behavior as a whole, from viruses to primates; through the tree of evolution we could trace the derivation of each behavioral pattern as it has been invented and perfected. Thus behavioral reality appears as a true universe in itself, an interconnected assembly of objects of knowledge. It is interconnected in fact, in the sense that (for instance) cultural behavior is influenced by the evolution of species; but more importantly it is interconnected *in our understanding*. We expect that the hostility of a person being assaulted, for example, is related to the general hostility of animals under threat, and helps make up the hostility of a nation being invaded. They are "the same sort of thing" and naturally fall together in our understanding of reality. Conversely, hostility and (say) a stone are *not* "the same sort of thing": one is behavioral, the other physical.

The idea just introduced—that there are natural divisions in our understanding of reality, that we are compelled to regard (for example) emotions and stones as belonging to two different kinds of existence—will be a recurring theme in this discussion. Evidence for it is everywhere, once we know how to look. In some ways this idea is so obvious that we might assume it merits no discussion or analysis. But I will show that it is not mere accident, or the result of ignorance about how such kinds of existence are in fact connected; instead, *it is a necessity built into the very foundations of understanding*. Without the recognition of such divisions knowledge stagnates and theorizing becomes impossible.

I now associate two quite different objects with this book before me. One is a physical assemblage of paper, ink and glue; the other is the behavioral object called "Plato's *Dialogues*." One is embedded in a physical universe where it can be weighed, burnt, etc.; the other is embedded in a behavioral universe, where it may be thought about, criticized, etc. The distinction between these two objects becomes evident when we consider destroying one or the other. If I destroy the physical book (or even all copies resembling it) I do not thereby eliminate the *Dialogues* or the manifestations they have left in human behavior. On the other hand if Plato (or even the whole Greek civilization) had never existed it would still be possible to assemble the physical book with all its markings; it would just be regarded as fictional or meaningless. In other words the physical book (and all the things with which it might react in the physical universe) is known independently of the behavioral work and all behavior connected with it.

The foregoing observation is made possible by my adopting a maximalist viewpoint, whereby any object—physical or behavioral—is understood in terms of the reality within which it is found rather than in terms of the constituents that can be dug out of it. The distinction between the two books is *not* based on our finding different minimal elements in them; it is based on our understanding that physical reality as a whole is different from behavior as a whole.

Has the potential of this book as a starting point for exploring reality now been used up? The answer is no; there is at least one more universe with which it is associated. Let us turn to one of the dialogues, called the *Timaeus*. It starts with a summary of part of the *Republic*, after which one of the persons of the dialogue, Critias, recounts the legend of Atlantis. Here there is no problem of understanding, even though as far as we presently know Atlantis never actually existed. The physical references—the size of the island, the earthquake and flood that destroyed it, the mud remaining where houses had been—are all comprehensible because they refer to the sorts of things we encounter in physical reality. The references to behavior—the bravery of her warriors, the magnanimity of her leaders—are similarly comprehensible in terms of the behavioral reality we understand. But then Timaeus starts unfolding an elaborate cosmogony, including a scheme for associating the elements of Empedokles (fire, air, water, earth) with what are now known as the "Platonic solids." Geometric solids bounded by identical regular polygons were a novelty in Plato's day; it was relatively recently that Euclid had described some of them in the 13th book of his *Geometry*. Theatetus, who was contemporary with Plato, was said to have proved there could only be five such. The theory of regular solids was a largely unused intellectual tool, much like the tensor calculus in Einstein's day. Intrigued by the solids' property of decomposing into one another under simple geometric transformations, Plato assigned four of them to what were then the "traditional" elements: the tetrahedron to fire, the cube to earth, the octahedron to air, and the icosahedron to water. The dodecahedron was taken to represent the whole cosmos. A geometric calculus could then be formulated in which the decomposition of each solid into sets of the others would parallel the transmutations supposed to occur among the physical elements. All this is set forth in the dialogue.

I mention this theory not for its intrinsic explanatory value, although it enjoyed a lengthy vogue during the Middle Ages. I mention it to illustrate this question: how do we understand the Platonic solids that it discusses? Are they part of physical reality, or part of behavioral reality?

Of course it is easy to manufacture physical objects "in geometric shapes": a "cube of sugar," for example. But a "cube of sugar" is not in any sense a geometric cube, because the sugar does not have any properties required of the geometer's object. Its faces are not perfectly flat, its edges do not meet in exact points, and so on. When we prove a theorem about a geometric object we never refer to any physical thing; in fact it is just as easy for us to prove theorems about shapes that cannot be represented physically at all, such as the tesseract. When we create physical things "in geometric shapes" as an aid to visualization, it is always clear that they are not perfect. Since perfect correspondence to description is a necessary property of anything subject to geometric proof, such things cannot be physical objects. This argument has been stated many times before, but it is easily forgotten.

A more subtle explanation for geometric objects is that they are figments of behavior. In this view Platonic solids, for instance, exist just to the extent that we think about them. Certainly all we know about them (and about all other entities of geometry, mathematics, and logic) we have learned through strictly mental operations. The proof that there are only five possible regular convex solids does not require that we examine the shapes of all possible things, or indeed that we use our senses in any way. It follows from the axioms of geometry by logical processes. It is a truth we acquire by sitting quietly in a chair and thinking: the sort of knowledge some classical philosophers called "a priori." Because the whole process begins and ends in behavior, it is natural to suppose that it refers only to more behavior—that Plato's statements about the tetrahedron, for example, refer only to an idea that was thought up and publicized by Euclid.

To be sure, an element of behavioral choice lies at the beginning of any logical discipline. This was nicely illustrated in the nineteenth century when the mathematician Riemann (and later Minkowski) showed it was possible to construct consistent but different geometries by altering the fifth postulate of Euclid's system, the famous "parallel postulate." The resulting "non-Euclidean geometries" were actually generalizations of Euclid's system, introducing certain constants to create a more detailed characterization of space. Euclid's parallel postulate had amounted to a tacit assumption that these constants were zero. By assigning them various values in what is now called a "curvature tensor," it became possible to describe different varieties of space, each with different geometric properties. For instance the sum of the angles of any triangle (which Euclid thought must always be 180°) varies in non-Euclidean space as a function of the curvature tensor. Thus it seemed that Euclid's "a priori knowledge" had been *wrong*, particularly after Einstein showed in 1915 that actual astronomical space could usefully be described as non-Euclidean, that we could associate non-zero values of the curvature tensor in physical space with the phenomenon of gravity. It seemed that Euclid had unwittingly regarded a behavioral decision—to regard space in one way and not in any other—as a geometric truth.

The actual situation, however, is this. No one has ever successfully argued that Euclid's theorems do not follow from his definitions, axioms, and postulates. What is argued is that some of these beginnings are not as "self-evident" as Euclid thought they were. Once we admit them the rest follows. The behavioral factor in geometry (and generally in any abstract discipline) is exhausted at the very beginning, when we formulate descriptions of what we are going to think about and how we are going to express our conclusions. After that the conclusions are independent of behavior. But this does not mean that the conclusions are *obvious*, or that we always think of them. The conclusions of a logical system do not necessarily "lie within" the premises in the sense that it merely takes a little juggling to expose them all. In 1895 Peano published an axiomatic basis for mathematics that can be conveniently summarized on a single page; but the consequences that can be deduced in his system are so voluminous it is unlikely they will ever be fully revealed. In terms of the *knowledge* generated by such a discipline, all the development of our understanding occurs after the initial formal decisions have been made. Only a few mathematicians spend their careers thinking about foundations: they are like prospectors who spot a vein of ore and say "dig here!" Following them come armies of other mathematicians who mine the lode, who devote generation after generation to exploring the consequences of the few basic ideas with which they start. Thus it is proper to treat abstract disciplines as processes of developing the consequences of initial decisions, rather than of making the decisions themselves, in which case behavior ceases to determine the results. This does not mean that no decisions are made in mathematical research. At every point it is necessary to decide where to look next, to judge which consequences of the premises are important and which are trivial. But such decisions do not change the conclusions, they only influence which conclusions are discovered.

The independence of mathematical truths with respect to our behavior stands out clearly in some of the classic problems in the field. For example, when Fermat died a notation was found in one of his books which has become known as "Fermat's last theorem." It states that for every set of integers x, y, z, and n not equal to zero, $x^n + y^n \neq z^n$ when n is greater than 2. Laborious analyses have established this proposition for some values of n, but no general proof has been found. Yet it is either true or not true. Any mathematician could achieve instant fame by quoting values for x, y, z and n for which the theorem does not hold. None has yet, but one might tomorrow. The point is that three centuries of speculation about this matter have so far failed to resolve it, which could not be the case if it merely involved behavior. There is "hard reality" here, outside our thoughts about it, which Fermat claimed to have seen but which has not been rediscovered since.

Those not in the field often fail to realize how extensive the disciplines of logic and mathematics are. Whole libraries are devoted to housing their conclusions. In an address delivered in 1900, Hilbert set 23 fundamental problems as a background for twentieth century mathematical research. Most have yet to be satisfactorily resolved, and some have yielded the remarkable conclusion that they are undecidable within present conceptualizations. It is clear that for each of Hilbert's propositions, determining whether it is true or false or undecidable on the basis of presently accepted premises is truly a search for knowledge. Yet it is not a search of behavior, for we have no control over its outcome. The only way we can influence the outcome is by changing our definitions and axioms, in which case it becomes a new and different search. Thus our understanding is enriched by such work, but what we end up understanding is neither physical nor behavioral. We come to know a third universe, an area of reality containing objects that I call "*ideals*."

Ideals in this sense are real maxima we come to know by logical processes. The objects mentioned in Plato's *Timaeus*—tetrahedron, cube, and so on—are discovered by certain explorations that also yield a wealth of other objects of knowledge. Just as the physical book before me is a point of entry for understanding physical reality, and Plato's *Dialogues* is a point of entry for understanding behavior, so the regular polyhedra provide a convenient (although arbitrary) starting place for understanding ideals. From them we can branch in many directions into geometry, mathematics, logic, and beyond.

As I will discuss more fully later, the field of ideals is not limited to entities such as numbers and geometric shapes. In this century the development of powerful general concepts in semantics and symbolic logic have indicated how most abstractions can be connected in our understanding. In particular, the concepts of "form," "essence," and "universal" that pervaded classical philosophy refer to what I call ideals. It is now possible— through an understanding of relations, functions and classes—to demonstrate the kinship of purely philosophical ideals to more rigorously described logical abstractions. They are all "the same sort of thing" in our understanding.

I now envision a tripartite division of reality. There is a physical reality composed of things such as stones and pencils, which are able to react upon one another in certain ways. There is a behavioral reality, composed of certain patterns associated with living things: the actions of organisms, human thoughts, cultural institutions. And there is an ideal reality composed of the objects of logic and abstraction. In the formal routines of human knowledge these areas of reality are explored typically by the physical sciences, the humanities and biological sciences, and the abstract sciences, respectively. Such scientific routines are usually dedicated to dissecting and analyzing reality into minima; here I am trying to build up a picture of reality in terms of maxima. In this sense, therefore, the three areas of reality—the physical cosmos, behavior, and ideals—are themselves the ultimate maxima. Each represents the largest possible unit of our understanding in a particular region, the farthest we can go when trying to grasp total reality from any single viewpoint. Hence I will call them *"orders of reality."*

At this stage it is important to pause briefly for a clear exposition of what the three "orders of reality" are—otherwise the rest of my discussion will not make sense. By referring to them I am pointing out the most absolutely fundamental way we understand reality. I am saying that everything in our world is part of one and only one such order. So let us now examine these entities as plainly as possible.

PHYSICAL REALITY is the easiest of the three to describe because many people think it is all there is. They equate it with existence itself. Thus the first requirement for apprehending physical reality is to realize that it is *limited*, that there are real entities which are not a part of it. In an earlier discussion I cited the Greek language as an example of one such entity; anyone who doubts either that such a thing as a language is real, or that its existence is non-physical, should think carefully about it.

When we go to school we learn about many aspects of reality, one of which might be the Greek language. It is typically taught to us in much the same way as the multiplication table or the anatomy of the frog. When examination time comes there are right and wrong answers to questions about Greek, just as with other subjects. This does not mean that the answers are absolute, or that counter-instances do not exist, or that further research won't turn up wholly different answers. But it does mean that we regard Greek as having some basis in reality, otherwise we would not tend to classify our assertions about it as right and wrong. When I ask a person "do you speak Greek?" and he understands what I am asking, we mutually presuppose the reality of such a thing in the same way that if I ask him "do you own a pencil?" our understanding mutually presupposes the reality of pencils. In short, there is no generic difference we can find between Greek (as an object of knowledge) and any indisputably physical thing (as an object of knowledge) which would justify our claiming that one is more real than the other.

Nevertheless there are very clear differences between Greek and any physical thing. About physical things we recognize a large cluster of characteristics, all of which they have and none of which are possessed by Greek or any other language: characteristics such as mass, motion, the ability to reflect light and be handled, the ability to be corked up in a bottle, and so on. These characteristics and our concept of physical reality itself are in some sense reciprocal; that is, the characteristics are found in the things we call physical, and the things we call physical are just those entities in which we find the characteristics. I will discuss this relationship in more detail later. The point here is that we cannot avoid recognizing a broad gulf between such things as languages and all the things we call physical, because the latter share so many characteristics not found in the former. In fact the only basic characteristic they share is that they are both objects of knowledge. We can find no other connection between them. Thus it is appropriate to regard them as both real, but assign them to different "orders" of reality.

Earlier, in contrasting a physical book with its contents, I touched on the possibility that we might treat entities such as languages as special parts of physical reality—parts that do not share the characteristics we find in other physical things (ponderability, motion, tangibility, etc.), but which still could be shown by very careful investigation to be inherently connected to things that do. One embodiment of this idea would describe a language as a complex, subtle arrangement of the brains in many human beings. It is a product of mental processes, and mental processes boil down to physical events taking place in brains. I discussed a similar viewpoint earlier, when trying to translate the hardness of a pencil into statements about physical minima. Here again the result is of no practical use—no one will ever learn a language by dissecting human brains—but more fundamentally it tends to violate our grasp of reality itself. We comprehend languages in a basically different way than we comprehend brain tissue. There is an old philosophical conundrum about a tree falling in an uninhabited forest: if no one hears it, does it make a sound? A popular answer is that it agitates the air but does not make a sound, for "sound" is a term we apply only to the internal sensations of hearing. This answer asserts that sound is a separate thing from air movements, such that the latter can exist without the former. But conversely sound can exist for us without air movements. We can talk about the sound of a falling tree (the crack and squeal of the fractured trunk, the whoosh of its fall, the crash of branches) without an actual tree falling. We would say of any theory that denied this possibility that it was "unrealistic." Similarly we can talk about a language without speaking it; in fact scholars talk about languages such as Indo-European that nobody speaks. Yet in these cases we are not just discussing our thoughts of the moment. We are discussing real things that happen to have no physical embodiment.

Thus physical reality is a limited part of total reality. It is that part, in fact, wherein certain things that are indisputably physical interact with other things—which are therefore also physical. I do not delimit this order of reality by providing a definition, a crucial test to be applied to each proposed entity to determine "is it physical?" Rather, I suggest we start from something—anything—that we will all agree to call "physical": this pencil, that stone, the light of the sun, or whatever. Then we ask "with what other things might it interact, as we understand the world?" Through such questions we quickly gather a large mass of objects, all of which fit and work together, into the whole called "physical reality." It includes manufactured objects such as pencils and natural objects such as stones; the energy of a beam of light and the energy of a falling weight; the bodies of living things as well as the remains of dead ones; in short, everything that can affect whatever object we have chosen at the outset as indisputably physical. *But it does not include everything.*

BEHAVIOR, the next order of reality, can be delimited in the same way. We start from an indisputable example—say, the thoughts that are presently in your mind as you read this—and proceed outward, identifying everything that is directly connected (or might be directly connected, as we understand the world) with one's thoughts. At the outset we find a complex mass called "consciousness": thoughts, sensations, attitudes, ideas, wants, feelings, plans, theories, memories, and so on. These are all our own personal

23

behavior patterns, and constitute the most indisputable pieces of behavior we know. But among them is also a consciousness of the same events in other minds. These events in other minds influence those in our own. For instance, my present plans and theories exclude eating ant poison because I have read or heard that other people have suffered after doing so. Their sensations are not part of my experience; rather I have borrowed them, or the idea of them, from the minds of other people. Similarly psychologists have unearthed much evidence that our behavior patterns are decisively influenced by the images we have of the attitudes of other people, particularly our parents. The interaction between the behavior of our parents and our own behavior is fully as real as the gravitational interaction between two planets; but it belongs to the behavioral order of reality instead of the physical.

From the behavior found in our minds and the minds of other human beings we proceed further to the behavior of animals. Limited communication, similar to that with a human infant, is now possible with chimpanzees; there is no natural break, no difference of kind, between our interaction with the ideas and wants of a chimpanzee and with those of another, albeit immature, human being. In the same way, when we ride a horse or train a dog we "relate" on a behavior-to-behavior basis. We understand that the animal wants certain goals and that it lays plans on the basis of certain conceptions it has; we then adjust *our* plans to aid or thwart the animal's behavior in order to achieve our own goals.

From our understanding of behavior in animals we can then proceed outward through the whole realm of life, finding a variety of behavior displayed by creatures of every size and description. The amoeba under our microscope exhibits, in a reduced way, the same kind of behavior as ourselves: it seeks and consumes food, avoids harm, reproduces when it can. By understanding its behavior we can "fool" an amoeba into doing what *we* want rather than what "it wants," as when we experimentally lure it to destruction with a scrap of artificial food. We can trace through a train of evolution the connections "upward" between the behavior of amoebas and that of multi-celled animals, ending in man; or "downward" to that of bacteria and viruses. In this way we can explore the whole realm of behavior, starting from an indisputable instance, to its fringes and questionable areas, such as the "behavior" displayed by crystals of tobacco mosaic virus.

In doing this we must take care to observe the separation between behavior and physical reality, for they are easily confused. To return to an earlier example, when a falling tree creates physical vibrations in the air is this not connected to the sound that is part of my behavior? Shouldn't any depiction of reality jump naturally from one to the other, thereby delimiting a single realm in which physical reality and behavior are mixed together? In Section

2.2 I will develop arguments to show that at every point our understanding of reality depends absolutely on the clarity with which we make separations such as this one between physical reality and behavior. Similar considerations are applicable here. When we start from the most typical, indisputable part of physical reality on the one hand, and the most typical, indisputable part of behavior on the other hand, by the time we reach their supposed meeting (such as the sound of a tree falling) we find ourselves talking in two entirely different ways. Air vibrations are physical things, to be understood one way; sounds are behavioral things, to be understood quite a different way. Air vibrations have frequency and amplitude, affect instruments, and can be displayed on an oscilloscope. Sounds are pleasant or unpleasant, trivial or frightening, meaningful or just noise. The physical-behavioral distinction is obscured when we only try to sort out the factors present in the event "tree falls"; but it emerges clearly when we approach this event from two different viewpoints, one of which has definitely started with physical reality and the other of which has definitely started with behavior.

It is essential to grasp the fact that behavior is an order of reality in its own right—it is neither reducible to other kinds of reality nor a mere theoretical construction. The primacy and independence of behavior, particularly of the individual human consciousness, has often been maintained by philosophers, of whom Berkeley was perhaps the most assertive. Taken to its extreme, this position is called "solipsism," and consists of the view that nothing is real except one's own experience. Solipsism has been called the only unassailable philosophical position because it seems to have an absolute minimum of assumptions. Nevertheless it is clearly sterile and impractical. It invites the sort of summary criticism that Dr. Johnson made when he kicked a stone and said "thus I refute Berkeley." Under the title of "phenomenology," Husserl and later philosophers have tried to show how a picture of reality might be built just out of the internal relations among the contents of consciousness; but such systems tend to seem strained and remote. I mention them here only to point out that some thinkers have maintained that behavior is all there is, just as others have maintained that physical reality is all there is.

IDEALS, finally, constitute the third order of reality that appears in our understanding of the world. Western philosophy might be said to have begun with a recognition of the independent reality of ideals in Greece two and a half millenia ago. The train of speculation that started with Pythagoras, Plato and Aristotle can be traced primarily to an overwhelming realization that there exists a realm of truth to which human reason has *direct access*. To cite a classic example, knowing that the square root of two is not a fraction does not require any other knowledge about the world; it can be deduced by anyone who is clever enough and who takes the time and trouble just to think about it. Plato tried to show that even a slave boy could invent geometry, with a little help. The force of his "Allegory of the Cave" is that true reality is populated by eternal ideal forms—what we customarily take for reality consists only of their shadows. In this way Plato maintained the primacy and independence of ideals as fully as solipsists have done with behavior or naive materialists with physical reality.

As before, we can develop a delimitation of the realm of ideals by starting with a typical, indisputable example and working outward, showing how other entities are linked to the starting point. For many ideals this procedure has already been carried out meticulously and in great detail. It is in fact the method of axiomatic exposition in mathematics, geometry, and logic. Starting with a very few agreed principles, applying them repeatedly in different combinations, all the discoveries of these disciplines can be generated. A good example (and practically the earliest one) is Euclid's geometry. His definitions, axioms and postulates can easily be written on one page; but from them flows the whole of classical geometry. When alternatives for the "parallel postulate" are substituted, completely new and different geometries result. At the core of this order of reality—while we are still in the realms of "pure mathematics" and "pure logic"—there is usually little question of distinguishing the entities we are considering from both physical reality and behavior. Establishing that 68921 is the cube of 41 clearly requires neither manipulating that many physical objects nor consulting our attitudes about the matter. It is either the case or not, and if it is the case it is so not just today or just for us, but everywhere and forever and ever. Few matters can be so decisively determined, and once determined are so hard to deny, as a mathematical calculation. It is little wonder that the Greeks found absolute reality in them.

Yet as we proceed to the fringes of the ideal order we encounter seemingly questionable cases. Plato made much of ideals such as "beauty" and "justice"; are these not merely sophisticated references to physical phenomena or patterns of human behavior? It was Plato's objective to show that they are not, to show that it is possible to generate truths about them in the same way that we generate truths about the square root of two. His attempts were much less successful than mathematicians' manipulations of numbers. But Plato *did* do a good job of demonstrating that beauty and justice themselves (whatever they may be and whatever else we may be able to say about them) have a subsistence apart from any specific beautiful thing or just act. In other words he showed that ideals must be distinguished from the things that "participate" in them if we are to make any sense of them at

26

all. He established what might be called the "principle of abstraction": that ideals common to several things must be treated as having a different kind of reality from the things they are common to.

The foregoing three realms—physical reality, behavior, and ideals—thus constitute distinct and independent orders of reality in our understanding. Do these three then cover *all* possible objects of knowledge? I believe they do at the present time. In Section 3 I will sketch the process by which living things have evolved a grasp of these three orders: first physical reality, then behavior, and lastly ideals. There is no compelling reason to suppose the process will end here, but neither is there clear evidence that it is going further. All the maxima of ordinary common sense belong to one or another of these three orders. For present purposes I shall assume that they cover all the reality we know, and will discuss the possibility of additions in Section 6.3.

Why is it important to recognize separate orders in reality? A first answer is simply that this is the way we in fact understand maxima. As we conceive of the world, at least some parts are clearly distinct from other parts—not just distinct as individual objects, but generically different, absolutely unlike kinds of things. Stones are not in the same realm as emotions, and neither are in the same realm as triangles. When we use these entities as starting points, exploring their connections to other entities, it may seem that the resulting systems of maxima approach one another. My copy of Plato's *Dialogues*, for instance, is a physical book with a behavioral content mentioning ideal geometric solids. Don't all three orders thus meet in one object? But on closer inspection the idea that they are all present in one location evaporates. This physical book shares no properties with Plato's thought. Plato's thought is not blue, flammable, ponderable, and so on, nor is the object I hold in my hand discursive, profound, tolerant, or the like. Similarly, Plato's thought has no geometric properties: it does not contain any points, lines or surfaces. A tetrahedron, Plato's thoughts about a tetrahedron, and a book in which I read about Plato's thoughts about a tetrahedron are all very different things, even though we may at first think they co-exist. On the level of natural experience I cannot be more specific than this; each person must consult his own understanding of the world.

But beside this empirical argument there are deeper reasons for separating the orders of reality, which I will discuss in Section 2.2. It turns out that divisions within reality are a precondition for theorizing. They are not a defect of understanding, but an essential requisite for the development of knowledge.

Hence the exploration of maxima yields a surprising result: reality, as we

27

understand it, is not a single system but rather at least three separate systems. Each order is an internally connected whole, but is isolated conceptually from the other two. Our knowledge may roam among physical things, observing the way they act upon one another; or it may survey behavior, appreciating the relations between primitive and advanced patterns, between individuals and groups; or it may study ideals, determining the properties of such things as sets, functions, and numbers. But it may not conceive of any thing that is simultaneously part of two systems: no physical objects that are also patterns of behavior, no behavior patterns that are also abstract ideals, no ideals that are also physical objects. At the level of maxima our understanding is ineluctably divided—we cannot even frame the concepts necessary to erase these divisions.

Yet obviously knowledge is not totally fragmented. We *do* relate the separate orders of reality, even if not by direct connection. The mechanism for accomplishing this is theorizing. When theorizing, as I will show, we force the orders of reality to assume a series of unnatural relationships, to further our explorations of each one. The basic tools for this process are *minima*—those products of our attempts to dissect and purify reality that I mentioned earlier. So before going on to a full discussion of theorizing it is necessary to consider these bits of conceptualization, and say something about the reasons for their generation.

1.2 Minima

> There are no whole truths; all truths are half-truths.
> It is trying to treat them as whole truths that plays the
> devil.
> WHITEHEAD

In exploring our understanding of maxima we eventually arrive at a series of largest limits—the orders of reality just discussed. Within the realms of physical reality, behavior, and ideals we strive to grasp an increasingly wider scope of relationships, progressively knowing more and more about that particular type of thing. But our understanding does not naturally jump between these universes. Combining the separate orders of reality is the job of *theorizing*; when we theorize we try to build bridges between maxima in the form of concepts of minima. Minima are therefore theoretical tools.

Earlier I mentioned the physicist's depiction of solid objects as "really" consisting of particles whirling in empty space. Such particles are conceived of as simultaneously physical and ideal. They are typical minima, generated by a process of theorizing. To illustrate how such an idea may arise, let us consider in outline the steps whereby human speculation has arrived at modern physics. It is a remarkable odyssey of thought, starting with the solid objects of everyday experience (such as pencils and teacups) and ending up with the invisible and incredibly tiny particles of physics that whirl through empty space in our hands.

The story starts with a naive, unanalyzed view of physical reality shared by most of mankind. This view is not necessarily typical of "primitive" people, for they often theorize in a highly developed animism, a theory combining physical reality with behavior that I will discuss in Section 2.1. Rather, we find it latent in everbody before they have been exposed to the sophistications of science or religion. From a commonsense standpoint, our first efforts to express an understanding of familiar physical maxima result in descriptions falling under three basic heads, which I will call "things,"

29

"changes," and "regularities." Thus ordinary people describing physical maxima will usually start by asserting that certain *things* (which can be named or pointed out) *change* in certain ways, and we can recognize certain *regularities* among the changes. People in all situations understand physical reality effectively on this basis.

But when people begin to think about their commonsense notions of things, changes and regularities they find that the material falling under these heads is too various and unwieldy to be conveniently interrelated. What they come up with is not a theory but rather a technology—a set of rules-of-thumb. There are thousands of different things and thousands of ways they can change, with varying degrees of regularity: the best one can make of this jumble is a body of observations and recipes. Thus people generate something like the ancient "arts and sciences": an astronomical prediction here, a formula for glassmaking there, but no comprehensive schematization of the whole. Such schematization as exists is (as I mentioned) animistic, lying in the province of magic and religion. The notations and recipes that first arise when we start to think about physical maxima are often valid and effective; but they don't yet comprise a theory.

In Western thought, the first departure from these commonsense notions was stimulated by the insight that there might be universal facts hidden among the variety we observe in things, changes, and regularities. About the sixth century B.C. the Greeks began to theorize on the basis of conceptualizing ideals. I have already mentioned Plato's attempt to associate the five regular polyhedra with physical elements. Fragmentary records survive of a variety of prior schools of thought, all of which tried to achieve a few simple reductions in physical observations to make them fit an ideal mold. Thus Thales of Miletus declared that "things" were all forms of water, and Anaximenes that they were all forms of *pneuma*, a stuff resembling air. For Anaximander all things came from a characterless neutral basis by a sort of "separating out" of opposing qualities. Empedokles abandoned such unitary schematizations for things, declaring that they were composed of mixtures of earth, water, air and fire—an idea that survived more than two thousand years. On the subject of change, Heraclitus promoted this notion to first place, treating "things" as simply illusions resulting from the successive configurations of a universal constant flux. With respect to regularities, the Pythagoreans were convinced that their newly-developed ideas about relations among numbers and geometric shapes must be the key to the underlying principles of physical events, the chords and melodies for the "music of the spheres." This rudimentary concept was later twisted into a declaration that "things are made of numbers," an attribution for which they were twitted by Aristotle:

30

There are some people who would even construct the whole universe out of numbers, as do some of the Pythagoreans. Yet manifestly, physical objects are all heavier or lighter, whereas unit-numbers (being weightless) cannot go to make up a body or have weight, however you put them together.[3]

The point of all these speculations, which have mainly historical interest today, is that they reflected a growing conviction that the worlds of physical reality and ideals should not—*cannot*—be unrelated orders of reality. Ideals exhibit just the characteristics of simplicity and rationality that physical maxima seem to lack. Triangles, for instance, come in all shapes and sizes, but their angles always add up to a straight angle; might not physical things, which also come in a variety of shapes and sizes, also have fixed common properties? The fact that the angles of any triangle have a common sum is not obvious from mere observation or common sense; it must be dug out by reasoning. Some such inspiration apparently started the Greeks reasoning about physical reality.

But Greek reasoning did not get very far. Neither their explorations of physical reality nor their understanding of ideals were sufficiently well developed to create the "fit" enjoyed by modern physics. For the next two millenia their principal legacy to Western thought was the work of Aristotle, who arranged and codified many of the ancient observations about physical maxima. It was a useful *corpus* of data, but not quite a physical theory. However, one idea developed by Greek reasoners survived and became the philosophical core of a new approach during the eighteenth century. This was the concept of *atoms*, attributed to Leukippos and Democritus. Even without further physical data to support it, the "corpuscular philosophy" remained alive through the Middle Ages because of its attractiveness as a point of contact between physical reality and ideals. *Particles* became the first minima of a new science, one that ultimately embraced also *forces* and *laws*. The theoretical relations among these new concepts were developed in some such way as the following.

A piece of wood is a thing; burn it and it becomes a piece of charcoal, which is another, different thing. If they were "really" the same, then we wouldn't be able to tell them apart; but if they are not "really" the same, where did the wood go when it burned and where did the charcoal come from? This puzzle illustrates a basic difficulty in reasoning about the "things" of common sense: they appear and disappear. Certainly *something* must remain throughout the burning process. But that something must be neither wood nor charcoal nor any other thing we observe directly. Just as certainly, something disappears: whatever it was that we called white and hard was annihilated, being replaced by something we call black and crumbly. To make this occurrence "amenable to reason" we must describe it in such a way that certain "basic" entities remain unaltered, while the things that come and go turn out to be unimportant. Thus we envision immutable "particles" (atoms in this case) which are in both the wood and the charcoal but which are neither wood nor charcoal by themselves. Burning them becomes simply a process of rearranging these particles; it is of no theoretical importance that we choose to call one arrangement "wood" and another "charcoal." By envisioning particles, theories about physical reality are saved from having to cope with something inherently inexplicable— namely, the incessant appearance and disappearance of their subject matter. "Things" become treated as incidental; only particles are *real*.

The essential requirement of any particle is that it be immutable; if it changes we lose our theoretical reference for the changes we are trying to explain. Yet particles, without themselves changing, must be capable of producing all the varied appearances of things. So stated, this requirement sounds like a paradox; and in fact it can be fulfilled only if we reinterpret our notion of "change." Thus the refinement of things into groupings of particles immediately entails a refinement of change.

Wood burning to charcoal is a change, but a complex one; a simpler example is the pure motion of any thing, such as the flight of an arrow. Nothing would seem to be easier to observe—nor more difficult to describe in terms "amenable to reason." If an arrow occupies precise positions during its flight, how does it get from one to the next? If it does not occupy precise positions during its flight, where is it? Moreover, why should it follow a predictable trajectory? Why not stop halfway, or suddenly turn around and come back? We find that our idea of "arrow-here to arrow-there" does not contain motion itself objectified; it is just a combination of two ideas of the arrow in two different places. It is not an idea of "something out there"—a "change-entity"—that guarantees a continuous trajectory from position to position. From such examples we see that raw ideas of change are theoretically sterile because they simply group ideas of things in various situations without themselves referring to any physical entities. What is needed, therefore, is a concept explaining change as an integral part of any physical event, a concept that describes entities we can identify and measure in their own right. These requirements are satisfied by the concept of *forces*. A force is a physical entity which, when applied to a particle, results in what we observe as change. By envisioning forces, theories are given something "objective" to refer to when explaining change.

A force is something independent of particles, which "acts on them." We say, for instance, that a force of one dyne is what makes a particle (or group of particles) weighing one gram accelerate at the rate of one centimeter per second per second. Yet at the same time a force cannot be observed alone; it manifests itself only by affecting particles. Nor can a particle be observed without impressing a force upon it. The two, particles and forces, are *theoretically* interdependent.

From this scheme of thought arose the notions of "mass" and "energy," which became ideal terms in which the basic characteristics of physical particles and forces were expressed. A moving particle was said to "have" a certain mass and a certain energy. The energy could be transferred from particle to particle but the mass remained constant (in pre-Einsteinian physics) until the particle was divided—hence was no longer a particle. Thus things undergoing changes became reinterpreted into transfers of energy among immutable bits of mass. The job of physics became one of explaining regularities among these transfers.

But mere ideas of regularity, like raw ideas of change, do not seem to denote anything "objective." They are only a catalog of associated events; Hume argued this point with merciless logic. Moreover, raw regularities display the same theoretical weakness as "unrefined" things: they appear and disappear. In the centuries before Newton, astronomers devised an elaborate description of planetary motion in terms of layers of "cycles" and "epicycles." This scheme, successively refined by Aristotle, Ptolemy, Copernicus, and Kepler, was a highly organized observation of regularities; but it does not today seem to us to describe anything "out there." It was all arbitrary and ad hoc, needing frequent modification to cover new data. Newton, on the other hand, broke planetary motion down into two mechanisms (gravitation and inertia) which by their interactions accounted for virtually every regularity that had previously been observed. The value of Newton's scheme was not that it was shorter or more comprehensible than the system of cycles and epicycles, but that it seemed to refer to "real mechanisms." It was more than just a reconciliation of regularities. This became increasingly evident over the years: Newton's scheme stood as written, while the other would have required constant tinkering to force it into line with new observations. Newton's explanation of regularities seemed universal; it applied as well on earth as in the heavens and did not "appear" or "disappear" in specific cases. As a result of successes such as this, physics began to replace the regularities observed by common sense with new, more refined pronouncements called *"laws."* By the late nineteenth century those laws that had become "established" in physics were thought by most scientists to be valid because they pointed out "mechanisms" of physical reality, not just associations among data. For this reason they were regarded as inviolable, since they were treated as *real* in their own right, not just as assemblages of predictions. Inviolable laws named "something out there."

This set of "refinements" of common sense—particles, forces, laws—formed the basis for modern physics. It has a logical coherence centered around an attempt to describe physical reality in terms of minimal elements. It starts with the monadic immutable particle, which is the "nexus" of any physical event. Forces "act upon" particles, resulting in what we observe as change. And the occurrence of forces corresponds to the "operation" of inviolable laws. At every point in this new scheme, physical reality has picked up ideal characteristics.

It is now traditional to regard the entities of physics as having been "discovered," as if they had always been lying around waiting for us to recognize them. However, we might equally well regard them as having been *invented*. A clue to the latter viewpoint lies in the way these entities proliferate in our understanding. To start with, a particle never identifies itself as such; at best any specific item in physical reality can only be assumed to be an immutable particle until proven otherwise. This is the same as saying that a particle is immutable with respect to certain laws—those denoting mechanisms in which the supposed particle in fact remains unchanged. There may be other (as yet unknown) mechanisms in which the supposed particle turns out to be a collection of more basic particles. Atoms, for instance, are particles with respect to the laws of chemistry but collections with respect to the laws of nuclear physics. Hence the recognition of particles is relative to the statement of laws. But a law referring only to immutable particles would have to be empty, for they do not (by definition) change. An agent of change—a force—must be introduced to give "content" to the law. The law then becomes meaningful only to the extent that it is a statement about arrangements of forces or transfers of energy. Thus our formulation of laws becomes a function of our identification of forces. But forces and energy are so conceived that they manifest themselves only by influencing particles; without particles to "act upon" they are unknowable. In this way the particles depend on the laws, the laws on the forces, and the forces on the particles.

This effect, in which concepts of minima tend to generate one another, is not uncommon. Because minima are artificial bridges between separate orders of reality, more are required as we explore reality further. In modern physics this happened after the discovery of the electron in 1897 and again after the introduction of the quantum concept of light in 1899. Before these developments, physical explorations had left atoms unaltered; what evidence there was of subatomic phenomena was minor and could be ignored.

Subatomic particles were thought to be impossible and light was treated as pure energy propagated continuously in the "ether." But electrons turned out to be just as surely particles as atoms, although incredibly smaller. To describe them new laws were needed, and then new forces to give meaning to the new laws. With light a complementary movement took place: when radiant energy was shown to be discontinuous a new particle (the photon) was needed to explain it, followed by new laws to define the new particle. With the development of atomic energy, and its consequent boost to research into subatomic effects, the proliferation of minima in physics became intense. This trend continues today, although there are now efforts to consolidate particle theorizing around a few even tinier entities called "quarks."

In the foregoing example we see displayed the basic differences between maxima and minima as units of understanding. Physicists explore physical maxima in their laboratories: they induce specific effects, put materials into unusual environments such as high pressure or low temperature, and make measurements. To assist this process they create a series of increasingly specialized machines, from spectroscopes to particle accelerators, that widen the scope of the physical effects and measurements they are able to observe. Simultaneously mathematicians develop increasingly sophisticated disciplines for handling abstractions, from the infinitesimal calculus to theory of groups. Both scientific communities are exploring reality, but their explorations can never meet directly. Still it is clear that mathematics and physics are able to help each other. So theorizers postulate the existence of minima—*objects of knowledge that are supposed to lie in both orders of reality*. In the present instance, physics treats particles as physical because they are the locations for mass and energy, but at the same time as ideal because they are uniform, immutable, and precisely definable. Forces are physical because they produces changes in things, and ideal because they are always metricized. Laws are physical because they govern physical events, and ideal because they are eternal, inviolable, and expressible mathematically. The complexities of maximal reality have been boiled down to hypothetical points at which different orders are supposed to coincide. Everything outside these points of intersection is now regarded as extraneous.

My description of scientific theorizing might be construed as implying that minima are not real, at least not in the same way that maxima are real. Since that sounds like a radical pronouncement, let me state carefully what I mean. There is some physical reality associated with what we call particles, forces, and laws—otherwise we could not observe physical effects from them. But the physical reality associated with them has no natural ideal properties. Conversely, the mathematical concepts in which physics is couched express some ideal reality; but there is no trace of physical reality about them. We can treat any of these minima as being either wholly physical or wholly ideal, and thereby grasp a part of reality: it is when we treat them as being partially or wholly both that our conceptualization goes astray.

Nevertheless minima are useful. By pinning two orders of reality together they enhance our explorations of both. If physicists had never conceived of particles, forces, and laws, they would never have thought to build the machines or conduct the investigations from which a great deal of knowledge has flowed. Similarly mathematics has been enriched by the concepts of physics, which have stimulated mathematicians to investigate many areas of ideals they might otherwise have never discovered. Each program of exploration acts as a lever upon the other, with minima acting as fulcrums. The general interplay of the orders of reality—physical, behavioral, ideal— in this process deepens our understanding of all three. This is why we bother to build theories at all.

2. Theorizing

A theory is no more like a fact than a photograph is like a person.

EDGAR HOWE

In the last section I began to discuss how theorizing fits into our general development of knowledge about the world. Our basic grasp of reality is a grasp of maxima, and it expands in the direction of ever larger and more comprehensive parts. The natural trend of my understanding of the pencil in my hand, for example, is toward the trees and minerals from which it came and toward its effects upon paper, my hand, and the other physical objects it touches. The natural trend in understanding my thoughts is toward the whole behavior pattern of which they are a part, toward the behavior of other persons with whom I interact, and toward living behavior in general. And the natural trend of understanding ideals is toward greater generality: toward showing how a specific geometric form, for instance, is related to a class of such forms which in turn can be described by an analytic function, which is one of a class of functions, and so on. In other words, our natural understanding of reality expands outward from whatever common objects we encounter, building increasingly complex pictures of maxima. But while so doing, our understanding discovers that it is channeled into three separate areas: physical reality, behavior, and ideals. The more we know about these types of reality the more it is clear to us that they are different in kind. Anyone who dispassionately examines his understanding must agree that physical objects are ''a different sort'' of reality from thoughts, and both are ''a different sort'' of reality from geometric figures. This holds throughout reality, so we must ultimately treat knowledge as referring to three separate orders.

But we do not always act as if they were separate. In practice, we conceive of parallelisms everywhere between the orders of reality. Printed books are treated as representing thought processes; numbers are treated as descrip-

37

tions of physical events; ideal formulas such as the syllogism and symbolic logic are treated as codifications of mental reasoning. Such parallelisms do not occur to us entirely naturally, as an inherent part of the world we explore: they are products of theorizing, and our understanding of them is therefore "theoretical knowledge."

Theoretical knowledge, the positing of parallelisms between the orders of reality, cannot be considered knowledge of reality in a strict sense. But it is not just game-playing either. It serves to enlarge our grasp of reality, to make us aware of maxima we would not otherwise have encountered. Without an understanding of writing our ability to transfer thoughts from one person to another through physical reality would be severely limited. Without mathematical theories physicists would seldom discover new physical realities; like ancient artisans they would spend most of their time stumbling across isolated effects. These parallelisms work in the other direction too. Writing enriches physical reality in that it helps organize people to produce the artifacts of civilization. Physics enriches our knowledge of ideals by suggesting new problems to be solved mathematically. In short, there is a strong "cross-breeding" effect in theorizing, whereby the interplay of one order of reality with another widens our grasp of both.

Minima might be described as the gametes of this cross-breeding. Positing a bare parallelism does not yet give us a tool for increasing our understanding of reality. To say in general that marks on paper can correspond to thoughts does not give us a system of writing; we must specify which marks correspond to which thoughts. To say in general that mathematical numbers may represent physical quantities does not give us a system of measurement; we must define physical parameters and institute standard units. At first such correspondences, each of which is a specific instance of parallelism, may be treated just as arbitrary associations among maxima. But as they proliferate we begin to treat them as inherently real. The parallelisms themselves become new objects of knowledge.

At this point, however, the tendency of our understanding begins running toward smaller and smaller bits. We want to know the *minimal* units of correspondence. What is the smallest written mark that has a behavioral meaning? What is the smallest piece of physical reality for which we can measure mass? What is the simplest law that describes gravity? These become the ultimate questions answered by theoretical knowledge. It may be possible to answer such questions without hypostatizing minima: but the normal procedure hitherto has been to translate the answer into the "discovery" of a new type of reality. The smallest pieces of physical reality for which we can measure mass are particles which (because they answer this question) are therefore assumed to be newly discovered realities. Similarly

38

the "law of gravity" is assumed to be a real mechanism. In this way the focus of our attention shifts from the maxima of natural knowledge to the minima of theoretical knowledge: from the reality that has always been the objective of our understanding to the manufactured tools by which that understanding is now developed.

One way to visualize the relationships between maxima, theories, and minima is to consider the differences between the questions "what?," "why?," and "how?" When we explore maxima we discover *what* reality is. We apprehend its physical, behavioral, and ideal parts in all their particularity and diversity. Nothing is "explained"; everything must be taken just as it is or we risk losing sight of it. We are led on to the far reaches of reality without further analysis of what we find along the way. But it is also useful for us to understand *why*. Reality by itself does not explain "why." Physical objects do not measure themselves, behavior patterns do not automatically include self-consciousness, ideals do not systematize themselves. Our "why" questions are answered by theories. Why do physical objects move the way they do? Because they obey Newton's (or Einstein's) laws of motion. Why does the pencil feel hard to me? Because when I touch it my finger deforms, setting in train a series of events that culminate with certain electrochemical happenings in my brain. Why is the square root of 2 not a fraction? Because when we assume that it is we are led to a contradiction, which we have decided beforehand indicates impossibility. In all these cases the "why" of some maximal fact is established by relating it to facts in another order of reality. The why of moving physical objects, for instance, amounts to a statement of ideal relations that we believe physical objects "obey." Our behavioral reaction to grasping a pencil is explained by citing physical events. The square root of two is not a fraction because when we assume it is we get into a behaviorally unsatisfactory position. Setting up parallelisms among the orders of reality has provided answers to our "why" questions about the things we observed when asking "what" questions.

But we do not stop at this stage. The "why" answers seem to be sterile unless we can further break them down into details, unless we can describe how the parallelism works at each step. Hence the "how" questions. How do physical objects change? By particles rearranging themselves under the influence of forces. How do my thoughts occur? By the interplay of sensations, emotions, memories, drives, and so on. How are geometric shapes composed? By combining points, lines, and surfaces. "How" questions ask us to identify minima, which are then supposed to be the elements that give life to the "why" answers. In effect, by going from "what" to "why" we

have left reality; it is now necessary to return to reality with a description of "how." But we do not actually attain reality; rather we define new artificial objects, the minima, which by this process are now taken to "underlie" or form the basis for the original maxima of natural knowledge.

In this way theorizing transmutes our knowledge from that of maxima to that of minima. It starts with the observation that certain threads of reality (certain systems of maxima) seem somehow cognate, although they lie in different orders. It fits these threads to each other in what I call a "parallelism" and is gratified to observe that the development of our knowledge of each one suggests a development of the other; they "cross-breed," the combination producing more total knowledge than two separate explorations would have. Finally it supports the parallelism by positing new entities— minima—that are supposed to be links between these maxima from separate orders of reality. The minima become the "explanation" of how the parallelism works, as well as our justification for adopting it. We thus acquire a new knowledge of these minima (what I call "theoretical knowledge"), which has not been generated from a natural exploration of reality but is more like an understanding of things we have created, a contemplation of our own tools. Nevertheless minima reflect back through the theorizing process, so that we come to treat them as "actual" or "basic" reality. We cease treating as basic the maxima with which we started. By such a process, for instance, the solid objects of everyday experience become transmuted into the particles whirling in empty space of modern physics.

It is characteristic of theoretical minima that we must think of them as located beyond the grasp of ordinary experience. They are generically different from maxima, and so cannot be found in the maximal world. For instance, as I noted in Section 1.2 the concept of particles (initially, atoms) was adopted to provide a stable theoretical basis for explaining the variability of physical "things." Atoms were conceived of as radically unlike all other physical objects in that they alone were immutable. This meant that these entities had to be incapable of direct observation, for every physical thing we know directly is variable. So theory placed them in the world of the invisibly tiny, where we could suppose they existed without contrary evidence from common experience. It was to be expected that as soon as the machines of physics became able to isolate and manipulate atoms, it turned out that they were not particles at all, but were as complex as larger physical objects. The theoretical location of "true particles" then had to be pushed farther into regions of unattainable smallness: first into the subatomic structure of electrons, protons, etc., and then, when these turned out to be too various, into the mysterious microworld of "quarks."

40

Transmutations from knowledge of maxima to that of minima occur quite generally in all phases of theorizing. I have used the example of ideal-physical theorizing because it is particularly clear, and also because laymen (for whom physics is somewhat remote anyway) can easily hold it in perspective. But an equally important example, closer to home, comes from physical-behavioral theorizing. Here the most characteristic resulting minima are called "causal links." A causal link is a physical event—physical configuration A causes physical configuration B. Yet it is also behavioral in the sense that we think of it in life-like terms: A "made B happen," once A had happened B "couldn't help but happen," and so on. Thus the causal link (the relationship itself between cause and effect) is hypostatized as simultaneously physical and behavioral. It is the product of a theoretical parallelism between these two orders of reality. When we carefully examine "causal links" (as Hume did) we find a clear distinction between the successive physical states supposed to be cause and effect and the behavior we suppose they exhibit in their connection. But by positing the link we artificially join these two separate kinds of reality together into one unanalyzable unity and treat it as real. This "new reality" then provides both an explanation and a justification for the original physical-behavioral association.

Is theoretical knowledge, therefore, just an illusion? One cannot object to the theorizing process in general, for it stimulates the search for much natural knowledge. We would never have stumbled across most of what we understand about reality if we had not had theories to spur us on. My objection to theorizing arises from the last stage of the process—the assumption that minima are more real than maxima. Not only is this based on a misconception, it is also counter-productive. It diverts our scientific explorations from understanding reality to examining our own research tools. An instance already mentioned is the self-generating proliferation of particles, forces, and laws in physics. Beyond a certain point the effort expended on "discovering" new particles is effort diverted from significant investigations of physical reality. It is tools being used to make more tools, rather than to dig around in the real world.

This does not mean that scientists must rigorously abjure calling their explanatory minima "real." A limited amount of such fiction has a salutary effect on research. By calling minima real we bring our hypotheses to life and give our theorizing a solid feeling. But here the justification ends. There is an old nursery riddle: if you call a dog's tail a leg, how many legs does it have? The answer of course is still four; calling a tail a leg does not make it one. Similarly, calling minima real does not make them so. At best such usage is only a psychological stimulus to explore reality; at worst it stultifies the same exploration by seducing us into ignoring maxima.

So my judgment about theorizing is that it is valuable as long as we limit the conclusions we draw from it. Theories by themselves do not reveal reality; they only help us look for it. Even in such a purely instrumental role theorizing is an important human task. At the same time it is a somewhat mysterious one. What sorts of things are theories anyhow? Why do we create them the way we do? How do they accomplish their task? These are the "what-why-how" questions asked earlier, but now directed *at* theories instead of being answered by them. They form the subject of the next three sections.

2.1 Theories

> Many shall run to and fro, and knowledge shall be
> increased.
> *Daniel 12:4*

Theories are patterns of human thought. We encounter them when we explore the behavioral order of reality. Earlier I mentioned Plato's theory that the four "elements" of Greek physics (earth, water, air, fire) could be associated with regular polyhedra. This was a thought in Plato's mind which he expressed in one of his written dialogues, from whence we can reconstruct it as a thought in our own minds. Thus a first approach to answering the "what" of theories is to say that they are parts of behavior, and specifically that they are objects in human thought.

Every theory is "about" something. Within human thought we find theories about stars, electrons, chemicals, and light; about plants, insects, and primitive men; about surfaces, numbers, and sets; about languages, history, art, morals, and existence; and about human thought itself. Not only is every theory about something; for practically every thing we discover in reality someone has constructed a theory about it.

Examined as real objects in behavior, theories exhibit various characteristics to us. They are frail or durable, elegant or crude, natural or artificial, satisfying or frustrating. Euclid's geometry is an elegant and durable theory. The kinetic theory of gases appears natural and satisfying. The phlogiston theory of combustion is crude and artificial. Philosophical solipsism is a durable but frustrating theory. On the one hand these characteristics seem to be a part of each theory, just as the characteristics of being hard, smooth, yellow and so on seem to be a part of the pencil on my desk. On the other hand, our perceptions of the characteristics of a theory may change radically when we compare it with another theory. Before this century, for example, the physics developed by Newton, Maxwell, and Dalton was generally thought to be elegant, durable, and satisfying; but by 1935 its basic concepts had been largely abandoned. A theory believed to be exceedingly durable and elegant had turned out to be frail, artificial, and crude.

The traditional explanation for many theory characteristics is that they are a function of its "faithfulness to nature." On this view a revolution such as the one just mentioned results because the old theory was found to be "incorrect"—it did not cover all the facts and contradicted some. We were wrong about its characteristics because we did not have the whole picture in mind. But Kuhn has pointed out that this traditional explanation is largely fictional; theories are replaced primarily because a more attractive scheme has been formulated, not because nature calls the turn.

> ...a scientific theory is declared invalid only if an alternate candidate is available to take its place. No process yet disclosed by the historical study of scientific development at all resembles the methodological stereotype of falsification by direct comparison with nature. ...The act of judgment that leads scientists to reject a previously accepted theory is always based upon more than a comparison of that theory with the world.[4]

Kuhn elswhere mentions "personal and inarticulate esthetic considerations"[5] as frequent grounds for switching theories. It is as if our tastes in theorizing change, and when they do we see our previous products of this occupation in an entirely different light.

There are many instances in which large changes in theorizing have followed small changes or additions to their subject areas. Most of the phenomena of optics, for example, had been observed and explained by the late nineteenth century; one would have expected that additional data such as the photoelectric effect and discontinuities in black body radiation could have been fitted into existing theories. But these new observations were shortly followed by a profound change in theoretical concepts about light—from wave models to particle models—which has been seesawing in both directions ever since. Similarly, calculations of astronomical motions using Einstein's mechanics are only triflingly different from those using Newton's. But the theoretical foundations under them are radically distinct. In this case the "esthetic" differences between the two theories are fairly clear. Instead of Newton's absolute space and time, Einstein (in the Special Theory) substituted an absolute propagation of light. Nowadays we do not easily envision space and time as physical "things"; it is more natural to treat them as a perceptual framework or a pair of intuitive preconceptions (as Kant did) about how the physical world should be arranged. Hence to have space and time dominate a theory about physical things (while at the same time being themselves totally passive, impalpable, and incorporeal) is in retrospect a strained viewpoint. A beam of light, however, is clearly a physical "thing." It is easy to imagine that its velocity of propagation is absolute, even if that means relativizing our measurements of space and time. It is historically more accurate to say that Einsteinian mechanics won out because of these considerations, than because it yielded more accurate astronomical predictions or explained the Michelson-Morley experiment.

The significance of the foregoing is that we cannot attribute the characteristics of theories (whether they are durable or frail, elegant or crude, etc.) solely or even primarily to their ability to "cover" their subjects. The notion that theories rise gradually from studies of their subjects, steadily improving as we learn more, is fantasy. Reality does not lead our understanding in such a straightforward way. Instead, theories have a certain fashionableness about them; how we judge one depends largely on whether it conforms to a preconceived theorizing *style*. Its "faithfulness" to its subject is only one factor, and frequently a minor one, in its appearance to us.

What is there about theorizing that determines its "style"? Let us return once more to the example of solid physical objects (things like this pencil) and compare two theories of radically different "style." The starting point is our natural grasp of physical maxima, of objects that we hold in our hands and move around in the physical world. By theorizing in one direction we arrive at modern physics—the scheme of particles, forces and laws that I sketched in Section 1.2. The style of this type of theorizing grew from the realization that mathematical truths could be discovered just be reasoning about abstractions. From there it was an easy jump to the supposition that truths about physical reality could be similarly reasoned out. Thus ideal properties were found "underlying" physical maxima: immutable particles as bases for the variety of things, metricizable forces as agents changing particle arrangements, and mathematically expressed laws to describe regularities in the distributions of forces. In order to verify that we understood a physical event we simply fitted it into our ideal framework by identifying the particles, forces and laws involved, made a few mathematical calculations from measurements and pre-determined constants, and made a prediction. If the prediction was fulfilled then we said we understood the event. Under this scheme the basic criterion for knowledge was the ability to correlate physical reality with mathematical (or more generally, abstract) models.

Now compare this with another style of theorizing about physical objects. Dobu is a rocky island off the eastern tip of New Guinea, inhabited by Melanesians. Dobuan life is relatively difficult, food is scarce, and competition between individuals and between family lines is keen. Success requires wits, planning, and knowledge. The knowledge by which a Dobuan gets ahead is derived from an extensive body of magical theory, which is generated within each family clan and passed down in great secrecy; it is knowledge of *incantation*.

> The ritual of Dobu consists essentially in the use of incantations in the performance of certain activities such as canoe making and fish-net making, in agriculture, in soliciting presents of valuables in the annual exchanges made by the long overseas expeditions, in the creating of love, in the making of wind and rain, in the causing and curing of disease, and in the causing of death...
>
> Behind this ritual idiom there stands a most rigid and never-questioned dogma, learnt by every child in infancy, and forced home by countless instances of everyday usage based upon it and meaningless without it or in its despite. This dogma, in general, is that effects are secured by incantation, and that without incantation such effects cannot come to pass. In its particular application it is most strongly believed that yams will not grow, however well the soil is prepared and cared for, without the due performance of the long drawn-out ritual of gardening incantations; canoe lashing will not hold the canoe together at sea, however firmly the creeper may be wound and fastened without the appropriate incantation being performed over its lashing; fish nets will not catch fish unless they have been treated with incantation...[6]

Other rituals are directed toward improving the weather, calming the ocean, and preventing natural disasters. This is clearly more than just the manifestation of a "technology" to improve such activities as agriculture and seamanship; it represents a firm belief that incantation, a personal interchange between man and nature, is an essential part of the workings of reality. When asked how European missionaries were able to grow yams without ritual, the Dobuans flatly refused to admit that such events occurred: they were inherently impossible. Once yams had started to grow, a function of the ritual was to coax neighbors' yams into one's garden and at the same time talk one's own yams into staying put. Supporting the incessant labor directed to this end was a perfectly serious conviction, everywhere asserted and never questioned, that in the middle of the night the tubers regularly left their vines and walked about from plot to plot. When asked how the yams could hear their daily exhortations, the Dobuans indicated the buds at the vines' growing points and asserted they were "ears."

Field reports of anthropologists are filled with examples such as the foregoing. In 1871 E. B. Tylor revived the term "animism" to denote the attitude of mind that supports them. He wrote:

> Conformably with that early childlike philosophy in which human life seems the direct key to the understanding of nature at large, the savage theory of the universe refers its phenomena in general to the willful action of pervading personal spirits. It was no spontaneous fancy, but the reasonable inference that effects are due to causes, which led the rude men of old days to people with such

ethereal phantoms their own homes and haunts, and the vast earth and sky beyond. Spirits are simply personified causes.[7]

The idea of a self-consistent animistic world-view, parallel to that of discursive Western science, was pursued by many anthropologists, culminating (1910) in Lévy-Bruhl's controversial concept of "pre-logical" mental processes:

> ...primitives perceive nothing in the same way as we do. The social *milieu* which surrounds them differs from ours, and precisely because it is different, the external world they perceive differs from that which we apprehend. ...The mystic properties with which things and beings are imbued form an integral part of the idea to the primitive, who views it as a synthetic whole.[8]

The importance of Lévy-Bruhl's work is that he treated the animistic world-view as a complete system of thought, instead of as a fragmentary tissue of errors and misunderstandings. His subsequent unpopularity arose because he at first maintained that it was an inferior world-view, and implied that it was one from which his "primitives" could not escape.

A typical current view is that stated by Malinowski, one of the pioneers of modern field anthropology. He points out that primitive people have theories which we would regard as "scientific" as well as those that are animistic or magical. The two co-exist and can be contrasted:

> Magic is based on specific experience of emotional states in which man observes not nature but himself, in which the truth is revealed not by reason but by the play of emotions upon the human organism. Science is founded on the conviction that experience, effort, and reason are valid; magic on the belief that hope cannot fail nor desire deceive. The theories of knowledge are dictated by logic, those of magic by the association of ideas under the influence of desire.[9]

In other words, animism is "wishful thinking." It would be nice if I could lure yams from my neighbor's garden into my own; therefore I will assume that this is possible and strive to make it happen. I want my boat to withstand the waves and my fish-net to catch fish; therefore I will speak to them as if they were conscious beings and influence them with my pleas. But how different in form is this state of mind from that of (say) a modern physicist? We might epitomize his philosophy in the same terms. It would be nice if the phenomena of nature conformed to mathematical formulas; therefore I will assume that this is possible and strive to discover what the formulas are. I want the machines I build to function in certain ways; therefore I will treat them as if they were controlled by ideal laws, and build them accordingly.

Nothing in the foregoing proves there is anything inherently inferior about relating physical reality to emotional states rather than to abstractions, or about assuming that physical events are determined by the operation of spiritual agencies rather than impersonal laws. In fact, both approaches yield theories satisfying to their proponents. Both are widely used. We cannot dismiss one style of theorizing out of hand merely on the grounds that it is "improper."

Of course the most commonly cited deficiency of animism is that it "doesn't work," or at least doesn't work as well as abstract reasoning. We know the Dobuan's yams do not leave the earth and wander about in the night because our abstract classification scheme tells us that plant roots are not capable of that sort of action. Therefore all effort expended on wooing yams into one's garden is wasted, and any theory that tries to justify this effort is false. We might "prove" this by going out in the night with a flashlight, looking for ambulatory tubers. But from the tenor of anthropologists' reports of Dobuan theorizing we can surmise in advance that their world-view would not treat such a demonstration as conclusive. They would claim our presence had suppressed the movements of the yams, or another magic agency had blinded us to their actions, or in some other way animistic forces had intervened to nullify our experiment. This is the way it is with animism. In the case of universal abstract laws one can make demands on one's data: disprove a principle by exhibiting a single adverse instance, for example, or make a verifiable prediction by logical processes. But when events are in the hands of willful spiritual agencies such experimental methods no longer apply. Verification is now a matter of communicating with the agencies and discovering how to get along with them. When you accomplish this your theory is "working."

Consider the conflict between animism and science from the opposite point of view. In the fifth century A.D. Saint Augustine wrote:

It is not necessary to probe into the nature of things, as was done by whom the Greeks call *physici* ... For even these men themselves, endowed though they are with so much genius, burning with zeal, abounding in leisure, tracking some things by the aid of human conjecture, searching into others with the aid of history and experience, have not found out all things; and even their boasted discoveries are oftener mere guesses than certain knowledge. It is enough for Christians to believe that the only cause of all created things, whether heavenly or earthly, whether visible or invisible, is the goodness of the Creator, the one true God.[10]

At the time we would have had to agree with him, for abstractly based science was then a much less useful and satisfying body of knowledge than Christian doctrine. Its high points to date had been such theories as Plato's

48

association of physical elements with regular polyhedra and the Pythagoreans' vague idea of a "mathematical harmony" in the universe. Against
this the Church provided comprehensive and detailed theories about heaven
and hell, about the Eternal Source of all natural phenomena and about man's
role in the world. It did not cripple such theories to realize that we could not
(for instance) observe heaven and hell directly any more than it cripples
modern physics to be told that we cannot observe an electron directly.
Church theories were adopted because they provided better explanations
than any other. Many of them are still widely held today.

Here we see two different "styles" of theorizing about the same subject,
about the ordinary objects of physical reality. One style depends on abstraction and reasoning, on the identification of mathematically definable forces
and the statement of universal laws. The other depends on communication
and sympathy, on the recognition of vital agencies in the physical world with
which one must cooperate. When we compare the two approaches from a
neutral standpoint it is evident that in the first case theorizing presupposes
connections of some sort between physical reality and ideals, while in the
second case it presupposes connections of some sort between physical reality
and behavior. The laws, formulas, and measurements of physical science are
expressed in ideal terms. The spirits and agencies of animistic theorizing are
expressed in behavioral terms. It is this fundamental difference in
reference—each positing a parallelism between physical events and a different independent order of reality—that results in two distinct theorizing
"styles."

It would be fair to say that animism is more generally used, even today in
"advanced" cultures, than science. If I bake a cake, I think of the ingre-
dients as having behavioral properties, not ideal properties. Flour, milk,
eggs and baking powder each "do" something to contribute to the finished
product. A chemist might characterize baking powder in terms of the
potential decomposition of sodium bicarbonate into sodium carbonate, water, and carbon dioxide gas, which proceeds at a certain rate in the presence
of moisture and heat by virtue of ionization. I would say it simply "makes
the cake rise." To assure that the cake rises, the Dobuan will say an
incantation; for the same purpose I select a "reputable brand" of baking
powder. He is appealing to a behavioral agency immanent in his kitchen. I
am appealing to a behavioral agency (a manufacturer) who is supposed to
compound the powder so that "it works." Neither of us will be very
conscious of impersonal abstract laws embedded in the process. If the cake
fails to rise the Dobuan may blame a malignant spirit; I might blame a
careless manufacturer. An instance of the cake falling flat will not contradict
any beliefs we hold, at least not in the sense that the Michelson-Morley

experiment contradicted Newtonian physics. It will just mean that "something didn't work." It is clear that this attitude is generally adopted in our everyday commerce with physical things. As I stated earlier, the more we examine the actual uses of science the more we discover it is a discipline mainly confined to laboratories.

In fact it is clear that without a firm grasp of animistic thinking no human being, not even the most capable scientist, could long survive. When I put a bite of food in my mouth it is usually because I believe it will "taste good," "satisfy my hunger," and the like, not because it contains certain molecules or conforms to certain chemical specifications. When I take a step I expect the floor will "support me," without knowing its modulus of elasticity. Obviously these beliefs may be wrong: I can get food poisoning, the floor can give way under me, and so on. But if science had never been devised or if I had never heard of calories, elasticity, and other idealizations, I would still be able to get along satisfactorily through my animistic conceptions of physical reality. On the other hand if I had no such conceptions—if, for instance, I could distinguish a potato from a rock only by measuring its carbohydrate content, and dared not take a step until I had determined the engineering properties of the floor in front of me—I would quickly perish. While it may be argued that the ideal expressions of science yield advantages over behavioral animism, the fact remains that animistic theories are essential to human life whereas scientific theories are not.

What exactly does it mean to say that scientific theories about physical reality are "expressed in" ideal terms, while animistic theories are "expressed in" behavioral terms? A simple way to understand this is to borrow the concept of "categories" from philosophy. Aristotle introduced this term in his short work *Categoriae*, which had a lasting effect on medieval and later thought. For him, categories were headings under which all the single things we could talk about were classified. He listed ten, all quite abstract: substance, quantity, quality, relation, place, time, position, state, action, and affection. Briefly, the sort of thing he intended by this scheme was to be able to specify that when we say (for instance) "the horse runs" we can analyze our statement further by saying that "the horse" is an example of substance and "runs" is an example of action. A set of categories thus gives us an overall view of how we think and talk about anything, by outlining the pigeon-holes into which our terms may be put. In the *Critique of Pure Reason* (1781) Kant developed a list of twelve "fundamental concepts of the pure understanding," by which he meant an absolute framework within which anything we can imagine must be cast. These categories, forming the cornerstone of his "Copernican revolution in philosophy," were generated

50

by an essentially logical process. As we would anticipate, they were even more abstract than Aristotle's, and included such headings as unity, plurality, causality, possibility, and so on. Kant speaks of Aristotle as having "merely picked [categories] up as they occurred to him,"[11] whereas for Kant they represented the absolute forms of existence as we apprehend it, and hence were independent of any empirical justification.

When used in such cosmic applications the concept of categorization tends to become remote and academic. But the idea is useful in analyzing theories of all sorts, not just metaphysics. Listing the categories used by a theory tells us (in summary form) just how it deals with its subject matter. They constitute the key to understanding how a theory goes about its basic task of explanation. The first thing we want to know about any theory is the limits of its subject-matter: what it is a theory "of." The next thing we want to know is what categories it uses. When we have these two specifications in mind we are in a position to compare that theory with any other, and to locate it within any scheme that characterizes theories in general.

For example, consider a well-developed modern theory: say, the exposition of chemistry one learns in high school. On the first day of class students are commonly told that the subject of chemistry comprises all physical matter and the transformations it undergoes. Typical instances are given: iron rusts, candles burn, cloth bleaches, sugar ferments. Iron, wax, smoke, bleach, alcohol—these are the familiar maxima with which the theory deals. They form its *subject*. At first the theory seems almost cosmological in scope; but it is soon evident that there are limitations on its subject. To start with, chemistry recognizes no transformations of matter "below the atomic level": most events taking place in the sun, for example, are explained by physics, not chemistry. But more subtly, practical chemistry is also limited to relatively "pure" forms of matter. No chemist would undertake to analyze a whole housefly, because it is such a concatenation of compounds that overall analysis would hardly yield any meaningful information. It would be like trying to pursue botany by studying aerial photographs of forests. A chemist would assert that "in principle" a fly could be analyzed chemically, its matter becoming described as proportions of carbon, hydrogen, oxygen, nitrogen, and other atoms; but such figures would tell us very little. To understand a fly we must turn from chemistry to biology. Similarly most other objects of everyday experience—earth, air, wood, cloth, etc.— are too "mixed" or "contaminated" to figure conveniently in chemical researches. Even water is usually distilled to remove minerals before it becomes an object of study. This does not mean that chemistry refuses to recognize such mixtures or cannot ultimately understand them; I am only saying that practical chemistry displays a strong inherent tendency to set mixed matter aside as not being a fruitful area for inquiry. Thus for most high school students chemistry soon devolves into the study of relatively pure "chemicals," i.e. materials purchased in bottles from chemical supply houses. The subject becomes esoteric, removed from common experience; and later the student may be alarmed to learn that such "chemicals" are present in the food he eats. In this fashion the discipline of chemistry retreats rapidly from its ostensive subject (non-subatomic matter in general) to knowledge of rather special materials under highly controlled conditions. It becomes the study of chemicals in laboratories.

How does the modern theory of chemistry handle its subject? We say that it starts by "categorizing" matter. Of all possible purified materials that might be found on a chemist's shelf, some hundred-odd are "elements"; the rest are "compounds." Every compound is made of two or more elements. We can demonstrate this by subjecting any compound to various operations such as heating or electrolysis and noting that it eventually disappears, being replaced by an equal mass of elements. Alternately, we can usually create the compound by bringing its elements together under the right conditions. For any given compound the ratio of elements by mass is always the same. This schema, enunciated 180 years ago by Proust and Dalton, forms the bedrock of modern chemistry.

Since then, of course, more has been added to the theory. Compounds hold together because of "bonds" between elements—attractions with which we can associate a definite amount of "energy." Elements have "valence numbers" that tend to predict the ways they will react with other elements. Elements are composed of tiny identical "atoms" which make up identical "molecules" in compounds; this accounts for isomeric compounds, which contain the same elements in the same ratios but have different molecular "structures." And so on. For illustration purposes we need consider only a few of these concepts.

By categorizing matter (even the already somewhat specialized materials on the chemist's shelf) we alter our view of it. Iron and oxygen, although utterly different by everyday standards, are similar because they are both elements; whereas rust, which is everywhere associated with iron in common experience, is different because it is a compound. Red, black, and brown rusts are similar because they are made of the same elements but different because their combining ratios are different. Materials as dissimilar as graphite and diamond are the same element, whereas materials as apparently similar as carbon dioxide and argon are fundamentally different.

The categories of modern chemistry, at least at the level of sophistication discussed here, are thus "element," "compound," "bond," and so forth. But these headings are not physical things: there is no material object we can point out as "element" itself, pure "bond," etc. In fact they are *ideals*. Chemistry is a theory with a physical subject and ideal categories. As a consequence, familiar physical things are now treated as having ideal properties. For instance substances such as iron (because they are elements) are regarded as inherently immutable during chemical transformations—not just usually immutable, or not hitherto transformed, but by their very nature not capable of being decomposed into anything else. If we start with an element in a closed container, no matter what chemical operations we perform on it we shall still have exactly that much of the element. An element is thus like an Euclidean point or an arithmetic prime number: it has an inherent property that belongs to it by definition. We may discover that a material thought to be an element is not an element—as happened in 1894 with atmospheric nitrogen—but such a discovery does not affect the category "element." It only changes the area of subject matter that we find fits the category. Similarly a compound is matter that (when purified) always contains two or more elements in a constant ratio. We describe a compound by writing the symbols for its elements with subscripts indicating the combining ratio, e.g. Fe_2O_3. In chemical theory this totally defines the material (ignoring isomers): one physical sample will be identical in its properties to any other. The ratio is an inherent part of the compound. The recently discovered solid solutions, which are in many ways similar to compounds but do not have fixed combining ratios, are not considered to be compounds. They fall under the category of "mixtures." Had they been well known in 1800, modern chemical theory as we know it might never have gotten off the ground.

So chemical categories are abstract descriptions. To find the subject of modern chemistry we explore physical reality; to find its categories we turn to another order of reality, to ideals. The theory as it exists today began to take shape toward the end of the eighteenth century, when a few thinkers began to conjecture that certain ideal concepts could be correlated with parts of the physical world. An ideal-physical "fit" had been conceived.

For comparison, consider modern chemistry's precursor, alchemy. Working with many of the same physical materials (often equally purified) it came up with an entirely different understanding. The categories of alchemical theory were behavioral:

> The first starting point for alchemical theory was Aristotle's *principle of development*: the conception that all material things, unless interfered with, will naturally change and develop—turning, when properly fed and nurtured, from an immature to a ripe or adult form. Rather than treating elementary matter as naturally inert and static, they thought of all things equally in a fundamentally *physiological* way.[12]

It had been believed for centuries that minerals "grew" organically in the earth. As a practical discipline, then, alchemy strove to reproduce the terrestrial womb in the laboratory, initiating and nourishing the gestation of one material into another, such as mercury and sulfur into gold. When considered from the alchemist's viewpoint, it was a perfectly reasonable idea.

Were we to formalize alchemical theory we would come up with categories such as "seed," "womb," and "nourishment." The process of transmutation was one of preparing a proper womb (typically the carefully heated retort or alembic), infusing it with the correct seed (such as a portion of gold around which more gold was to grow), and adding nourishment over a period of months, much like cultivating a plant. The theory's categories do not describe these parts of physical reality by their abstract properties, but by *what they do*. The womb promotes growth, the seed grows, the nourishment sustains the process. The same mercury that modern chemistry calls an immutable element alchemy characterized as a "food" that helps metals mature. This difference in categories is the difference between ideals and behavior, between reality that we know through its description and reality we know through its action. Because they subscribe to these opposing sets of theoretical categories, the modern chemist and the alchemist see the same physical maxima in radically different ways.

We may now make a rough "what" characterization of theories. A theory is a pattern of thought in which part of one order of reality is categorized by part of another. In my examples, modern chemistry categorizes parts of physical reality by ideals while alchemy categorizes essentially the same parts by behavior. This theorizing pattern occurs generally among the orders of reality, each being regularly categorized in human thought by the others.

The foregoing characterization of theorizing, however, seems to raise more questions than it answers. Why draw categories from a *different* order of reality than the subject? Are the categories of one theory always drawn from only one order of reality? Why theorize at all? I have tried to show that theorizing is a somewhat special kind of occupation, which requires considerable twisting of reality if it is to succeed. Every theory tries to categorize one type of thing in terms of a wholly unrelated type of thing. At first this sounds like a recipe for futility. Yet theories are conceived, are followed, are argued, and are used to achieve valuable results. There must be good reasons why we theorize. To understand them we must go one step further, to elucidate in general the "why" of theorizing.

2.2 Error

Nothing is so firmly believed as what we least know.
MONTAIGNE

It may sound paradoxical to assert that one purpose of theorizing is to define error, but this is so. It is meaningless to ascribe error to the natural events and existences of reality—things are simply "the way they are." But by theorizing we step outside the normal conceptual pathways of reality, because we bring together two parts that would not otherwise bear any relationship. By theorizing we gain a kind of perspective that manifests itself in the emergence of an idea of error. This idea then becomes an important factor in the development of our understanding of reality. Definitions of error are thus essential products of theorizing.

Try to imagine a "theory" in which parts of one order of reality are categorized by other parts of the *same* order: say, a "theory" about physical things using physical categories. For example, imagine adapting the theories of chemistry and alchemy just mentioned to this form. In all cases the starting point is a subject area consisting of a variety of relatively purified physical materials: crystals, gases, metals, solutions, powders, etc. In modern chemistry we approach these physical maxima with a set of ideal categories. We look for certain of them to be immutable, others to contain mathematical ratios of more basic materials, and so on. In alchemy we aproach them with a set of behavioral categories: we look for materials which will grow and change, which will assist or nourish other transformations, and so on. In the "theory" now proposed we must approach them with physical categories. For instance we now look for certain "physical forms," such as solid, liquid, or gas. We distinguish the metallic from the earthy, the dense from the light, the hard from the crumbly. In a slightly extended sense we are categorizing what Locke (1690) called the "primary qualities" of materials. They are the properties of physical things that we can grasp solely in physical terms. In the scheme of categorization proposed here we would have to be careful to avoid "secondary qualities"—color, taste, and so forth. As Locke pointed out, they depend both on the material and on the person experiencing them: colors appear differently if we are suffering from jaundice, taste sensations depend on what we have eaten last, etc. Characterizing something as "sweet" would be admissible only if sweetness could be identified purely in terms of physical effects; otherwise it would only be a loose way of saying it "tastes sweet," meaning that it does something to our mouths, which involves applying a behavioral category.

A formal description of physical reality using only physical categories seems strange because it does not appear to tell us anything. It only seems to rearrange the basis of our knowledge without adding any new information. When we decide to call such things as stone and wood "solids," such things as water and oil "liquids," and such things as air and steam "gases," without giving them behavioral properties, we are hardly doing more than repeating ourselves. Such a scheme is a natural and handy way of thought, but it does not yield *understanding*; it only brings the subject into more convenient form for further explanation. It takes things uncritically "as they are." I suggest we should call such a scheme not a theory at all, but rather *common sense*. By means of it we simply envision more physical maxima, without discrimination or analysis. Thus in my discussion the term "theory" will apply only when one order of reality is categorized by another; any scheme of categorization using one order alone will be "common sense."

This distinction between theories and common sense extends the discussion of Section 1.1. There I described how we explore physical reality by starting with whatever maxima happen to be before us (a book, a pencil, a teacup) and discovering how they interact with other things. As long as our exploration stays within this order of reality, as long as we do not (for instance) "interpret" physical reality using concepts of causation or mensuration, the resulting knowledge is commonsensical. It grasps physical reality "in its own terms." The same holds for behavior and ideals: each can be explored alone, "in its own terms." A commonsense grasp of behavior, for example, includes our thoughts and emotions just as "given," without either ideal categorizations (morals, ethics, valuations) or physical categorizations (external causes). A commonsense grasp of ideals explores them in abstraction, without treating them either as physical "forms" (e.g. geometric shapes) or as formalizations of thought (logic).

Thus common sense (as I treat it here) is the pure exploration of reality one order at a time. To the extent that it might be said to categorize reality at all, its categories are an integral part of the process of exploration. "Categorization" of this kind does not seem to us to produce "new knowledge." In exploring physical reality (for instance) we might note that certain materials are everywhere present in a container; certain others are present only in the bottom of a container; and yet others are present in arbitrary parts of a container. For convenience we may refer to these as gases, liquids, and solids. But such characterizations add little or nothing to our knowledge; they only tend to gather existing knowledge together.

Another way of putting this is to say that common sense is "uncritical." When we merely distinguish gases from other materials without otherwise characterizing them, we have come no closer to understanding them. We have not suggested "why" they are different, as the physicists' kinetic theory does. When we come across something new in this scheme (such as the discovery in 1937 of the superfluidity of liquid helium) common sense simply adds it to our knowledge of physical reality; it is the task of *theorizing* to discriminate it from other things. Limited to using descriptions drawn from the same order of reality, common sense can only tell us where the new object occurs in our overall transactions with the world. In this way our commonsense knowledge of any order of reality provides us with a basis for understanding it, i.e. with subjects for theorizing; but it is only theories themselves that probe and analyze these subjects, resulting in new understandings. They do this by borrowing categories from *other* orders of reality.

Why theorize? If common sense—the unilateral exploration of each order of reality—is a natural process of knowledge, why add an artificial process to it? A first approach to answering this question involves noting some very basic varieties of theorizing. The survival of any living organism requires a constant interchange between its behavior and physical reality. Physical stimuli (events in the physical environment) show up in behavior as perceptions of some sort; the organism's behavioral responses are realized physically as actions in the same environment. When this process takes place in ourselves some of the behavior lies in thought, where we may be directly aware of it. A pencil rolls off my desk; my perception of this physical event starts a "train of thought." Do I need the pencil right now? Is there another within reach? How easy will it be to retrieve it? At some point these considerations usually result in my getting down and reaching under the desk, a physical response. Our daily life is filled by incidents like this. Most of them take place on an "unconscious" level: that is, we are not explicitly aware of all the considerations entering into our reactions to the physical world. Generally speaking, we become aware of the process only when a problem arises that we cannot solve unconsciously. When I am driving a car, for example, I do not normally "think about" my driving, although the activity itself clearly uses my mind. It is only when an unusual situation arises—a car unexpectedly pulling out of line, a red light ahead, the sound of a horn or whatever—that I "become conscious" of what I am doing.

It is under such conditions, when the flow of commonsense interchanges between human behavior and physical events is broken, that theorizing becomes necessary. John Dewey analyzed this process at length.[13] Equating "knowledge" with what I call "theoretical knowledge," Dewey asked why it was created and what ends it served. His answer was that such knowledge formed an intermediate step between two stages of "experience." The first stage is what I call common sense: for Dewey a blend of instinct with habit in which the human organism lives in a sort of symbiotic relationship with its environment. A conflict or "tension" in this situation produces the need for knowledge. Satisfaction of the need demands discursive intellectual thought, the consummation of which is the removal of conflict. Since knowledge is sought only for this purpose—dealing with one's environment—it is all literally "experimental." Moreover for Dewey it is never an end in itself but leads immediately to a higher stage of experience that is richer, more orderly, and more fully "aware" than the first:

> Speaking then from the standpoint of temporal order, we find reflection, or thought, occupying an intermediate and reconstructive position. It comes between a temporally prior situation (an organized interaction of factors) of active and appreciative experience, wherein some of the factors have become discordant and incompatible, and a later situation, which has become constituted out of the first situation by means of acting on the findings of reflective inquiry. The final situation therefore has a richness of meaning, as well as a controlled character lacking in the original.[14]

In Dewey's analysis theorizing "elevates" common sense to a new level of capability in dealing with reality. It does this whenever we find that common sense "doesn't work." The present analysis extends this concept: theorizing "reconstructs" common sense by permitting us to *question* it. When a problem arises in the interplay between my thoughts and physical reality (for instance), common sense fails to achieve a solution because it treats each order of reality in its own terms. I am forced to understand the problem either wholly physically or wholly mentally, and cannot adjudicate between these two independent positions. A theory allows me to compare the two viewpoints; when I do, one result of this comparison is a concept of *error*.

For example, suppose a penny and a dime are on the table in front of me. I want to know which is larger. My physical common sense tells me the penny is larger; in the behavioral common sense of my sensations the penny also appears larger. So far there is no problem and no need to theorize. But suppose the penny and dime are placed on a drawing of converging lines, creating an optical illusion in which the dime appears larger. My behavioral common sense (which is capable only of accepting my sensations uncritically) now tells me the dime is larger. Yet physical common sense still claims the dime is smaller. There now exists a conflict which can manifest itself in several ways: for instance I might find my efforts to cover up the penny with the "larger" dime frustrated.

To resolve the conflict I resort to a *theory of perception*. It states that my thoughts of a certain kind are "physical images"; in other words, it applies physical categories to my thought behavior. Among these categories will be "disc images" (or images of flat things or of coins themselves, at various levels of categorization), which separate and identify the sensations I have of coins, and in particular of these coins. The theory will also have categories identifying relative size, under which other parts of my thought behavior will fall. Using this theory, I will then be able to understand that one sensation I have refers to the physical penny and another refers to the physical dime, while the thought I have that the dime is larger than the penny refers to their relative physical size. Such a theory of perception (even in the rudimentary form sketched here) now provides me with a vital new piece of knowledge, for I already know from my commonsense grasp of physical reality that the penny is actually larger: therefore a conflict or error exists. Applying the theory further allows me to locate the source of the conflict: by moving the two coins around until the penny appears larger (i.e. the conflict disappears) I discover that the perceptual problem occurs only when they are on the drawing of converging lines. This may then become the starting point for enriching my common sense with an understanding of optical illusions, central to which will be a notion of erroneous perceptions.

It is important to realize that no understanding of just one order of reality by itself can yield any idea of error in a situation such as this. Suppose we had an elaborate body of knowledge about physical reality without any understanding of behavior. We would then have to describe my judgment about the relative sizes of the coins as a string of purely physical events. Such an understanding would assert that when discs of various sizes are placed before me, my mouth will tend to make certain sounds ("statements" about them). It will turn out that the sounds made by my mouth will be different if a converging line pattern is placed under the discs. But there will be no way (within purely physical knowledge) to decide that one sound pattern is "correct" and the other is "incorrect"; both must be regarded simply as natural products of the existing physical conditions. That is, the only description purely physical knowledge could make of the optical illusion would be to specify that my mouth makes certain sounds when discs are on a plain background and different sounds when they are on a lined background. The description could not be made to yield any specification of error, nor would it make any sense to label one pattern of sounds "erroneous." Similarly, suppose we understood behavior but had no knowledge of physical reality. Our knowledge would now specify that when I have a sensation of a plain background my image of the coppery disc appears larger than that of the silvery one, but when I have a sensation of converging lines in the background the reverse is true. Both cases would have to be treated as equally valid and complete sets of sensations; in the absence of *any* knowledge of physical reality neither could be identified as "erroneous." In general, every time we try to describe reality in terms of our knowledge of just one order we find that the very notion of "error" is extraneous and cannot be included.

The conclusion just stated is uniformly true throughout the whole of knowledge. When we explore reality our understanding expands within each of its independent orders—physical, behavioral, ideal. Within any one order we may come to know more and more, but can never frame an idea of error. These parts are simply connected as they are, and we must accept them uncritically. But when we *compare* two orders of reality—as in the example just given, when we compare our knowledge of our sensations (in behavior) with our knowledge of our physical surroundings—then we begin to comprehend that one may be "incorrect" with respect to the other. This is the case for all combinations of orders.

I have just illustrated how behavior may be understood to be erroneous with respect to physical fact. Conversely, physical events may be understood to be erroneous with respect to behavior, as when we intend to perform a certain physical act but end up doing something else. I wanted to pick up the pencil, but pushed it off the desk instead. Characterizing such an occurrence as "incorrect" becomes possible only when we simultaneously understand the behavior willed or intended and the physical actions done.

Theorizers frame ideas of correctness and incorrectness between *ideals* and physical reality in the same way. This is the starting point for modern science. Scientists assume that for any given set of physical facts there is an ideal description; and if the description is "correct" it will yield, by logical processes within ideals, other descriptions for which there must be corresponding physical facts. This, in capsule form, is the process of induction, prediction, and verification that is commonly taken to be the core of scientific method.

Depending on whether the scientist is a theoretician or a practitioner, when a discrepancy appears between ideal formulas and physical facts he will attribute the problem either to an erroneous description or an incorrectly done physical experiment. Either way the discrepancy spurs new investigations, leading to an enlargement of knowledge. It is part of the accepted folklore of science that when facts do not "verify" formulas the latter are re-written, although as I mentioned earlier this scenario is largely honored in the breach. A more common outcome is the revision of experimental technique under the same circumstances. The discovery of argon gas in 1894 (for instance) resulted when measurements of the specific gravity of nitrogen derived from its compounds and that of nitrogen extracted from the air turned out to be different in the third decimal place. At that late date it would have been too deep a violation of physical theory to allow a variation in specific gravity to result from the provenance of an element; so the only alternative was that cne or the other measurement was incorrect. Eventually it was discovered that atmospheric nitrogen as it was then extracted contained over two percent argon gas, a hitherto unknown material. Thus was our knowledge of physical reality enlarged. Similarly, Szent-Gyorgi discovered Vitamin C by observing a brief delay (less than a second) in the progress of a commonly performed chemical reaction. Such observations of events that are "incorrect" with respect to our ideal expectations are a frequent source of new data in science.

These examples illuminate the question: why do we need a concept of error? Common sense is capable of exploring reality without identifying error, by the separate development of our knowledge of the physical cosmos, behavior, and ideals. Why then do we press our commonsense knowledge into parallelisms, categorizing one order of reality by means of another, just to apprehend places where they conflict? The reason is that this is a highly efficient way to find "new reality." In the instances just mentioned (the discoveries of argon and Vitamin C) it is unlikely chemists would have stumbled across these materials without the impetus of anomalous occurrences. The error between fact and formula was crucial. In the earlier example, my awareness that the relative sizes of two coins in my perception can be altered by their background leads to the discovery of optical illusions. Many such examples could be cited.

What happens here is that theorizing provides us with a means, artificial but useful, for separating "old knowledge" from "new knowledge." Error is a sort of signpost that alerts us to the direction in which new knowledge lies. Through the scientific categorization of physical reality by ideals we encapsulate large areas of physical knowledge, treating them as "already known." The scientist does not have to determine the physical properties of everything he uses in an experiment, because scientific theory tells him that they will be the same as the properties of previously measured "like" objects. Thus his observations may focus on the new and anomalous. A theory of behavioral perception tells me I need not test the solidity of my desk before laying a pencil on it, because it is solid if it "looks" solid. Such a theory obviously saves me a great deal of trouble, and frees my understanding for circumstances in which my perceptions encounter difficulties. When we discuss the relations between ideals and behavior, as Plato frequently did, we need not constantly review the bulk of human life, because most of its ideal characterizations are commonly agreed. Instead we concentrate on the crucial or "poorly understood" instances (such as "true justice") where traditional ideal-behavioral correspondences do not seem to fit. In all such cases, when error crops up in our comparisons it is a signal that new knowledge is at hand.

Dewey noted that theorizing occurs in response to a problem in common sense. We can invert this slightly by saying that theorizing enlarges common sense by identifying its problems. Theorizing defines error, and error shows in which new direction our common sense may grow. This is the "why" of theorizing: it is an efficient means for indicating to us what we don't yet know.

Our understanding of any order of reality, however well developed, is of course an understanding of only *part* of reality itself. This is what is meant by separating reality into orders. As we explore any such part, eventually we must come to its "boundary," beyond which lies another order. At first we will try to fit what we find into our existing understanding. But in most cases this attempt will eventually fail; we must search for understanding in another order of reality. The signal that tells us this is necessary is our consciousness of error. At exactly those places where our knowledge fails as a full explanation of reality we become aware that something is "erroneous" with respect to something else—a thought with respect to a fact, an action with respect to an intention, a fact with respect to a formula, etc. The experience of error jogs us out of common sense and forces us to theorize. Thus we turn our attention from one type of maxima to an entirely different type, from one order of reality to another. Making this transition through an awareness of error is the principle outcome of theorizing, and the desirability of making it is the principle reason we theorize.

2.3 Method

> If a man begin with certainties, he shall end in
> doubts; but if he will be content to begin with doubts he
> shall end in certainties.
> FRANCIS BACON

How is theorizing done? I have discussed generally what theories are and why we build them; the last topic in this series of characterizations is an examination of the general theorizing method.

In Section 2.1 I mentioned theorizing "styles" and related them to the theorizer's selection of categories. For instance, a theory about physical reality using ideal categories (typical of modern science) displays a style wholly different from that of an animistic theory about the same subject, using behavioral categories. Ideal categorization, in this case, gives our understanding of physical events a quality of rigorousness and absoluteness, the security of knowing that ineluctable forces are everywhere and eternally operating in accordance with unbreakable laws. Behavioral categorization, on the other hand, produces a theory that is more flexible and dynamic, in which our relationship with physical events is an important factor in our understanding them. From a scientific viewpoint any theory that inspires the natives of Dobu to cajole their yams and mutter incantations to canoes and fishnets misses the point because it fails to touch on the absolute principles involved; while to a Dobuan the scientists' talk about invisible particles, forces existing in a vacuum, and laws enforced by no one would seem so remote and contrived a description of reality as to be utterly without interest. And it seems both are at least partly right. Just as a Dobuan could not run a scientific laboratory without adopting ideal categories, so no scientist could feed himself on Dobu (or anywhere else, for that matter) without using behavioral categories.

To the foregoing two styles we can add a third, resulting when we adopt physical categories. Physically categorized theories have a quality of being externally determined in a changeable, contingent way. They tend to follow

63

the subject matter, wherever it may lead. For example, consider language behavior. We can simply use a language without thinking about it, in which case to the extent we categorize it at all our categories are also behavioral; this constitutes the "common sense" of any language. Or we can theorize about it. When we theorize about language behavior we have two choices: ideal categories or physical categories

Ideal categorization in language theorizing leads to the discipline of *logic*. In modern symbolic logic, for instance, the "sentential calculus" interprets ordinary language expressions such as "grass is green" into "sentential functions" where a string of symbols is read in some such way as "for all x, if x is grass, then x is green." The intent of this theory is to "formalize" common speech by revealing its abstract underlying principles. The *physical* categorization of language, on the other hand, results in theories of grammar and lexicography. It discriminates language on the basis of the physical things or events words and phrases "represent." For instance we distinguish nouns, verbs, and adjectives because they refer to physically distinguishable entities—objects, actions, and qualities. A good dictionary usually attempts to relate specific fragments of language to physical facts even when words refer to pure behavior, such as emotional states. Without physical references that ultimately tie word meanings to things that can be pointed out, dictionary definitions tend to become vague and circular. The same holds when we try to learn an unfamiliar language without an interpreter: we point to things and indicate physical actions in order to elicit the kinds of language behavior that "represent" them.

For convenience in the following discussion I will epitomize the three general theorizing styles by three words that more or less connote their characteristics. I will say that physical categories make a theory "objective," behavioral categories make it "usable," and ideal categories make it "logical." Thus, for example, scientific theories that depend heavily on abstractions are logical but not very usable; they are not handy for everyday living. Theories that categorize things by their behavior are usable but not very logical. Dictionaries, in which language behavior is categorized physically, are objective but not very logical; they tell us what words "mean" even when the meanings are vague or contradictory.

These epitomizations of theorizing styles are not as arbitrary as it may at first seem. As I will discuss in more detail in Section 3, living things in general have evolved their tripartite grasp of reality to fill specific needs. Briefly, I will examine how life arose out of physical reality by the evolution of responsive machines (organisms) in a favorable thermodynamic situation. Such machines are physical and must constantly respond to physical events.

64

Objectivity—being responsive to facts—reflects life's earliest need to follow the exigencies of physical existence; any organism that is not objective perishes. At a later stage of evolution it became additionally important for organisms to understand each other's behavior. Those that did were more successful in capturing food, reproducing, and so on. Knowledge of behavior made life aware of a world that related directly to its needs and goals: it added the "use factor" to knowledge. Finally, first species and then individuals acquired a grasp of ideals, ultimately generating the human capacity to be logical. Logic is an efficient method for organizing very complex behavior, for classifying and setting aside all factors that do not pertain to present goals. Ideals make it possible for life to sort out behavior techniques "in general," remembering those that are successful and forgetting those that are not.

Thus we (as living things) have evolved three different approaches to reality, which show up in our common sense as a grasp of three separate "orders." Depending on circumstances, our understanding of reality must be in turn objective, usable, and logical. When we create theories we derive categories from common sense, applying them to otherwise unrelated areas. These categories carry with them the qualities we have learned to recognize in reality, lending them to new subject matters. In this way our selection of categories tends to give theories distinct qualities of being objective, usable, or logical.

Although apparent theory characteristics are derived primarily from their categories, subject matters also play a role. Because these are the sole characteristics of our commonsense viewpoints, *any* theory about physical reality must try to be objective, *any* theory about behavior must try to be usable, and *any* theory about ideals must try to be logical. If they are not, theorizing will ultimately challenge common sense and common sense will win. But such subject-oriented characteristics of theories appear principally in a negative form, as "warnings." It is a serious defect if a physical theory strays too far from objectivity or a theory about behavior is too patently useless or a theory about ideals is plainly illogical. Yet these defects are not always evident. Theories are "self-protective": they typically define potential defects in terms of their own categories, so that they retain control over the concepts of their own verification as much as possible. For instance, in scientific disciplines using ideal categories the ostensive test of "loss of objectivity" is the demonstration of a single counter-example. If a theory predicts event "A" and event "not-A" happens instead, then the theory is taken to be not objective, and should be revised. But this is a *logical* test for objectivity, based on a presumed applicability of the "law of contradiction." Compare this with the Dobuan theory of physical events (using

behavioral categories) described in Section 2.1. Their theory tolerates contradiction easily, and no demonstration of counter-examples alone will
destroy it. When European missionaries grew yams without incantations the
logical consequences of this fact did not drive the Dobuans to revise their
beliefs, because any threat to their theory would have to be *behaviorally*
characterized. Only the demonstration of the working of a more effective
incantation—i.e. a more usable theory—would convince a Dobuan that he
had not been fully objective in his approach, that he had not been appealing
to yams in the way they demand. Thus the scientist's criticism of animism as
being illogical is derived from his own view of reality, and is no more
inherently valid than the animist's criticism of science as being unusable.

An inspection of various theories shows that, in general, the characteristics they get from their categories tend to be dominant. In effect, each theory
promises to show us its subject in a new light, regardless of how we have
seen the subject before. Unless its new depiction is an outlandish violation of
our existing common sense about the subject, our tendency is to let the
theory work its charm. An important factor in its success is then the degree to
which it also revises our notions of verification. This is how (for instance)
science and animism can make the same physical events seem to be controlled logically from one viewpoint and explained behaviorally from another:
both approaches violate common sense (by mixing up our understanding of
the orders of reality) but cause us to ignore the violations by redefining our
methods for detecting error itself.

It is at this stage that the postulation of *minima* becomes essential to
theorizing. The problem is that categorization itself is a form of error. From
the viewpoint of common sense, categorization attempts to relate two parts
of reality that are *inherently unrelatable* because we understand them in
totally different ways. Theorizing tries to convince us (for instance) that
physical things have ideal properties when our entire common sense tells us
that physical things and ideals are two distinct kinds of reality. Were we
simply to propose a scheme of categorization in all its nakedness—"we have
decided to treat physical things as if they had ideal properties"—we would
just be laughed at, as Aristotle laughed at the Pythagoreans. But successful
theorizers are more subtle. *What they do is "bury" the inherent error in
theorizing by "discovering" minima.* Minima solidify categorizations by
providing concrete objects of knowledge for their justification. At the same
time, categorizations support minima by giving us reasons for treating them
as real. The end result is that in any theory we decide (usually implicitly) to
adopt a set of fictions in the form of concepts of minima. These constitute

66

fixed, unanalyzable points that "pin" the theory together and convince us to accept it.

Although minima are posited to "bury" the error of categorization in all types of theories—not just physical theories using ideal categories—this process is particularly clear in modern physics. We can even discover approximately when the burial took place, and who did it. Isaac Newton's unprecedented success in achieving a physical-ideal "fit"—his extraordinary ability to draw up correlations between the physical observations of his day and the elegant mathematical formulas that became their "laws"—obscured his shortcomings as a philosopher. The need to justify such correlations in general became ignored as his theorizing matured. In his early work Newton was meticulous in resisting all arbitrary "hypotheses," all guiding ideas not derived from unquestionable experience; but later he unwittingly compromised by concealing his "hypotheses" within the selection of the basic ways he would describe reality. They became embodied in his general choice of such minima as mass and forces. E. A. Burtt, in his critical work *The Metaphysical Foundations of Modern Science*, points out this transition (my italics):

> Do not the very initial experiments and observations, as a result of which the mathematical behavior of phenomena is defined, presuppose something which we can only speak of as an hypothesis, to direct those experiments to a successful issue? In the days of his early optical labors Newton would not have entirely refused assent; there are sometimes hypotheses which definitely 'can be an aid to experiments.' But in his classic writings even such guiding ideas seem to be denied place and function. Apparently we need an hypothesis only in this very general sense, namely the expectation that inasmuch as nature has hitherto revealed herself as being to a large extent, a simple and uniform mathematical order, *there are exact quantitative aspects and laws in any group of phenomena* which *simplifying* experiments will enable us to detect...[15]

Thus by selectively treating certain parts of reality as both physical and ideal Newton instituted a legacy that persists in physics to this day. He established the idea that a "search" for physical-mathematical minima was prerequisite to ultimate knowledge about physical reality.

Ordinarily such a search would violate common sense. Yet we tolerate it because it seems to be an integral part of the normal process of theorizing, which we accept. As I described it earlier, theorizing is a process of laying one order of reality alongside another to create a "fit." Because we understand any theory's categories in an entirely different way than we understand the reality categorized, the fit is never perfect. In fact we can find error at any point we choose. Under the rubric of "conventionalism" Henri Poincaré pointed out early in this century that for any given mathematical expression and any given set of physical facts, a set of ''operational definitions'' could be devised that would make the mathematical expression a ''valid'' description of the facts. Conversely, a set of operational definitions can always be written that will make the expression invalid or erroneous with respect to the facts. The obvious reply to this is that some operational definitions are immensely more complex than others, and we are justified in insisting on the simplest. For instance the operational definitions required to make the Pythagorean theorem $A^2 + B^2 = C^2$ represent Newton's law of gravity would be so complex and clumsy that no one would accept them in the foundations of a valid theory. In *Foundations of Physics*, Philipp Frank sums up this position as follows:

> The equations, by themselves, are said to be 'valid' or confirmable by experiments only if, by substituting 'simple and practical' operational definitions, they become confirmed physical laws. This does not exclude that, by admitting all imaginable operational definitions, almost any system of equations could be converted into confirmed laws, provided that the system is not self-contradictory. If we consistently make the distinction between 'simple and practical' operational definitions and arbitrary definitions which may be 'complicated and impractical,' it becomes clear in what sense the general laws of physics are purely conventional and in what sense they are valid assertions about facts.[16]

In rebuttal, P. W. Bridgman has pointed out by an elaborate analysis what the operational definition of even such a basic physicist's term as ''energy'' would have to be.[17] It turns out to be of staggering complexity and requires many of what he calls ''pencil and paper operations.'' Yet this has not driven physical theoreticians to abandon ''energy'' as a fundamental category.

Even in the highly rigorous discipline of theoretical physics, the inherent unbridgeable gap between its two orders of reality (mathematical ideals and physical events) is hardly ever admitted. When the parallelism seems to work, when new mathematical descriptions lead to new physical insights, the difference tends to be ignored. We read statements such as this by the physicist P. A. M. Dirac (1963):

> It seems to be one of the fundamental features of nature that fundamental physical laws are described in terms of a mathematical theory of great beauty and power, needing quite a high standard of mathematics for one to understand it... One could perhaps describe the situation by saying that God is a mathematician of a very high order, and He used very advanced mathematics in constructing the universe. Our feeble attempts at mathematics enable us to understand a bit of the universe, and as we proceed to develop higher and higher mathematics we can hope to understand the universe better.[18]

Yet when physicists are less sanguine, when their research uncovers mathematically intractable effects and their formulas seem to mock at common sense, their attitude may swing in the other direction. At these times their implicit standpoint might better be represented by Einstein's oft-quoted dictum: "So far as the theorems of mathematics are about reality they are not certain; and so far as they are certain they are not about reality."

A basic difficulty with the operationalist defense of physical science— claiming that its formulas are "valid assertions about facts" because their correspondences can be established by adopting "simple and practical" operational definitions—is that it begs the question. For any given set of facts and system of formulas declared to be valid assertions about the facts by virtue of "simple and practical" operational definitions, a set of *even more* "simple and practical" operational definitions can always be found that will *invalidate* the formulas. In other words, science assumes for a given set of physical facts that some system of formulas must be applicable. It then selects that system of formulas which can be applied by means of the simplest operational definitions, rejecting other systems that require more complex justifications. But it does not accept even simpler operational definitions if they result in no system of formulas being validated, because *its purpose has been to fit formulas, not to find simple operational definitions*. In this way the question of whether, for a given set of physical facts, there exists *any* system of formulas that are "a valid assertion" about them is begged.

The source of this difficulty becomes clear when it is expressed in terms of the present analysis. Any identification of "simple and practical operational definitions" requires the inclusion of behavioral categories in a physical theory, in addition to the ideal categories embodied in its mathematical formulas. "Simple" and "practical" are qualities that can be understood only by referring to behavior. But a theory becomes inconsistent when it uses both ideal and behavioral categories, particularly when their application is in a sense reciprocal—when a variety of different ideal categories could be "validated" by choosing suitable behavioral categories and vice versa. To achieve consistency any theory must draw categories from only one order of reality. If scientists retain the behavioral categories and follow them through, the ideal categories evaporate, because as I mentioned the simplest and most practical operational definitions of physical fact yield the conclusion that *no* ideal equations are "valid" for it. Conversely if they retain the ideal categories then these must be judged by their own logical characteristics; they may not be further discriminated in terms of our convenience in applying them.

In this dilemma, minima come to the rescue. By asserting the reality of a minimum we posit that two independent orders of reality actually meet at a certain point. This seems to establish an absolute justification for their parallel "fit" in that region. For instance in physics, where ideal formulas are being fitted to physical facts, asserting the reality of "particles" constitutes something like adopting an operational definition without seeming to. The particle concept simultaneously idealizes something physical and "physicalizes" part of our ideal formulas. Particles are physical because they are the ultimate constituents of matter, make tracks in our cloud chambers, cause scintillations in our detectors, and so forth; at the same time they are ideal because they are indivisible, always have the same properties, are immutable, and can be totally characterized by mathematical expressions. In a theory about particles we cannot doubt that physical reality and ideals meet. Do you doubt their physical existence? Then take your radium-painted wristwatch into a dark room and *see* particles bursting from the dial. Do you doubt their ideal nature? Then consider the numerical constants for their mass, charge, etc., which completely define them and which have been verified by a multitude of experiments. With evidence such as this, ideal-physical theorizing comes alive.

Positing minima satisfies the same need as adopting "operational definitions." Minima solidify a theoretical "fit" between two orders of reality; they promote the theory that hypostatizes them from mere supposition to an apparent description of actuality. So characterized, they may sound like simple conjurers' tricks. But minima are what make theorizing work, and theorizing does expand knowledge. For instance the particle concept does help enlarge our understanding of reality: not the "reality" of particles, for we have already crippled ourselves in this area, but reality elsewhere. On the one hand particle research encourages us to build new and hitherto unimagined machines for manipulating small masses at enormous energies, as well as instruments of great sensitivity for recording the histories of minute and brief physical events. On the other hand it stimulates mathematicians to investigate areas of ideals (such as theories of transformations) that would not otherwise be discovered or deemed to have interest. All this constitutes a genuine exploration of reality. Out of it comes new knowledge of highly unusual areas of physical and ideal reality, which we would never have thought to examine had we not first adopted the notion of tiny particles moving through space. Out of it will eventually come whole new insights to add to our present common sense, and from *them* will come new theories in which particle concepts will probably play no part.

What happens in actual theorizing is that minima are posited to justify our adopting a "fit" between two orders of reality, and subsequent explorations radiate outward (within each order) from those points. Later on these explorations may suggest a better fit. If the better fit is adopted we "slide" the correspondence and then justify it by positing new minima, often thereby abandoning the old ones. For example the eighteenth century theory of heat posited a minimum which Lavoisier christened "caloric"—a fluid that flowed from hot bodies to cold ones. Its reality was defended much as that of particles is today. Do you doubt the physical existence of caloric? Then put a poker in the fire and watch it soak it up. Do you doubt its ideal nature? Then examine Lavoisier's formulas, by which its motions are thoroughly described, quantized, and predicted. What finally killed caloric was the particle theorizing inspired by Newton and Dalton. With the development of principles relating the pressure, volume, and temperature of gases (by Boyle and Mariotte) it became clear that heat could be understood better as a manifestation of particle motions than as a monolithic fluid. "Kinetic energy" became a new minimum, and explorations of reality proceeded from that point. The theoretical alignment of ideals with physical fact had been altered in such a way that the existence of caloric was no longer needed to justify it, so the concept was dropped from physics.

Thus there is a process of mutual support between theories and the concepts of minima that they manufacture. Minima make a theory seem "realistic," while at the same time the theory supports our belief in the existence of its minima. Because the categorizations of any theory are potentially erroneous at every point of their application, we must destroy our sensibility of error at one or more points before a theory becomes workable. Minima do this job, which is why they have become a mainstay of theorizing. Using them as unquestioned "fasteners" between two different orders of reality, we establish a theoretical alignment; this then inspires us to dig about in neighboring areas, discovering new maxima that ultimately lodge in our common sense. Whenever we discover a better theoretical alignment we shift our categorizations, usually in the process dropping old minima and positing new ones. This (in most general terms) is how we theorize.

A philosophical point is worth noting here. Some epistemologists have placed a great deal of emphasis on defining a class of facts of which we can be "most certain." Claims have been made at various times for the absolute certainty of mathematical truths, of individual sensations, and of the existence of God. Now in comparing our ideas of maxima with our ideas of minima, one of their striking differences is that as maxima become larger (within the limits of our understanding) we become more certain of them, while as minima become smaller they become more problematic. Thus as I

71

sit here I am fairly certain that there is something I call a pencil lying on something I understand to be a table; my certainty is not absolute because it is tempered by the realization that I might be suffering from a temporary hallucination or someone might have arranged a clever illusion while I was out of the room. I am considerably more certain that there are pencils and tables somewhere, even if not here now. I am most certain that there is a physical world in general containing things like pencils and tables. That the whole physical world is not an illusion, although parts of it may be, is one of the most certain facts I know.

Going in the other direction, the fact that the wood of the pencil is made up of cells is something of which I am less certain than that it is lying on the table in front of me. The evidence for this requires me to make several assumptions about microscopes and optical theory. Finally the idea that it is "ultimately" composed of subatomic particles (or quarks) is the kind of fact of which I am least certain. For that I must accept a mass of theory "explaining" what would at first appear to be irrelevant pictures of cloud chamber tracks and records of pointer readings made by incredibly complicated machines.

The difference here is not so much the number of assumptions demanded by minima (as opposed to maxima), but rather *where these assumptions lie*. In the case of my being certain of the physical world as a whole my assumptions are all drawn from the same order of reality. My common sense has categorized physical things physically, in a picture that "all hangs together." But in the case of my being certain of such things as subatomic particles, I must apply a large body of non-physical "accessory" facts. If I do not believe it is valid to associate with every particle a number representing its "energy," for instance, then cloud chamber pictures will become meaningless for me as depictions of reality. Looking at them will not make me certain of anything. The key to successful theorizing is that we are willing to make such associations, and are led thereby to hypostatize minima. The key to common sense is that we avoid them, and are led thereby to understand maxima. As minima become more "fundamental," the association between separate orders of reality on which they depend becomes more tenuous, and we become less certain of their existence. This is a general epistemological defect that is intrinsic to theorizing itself.

2.4 Structuralism

> In a world in search of meaning and an understanding of itself, structuralism has given voice to a new view, a new 'myth' which has been recognized and seized by many people, each in his own way.
>
> DeGeorge

In recent years a style of theorizing has arisen, particularly among French thinkers, called "structuralism." Although frequently pursued in the confused state typical of methodologies in their formative stages, structuralism embodies ideas that purport to alleviate some of the theorizing defects I have been discussing. Thus it merits a brief review here.

At present the name "structuralism" is used fairly indiscriminately to cover a mixture of theorizing approaches, which accounts for the universal difficulty its practitioners find in defining it. Two of these approaches, although central to the structuralist idea and a subject of controversy to many thinkers, have already been treated here and so need only be mentioned.

First is the idea of an independent reality called "behavior," neither chimerical nor reducible to physical events. This attitude echoes Descartes, a primary source of French philosophy: in explaining his famous *"cogito, ergo sum"* Descartes defined the subject of *"sum"* (the "I" of "I am") as "a being which doubts, which understands, which affirms, which denies, which wills, which rejects, which also imagines, and which perceives."[19] Such a "being" is clearly a part of the behavioral order of reality, in the terminology used here. However, the independent existence of behavior is by no means universally admitted by philosophers and scientists. One of the struggles of structuralism (which originated in such behavioral disciplines as linguistics, anthropology, literature, and psychology) has been to establish the validity of making assertions about pure behavior. For instance Howard Gardner (*The Quest for Mind*) writes:

...the structurally-oriented social scientist typically models himself after a natural scientist. ...All these scientists may be said to be searching for the

73

structural components, and the underlying structure, of the physical or biological world; they do so by seeking units which they can see (like cells) or which, though invisible, can in some sense be said to have a physical existence (like atoms). The social scientist, by contrast, deals with behavior, with institutions, with thoughts, beliefs, fears, dreams. At various times, it has been claimed that these do not exist and therefore should not be studied, or, alternatively, that they do exist and are as physical as cells or crystals. The structuralists subscribe to neither view. They believe that behavior and institutions do have a structure, and not merely in a trivial or metaphorical sense, but that this structure will never be visible or tangible; nonetheless, that it is incumbent upon the investigator to ferret it out and to map its dimensions, in clear, preferably formal or mathematical language.[20]

The other part of the structuralist approach treated in the present discussion is the idea of categorizing behavior ideally. Note the reference to this at the end of the foregoing quotation. The elaborate formulations developed by Lévi-Strauss to define the "structures" of kinship relations and traditional myths are examples of this approach. They represent an attempt to achieve for theories of behavior what mathematical formulas achieve for theories of physical reality: namely to describe in symbolic and logical form the properties that a theory finds common to a variety of separate subjects. In this there is nothing extraordinary. In fact we might wonder that it has taken so long for studies of behavior to achieve the kind of "Newtonian revolution"—ideal categorization—that studies of physical reality enjoyed more than two centuries ago.

But there is a third approach arising from structuralism that is truly new. This is the idea of combining physical, behavioral, and ideal categories into a single explanatory device that will make *uniform* theoretical treatments of all subject matters feasible. One of the pioneers of structuralism, Maurice Merleau-Ponty, introduces the term "form" in this role. After delineating three separate orders of reality corresponding to those described here, but characterized from a phenomenological and Sartrean viewpoint, he writes:

It is here that the notion of form would permit a truly new solution. Equally applicable to the three fields which have just been defined, it would integrate them as three types of structures by surpassing the antinomies of materialism and mentalism, of materialism and vitalism. Quantity, order and value or signification, which pass respectively for the properties of matter, life and mind, would no longer be but the dominant characteristic in the order considered and would become universally applicable categories.[21]

Contained here is the germ of an idea: if we treat all reality structurally we might be able to theorize successfully from a single set of universal categories, because the structural approach combines physical, behavioral, and ideal viewpoints. This idea would occur naturally to theorizers who are trying to categorize behavior by ideals borrowed from the physical sciences. Since their data would tend to remain physical (sounds and marks in linguistics, the observed actions of primitive people in anthropology, etc.) any theory about the associated behavior that does not include some form of physical categorization is immediately subject to attack as "not objective." When wholly separated from physical embodiments, behavior theories either float off into mystical introspection or become moralistic, both of which tendencies type them as "unscientific."

Hence it is a clever approach to say that behavior is being characterized "structurally." The idea of structure has a sufficiently physical flavor to suggest objectivity, without losing the flexibility of categorization by ideal formulas. For instance when Lévi-Strauss finds two primitive myths to be similar because they can both be defined by the same string of quasi-mathematical expressions, he flies in the face of traditional anthropological theorizing, which would relate them (if at all) on the basis of the similar physical needs or situations of the mythmakers. Traditionalists will complain that his abstractions are pure inventions and that he is not being objective. But when he claims they have the same *structure*, even though his reason for saying so is that they "conform" to the same abstract formula, it sounds more concrete. If things like atoms and bridges have structures, why shouldn't myths and rituals also have structures? In this way the idea of structure permits abstract studies of behavior to flourish within a scientific community heavily dedicated to physical theorizing.

From another standpoint, structural theorizing is not all that new. The physicists' concept of a "field," which dates back at least to Maxwell, refers to a structure in the modern sense. Just as the structural notions cited above were devised to relate ideals and behavior without losing objectivity (the characteristic of physical categorization), so the physicists' field was devised to relate ideals and physical reality without losing usability, the characteristic of behavioral categorization. Maxwell discerned that the electromagnetic phenomena discovered by Faraday and others could be described by a set of equations, but these alone would not give us a usable concept of what was happening. Merely writing a set of partial differential equations on a blackboard does not satisfy our need to visualize what occurs (say) between the poles of a magnet. Calling them "field equations" did the trick. The equations became treated as defining a set of "potentials" for each point of space surrounding the magnet, which in turn determined what events might occur there. It is as if we had created a race of "behaving points'' around the magnet, instructed by the field equations how to perform physical actions. Eventually it even became legitimate to visualize the avowed fiction of "lines of force,"—tracks that events "tended" to follow—adding a further behavioral cast to the original abstractions.

In more formal terms, the physicists' field may be defined as a set of quantities closed under a set of functions. The quantities are what we are capable of measuring physically in any part of the field: space-time location, mass, electric charge, etc. They can be treated as determiners of all possible physical occurrences in the field. The functions relate the quantities to each other in a compact and continuous way, so we can describe abstractly their mutual variations. Usually we are specifically interested in how the other quantities vary with respect to space-time location: so we collect the quantities into "tensors" and thereby assign to each point of space-time a bundle of measurements, as if a tiny observer were reporting the potentials for physical action at that point. Note that the tensors are not understood to have tangible physical existence in themselves; instead, they describe how the field "behaves." The very important requirement of "closure" disciplines this arrangement. It forces us to make sure that the field functions do not describe any measurements that could not actually be made.

One of the attractions of field theorizing to some physicists is the possibility that it can dispense with traditional minima. A particle, for instance, shows up in the field picture as a "singularity": something other than a bundle of measurements, which by its very existence violates the closure of the field. Einstein's attempts to formulate a unified field theory for physics were never concluded because he could not achieve a single closed representation of both gravitational and electromagnetic effects. Nevertheless he envisioned the possibility of a structural theory freed from certain ideas of minima:

> ...What appears certain to me, however, is that, in the foundations of any consistent field theory, there shall not be, in addition to the concept of field, any concept concerning particles. The whole theory must be based solely on partial differential equations and their singularity-free solutions.[22]

To round out a survey of structural conceptualizations consider their oldest and commonest embodiment, the engineering treatment of complex physical objects. An engineer designing a scaffolding, for example, may start with a basically animistic approach: beam A "supports" platform B, while tie rod C "takes the strain off" member D. Even in an advanced technology this is a legitimate way of thinking, because if pressed to justify his design the engineer can always calculate (using abstract formulas) exactly to what extent A supports B and C relieves D. In other words the engineer's behavioral categorizations of the physical object he is designing are backed up by ideal categorizations. The justification for this approach is to call it a "structure": a logically coherent whole with behavioral parts. Justifying physical-behavioral theorizing by means of an ideal backup complements the two previous cases, where the French structuralists added a physical cast to their ideal treatments of behavior and where field physicists added behavioral concepts to their ideal categorizations of physical reality. In all these instances structuralism adds a "missing ingredient" to conceptualization and encourages us to theorize with all three orders of reality.

In its more general application to science, particularly among English-speaking theorizers, structuralism is sometimes rechristened as the study of "systems." In this guise much is expected of it; for instance Ervin Laszlo claims:

> Physical phenomena are now viewed as systems, in which subsidiary events are not separate particles but subsystems: subpatterns within the overall pattern which is the object of investigation... The remarkable fact is that contemporary science has effectively, though largely tacitly, abandoned the notion of isolated particular entities as its units of investigation.[23]

Again the elimination of minima is celebrated, but perhaps prematurely; it might be hard to find agreement with the foregoing statement at a congress of particle physicists. Systems theorizing is sometimes now contrasted with "reductionism," the latter referring to the prevailing tendency to regard maxima as no more than large collections of minima. Papers by reputable scientists have begun to crop up, expressing the general position that it is improper to treat wholes entirely as the products of their parts.

How valid is the structuralist approach? As a new technique in theorizing it may lead to hitherto unrealized areas of knowledge. But despite the claims of its proponents, it does not eliminate the inherent problems of theorizing I described earlier. The basic idea of a minimum is that of a theoretical entity proposed as a natural, absolute limit of inquiry. It may not be divided, analyzed, or explained in terms of its contents; it must be "swallowed whole." Traditional minima (as implied by my choice of the term) are small and elemental, and it is these that structural theorizing seeks to eliminate. But a structure, although "large" and wholistic instead of small and elemental, easily becomes just as limiting to our understanding. It becomes a new part of reality that cannot be analyzed, that must be "swallowed whole." Thus P. A. Weiss contrasts systems with "machines":

> In the system, the structure of the whole determines the operation of the parts; in the machine, the operation of the parts determines the outcome.[24]

Here the desire to get rid of monolithic elemental parts in theorizing has led to the hypostatization of monolithic elemental wholes: they determine other events but are not themselves analyzable.

In the traditions of theorizing I discussed earlier, minima were devised as "two-way fasteners" to pin together parts of reality from two separate orders, thereby justifying the parallelism of categories and subjects that we need in order to theorize. In structuralism as currently expounded, structures might be thought of as "three-way fasteners," serving the same function but applied to parts of all three orders of reality. As such they would offer no alleviation of the error-concealing problem of traditional minima, nor could they transcend the latter's inherently instrumental role. To the extent that structures themselves become treated as real objects of knowledge they re-introduce all the artificialities that departed with the abandonment of more familiar minima.

In some cases theorizing about structures might be *more efficient* than traditional theorizing; but it cannot constitute an absolute improvement. At best, structuralism can introduce new concepts to thought and give us new ways to explore reality. This can produce genuine expansions of our knowledge, as Piaget, Chomsky, and others have shown. But at their worst, structural ideas stultify the development of understanding, by creating a feeling that we have transcended problems that are actually still with us. The danger is perhaps more severe with structuralism, because of its protean ability to adapt to criticism. I cited how it insulates ideal categorizations of behavior from charges of non-objectivity, and how it makes physicists' idealized fields seem behavioral. When used in this way—defensively—structuralism can choke off what I believe is the most effective route to knowledge: the process of "comparative theorizing" I will discuss in Section 3.3. It papers over the artificialities inherent in theorizing of any sort; and to the extent that it does this effectively and imperceptibly, it can limit understanding as easily as it can expand it.

Theorizing is always instrumental. We do it because it will lead us to something else. That "something else" is knowledge. The foregoing discussions have been aimed at uncovering some of the characteristic ways we acquire knowledge; let us now consider some of the things that knowledge does for us, in order to understand why we seek it in the first place.

3. Knowledge

> All men by nature desire knowledge.
> ARISTOTLE

The overall process of exploring reality (as I have described it here) at first sounds peculiar. We start in common sense by perceiving three independent orders of things, each understood in a different way with no elements in common. We then seize unrelated parts of these orders and force them together in our comprehension, under the name of "theorizing." Finally we conceal from ourselves the inherent erroneousness of what we have done by inventing new bits of reality—minima—to pin together points of our theoretical parallelisms. We do all this not as a special procedure, or because a fancy has struck us at one time or in one area of knowledge, but as a universal and methodical ritual.

But yet it works. Theorizing increases knowledge. Relating the unrelatable and proposing objects of knowledge that are by their very nature incorrectly understood results in an ever-widening commonsense grasp of reality. Still, this program seems to work in spite of itself. Theorizers perform their rituals, create their artificialities, and talk us into believing what they have done. For a while we have the satisfaction of thinking that one area of reality has at last been utterly explained. Then it turns out that there is an even better ritual available, beside which the old one is now to be considered a clumsy and absurd tissue of misunderstandings; and we dutifully sack yesterday's "ultimate knowledge" in response to the new call. Yet yesterday's theory was never a total waste. We find that we emerged from it with our common sense enriched and our grasp of reality newly extended.

Why do human beings feel an urge to build theories? As any parent knows, a sequence of "why" questions has no natural end. For any process we observe it is possible to construct an infinite regress of explanations, each covering the one before. In Section 2.2 I discussed the first layer of the "why" of theorizing, which can be briefly summarized. Theorizing emerges from common sense as a process of using one order of reality to explore another. The order of reality being used appears as a source of "categories," by which the reality being explored is encapsulated into bundles of "known facts." Hitherto unknown facts then come to our attention because they produce in us an awareness that some part of reality is erroneous or incorrect with respect to another part. Minima are tools for this procedure: they dull our awareness of error in certain areas of reality so we will apprehend it more clearly in areas where "new knowledge" lies. The ultimate repository of what we have learned is common sense, our grasp of reality understood in its own terms, without theoretical treatment. Theorizing as a whole may be visualized as forcing an overlap between two disparate kinds of reality, holding them together by our acceptance of minima; our understanding then moves outward from the minima (which we define as points of perfect, natural overlapping) looking for discrepancies in the parallelism. In areas of discrepancy revealed by this procedure we learn hitherto unknown facts. Gathering these facts constitutes the "instrumental why" of theorizing.

But different types of theories lead us to different types of facts. As I mentioned, the qualities of any theory depend largely on which order of reality (physical, behavioral, ideal) supplies its categories. We can appreciate the effects of categorization in another way by asking "what kind" of new knowledge is revealed by various categorial schemes. When categories are drawn from physical reality, for instance, the resulting theories tend to make us aware of facts that are independent of us, that are "out there." Thus the most basic theory of perception (in which sensations are treated as derived from physical events) identifies certain ideas as "objective"—those that exist regardless of our volition and hence are felt to refer to externalities. If we never held a theory of perception we would regard dreams, hallucinations, and perceptions of physical things on an equal footing; but by virtue of such a theory large areas of our mental states are categorized as referring to an "outside world." When an idea comes along that does not fully fit the theory, such as Thurber's unicorn in the garden, we are in a position to gain new knowledge. The signal for this knowledge is the awareness of error between our sensation behavior, which sees a unicorn, and our physical categories, which do not include such a beast. The resolution of the error is either to add unicorns to our physical common sense (thus making them available as perceptual categories), or to adjust our understanding of sensation behavior to recognize strong hallucinations of a certain kind. In this way our physically-categorized theory of perception expands our knowledge of "external" objective reality. It forces us to decide whether or not unicorns exist "out there."

When categories are drawn from behavior the resulting new knowledge tends to makes us aware of reality in terms of our own needs, wants, and plans. Earlier I mentioned the common application of animism (the categorization of physical reality by behavior) to everyday living. Through animism we grasp a reality that operates much the same way we do, and hence can be directly related to our own life processes. We "get along" with the world; and when it does not "behave" the way we expect it to, this is a signal that we need more knowledge about it. Thus behavioral categorization gives us knowledge of how we and the rest of reality fit together, of objects and events that are in some sense directly "usable" by us.

Finally, when categories are drawn from ideals the resulting logical theories tend to make us aware of enduring and definable reality. For instance, by categorizing physical events ideally we identify and group their common descriptions. Large areas of physical reality become subsumed in our knowledge as instances of principles already known. Areas that do not fit the principles—that "violate scientific laws"—thus stand out as objects of exploration, as sources of new knowledge. The whole process of science is one of expanding our knowledge by sifting out of reality those parts that we regard as immutable and logically comprehensible.

In this way each distinct "style" of theorizing plays a different role in the totality of our transactions with reality. In various situations we need knowledge that is variously objective, usable, and logical. Theorizing occurs because it is a more efficient way than bare common sense for ferreting out new objects of knowledge from the mass of experience; it is an effective "knowledge-building" procedure. Each theory is like a platform we create in reality in order to have a firm base from which to explore. Without such platforms we would be unable to distinguish the known from the unknown and would find ourselves awash in a sea of fragmentary knowledge, piecing together bits of understanding at random. But ironically it is not theoretical knowledge—statements about minima—that are theorizing's principal product; rather it is the commonsense grasp of maxima that each theory leaves behind it. When adopting theories it is essential to recognize their inherently instrumental nature; they are important for the knowledge they help us find, not for knowledge of the theoretical platforms themselves.

Theorizing thus expands knowledge. But it is possible to inquire further, to ask why expanding knowledge is a desirable human occupation. If theorizing is explained as an effective ritual for acquiring new knowledge then the question "why theorize?" leads to the question "why acquire new knowledge?" To answer this, we must first note that theories are not only instrumental with respect to knowledge in general, but *also with respect to each other*. For example, a basic theory of perception is prerequisite to any animistic theory about physical events; and such animistic theories about things' "behavior" occur prior to any ideally categorized theory that finds universal "laws" underlying that behavior. In general, our knowledge of reality expands by means of a series of stepping stones: understanding physical reality precedes understanding behavior, which precedes understanding ideals. This important insight is the starting point for appreciating the acquisition of knowledge as an historical process. The kinds of knowledge we presently possess represent the descendants of earlier kinds, much as animal and plant species today represent the descendants of earlier stages in evolution.

In fact, comparing the acquisition of knowledge to a pattern of biological evolution is more than just simile. Understanding is part of behavior, which is the pattern of living things. Acquiring knowledge is part of the living pattern because successful evolution has depended on life's expanding grasp of reality. But the stages of understanding I am presently discussing—differentiating three orders of reality and using them in theorizing—are not late developments. They became established with the earliest formation of life itself. To grasp the reasons for them we have to go back to the very beginning and picture the emergence of life's most primal processes.

3.1 Evolution

> We have found a strange footprint on the shores of the unknown. We have devised profound theories, one after another, to account for its origin. At last we have succeeded in reconstructing the creature that made the footprint. And lo! it is our own.
>
> EDDINGTON

Pasteur's experiments in the latter half of the nineteenth century opened up the question of the origin of life on earth by effectively destroying the medieval supposition of spontaneous generation. Darwin outlined the general process of evolution by which its historical development could be explained. Disciplined speculations on the events involved in life's emergence were published by the Russian biologist A. I. Oparin in 1936 (*The Origin of Life*); but it was not until 1953 that laboratory experiments began to suggest a plausible scenario. In that year S. L. Miller published an account of an experiment in which a mixture of water vapor, methane, ammonia, and hydrogen (presently believed to have been major constituents of the earth's atmosphere when life arose) were circulated over an electric spark for several days. The result was a dilute mixture of amino acids, the basic building blocks of organic materials.

Amino acids are still far from living things. But this simple demonstration showed that strictly physical processes, given the right conditions and enough time, might randomly generate the complex molecules characteristic of viable organisms. If the conditions in Miller's experiment are at all representative of primitive earth, we must imagine its surface covered by a dilute broth of organic molecules—not just the size of a flask but the size of the oceans and not just circulating for days but circulating for millions of years. We can then speculate that life began when the right kinds of molecules "fell together" by chance. Along the same lines, Oparin suggested its origin in the known inorganic process of "coacervation," by which large molecules concentrate in colloidal droplets.

Knowing the end-result—living organisms—what can we imagine these randomly-produced molecules might do to start them toward becoming

83

alive? In the present state of knowledge, it appears that the first life-like process individual molecules might exhibit would be fermentation. From each gram of sugar available in the broth, a "fermentation molecule" could create half a gram of carbon dioxide gas and about 100 calories of energy. This energy would constitute the first appearance on earth of the "entropy reversing" process I will discuss presently, for it would be extracted from the environment and concentrated in the molecule. We must assume that the "right kind" of molecule would contain some high-energy bonds in which it could be stored. Admittedly the probability of all this "falling together" is quite low; but we must also suppose an extremely large number of opportunities as the ocean of broth was stirred for thousands of millenia.

Oparin suggested that the first such molecule would grow larger and larger, as it stored more and more energy. At some stage mechanical factors would cause it to break apart. With a little luck one or more parts would be able to reconstitute the processes of the original; in this way the phenomenon of fermentation could gradually spread throughout the nutrient sea.

Our best guesses indicate that at this stage the terrestrial atmosphere would have contained neither oxygen nor carbon dioxide. But the latter is given off by fermentation, and being heavier than methane or ammonia it would tend to concentrate near the surface of the fermenting waters. We can therefore imagine the random invention of photosynthesis (again after an extremely large number of opportunities) by some of the fermentation molecules. In an environment where fermentation has proceeded long enough to attenuate the naturally-produced supply of sugars, photosynthesis would have considerable "evolutionary value," for it converts water, carbon dioxide, and sunlight into sugar and oxygen. The sugar becomes immediately available for the production of energy in the photosynthetic organism; because it both creates sugar from sunlight and ferments sugar to energy, such an organism is in effect capturing the energy of solar radiation.

But photosynthesis releases oxygen into the atmosphere, where it would have begun to replace the carbon dioxide. This would have stimulated one final basic development: respiration, by which sugar and oxygen are converted into carbon dioxide and water. In addition respiration would have exhibited substantial "evolutionary value" over fermentation, for it generates 35 times as much energy while consuming the same amount of sugar.

The foregoing scenario hypothesizes only the development of "energy catching" techniques in life. To it one would have to add an account of the development of differentiation, cellulation, growth regulation, and (most importantly) molecular replication—all inventions produced along the way that gave organisms stumbling on them an edge over their competition. At present our grasp of this history can be no more than careful supposition. My

84

point is that it now appears possible to extrapolate evolution backwards, referring only to physical processes and occasional occurrences of low probability in a setting of very many trials, to arrive at an unbroken chain of events starting from the original inorganic state of the earth. There is no need to imagine an evolutionary "leap" (either vitalistic or extraterrestrial) from simple inorganic molecules to living organisms, which cannot be explained by known physical processes.

Supposing this account to be plausible, at what stage should we claim that *behavior* first appeared on earth? Answering this question illuminates our whole grasp of reality in which we comprehend distinct, independent orders. Imagine that we are present to observe the beginning of the process just described. We have arrived, say, from another planet with a highly advanced technology, and are able to observe these molecular events with powerful microscopes. At first our inspection of the primordial broth would reveal only an immense collection of molecules of various sizes and complexity all bumping into one another—now briefly linking, now fragmenting into other molecules, in no apparent pattern. From the viewpoint of our advanced technology all we have observed is a strictly physical process. But presently we notice a recurring pattern among certain large molecules: they attach themselves to sugars, break them into alcohols and carbon dioxide, and store some of the released energy as bonds in their structures. From time to time these large molecules divide in half and the halves take up the same process. Now, our recognition of this pattern is optional: it is a product of theorizing upon what we see. We might equally well discern a pattern in the occasional collisions of sugar molecules, or in the random formation of any class of large molecules that do not exhibit "metabolism" as we know it. But now let us imagine that we see one of these large sugar-breaking molecules do something "wrong." It attaches to a sugar in the wrong place, or fails to get rid of its alcoholic waste, or fissions in a way that does not allow the two halves to continue the process we have observed. We could choose to ignore such "error." But if we treat it as significant, the only way we can explain it is by reference to *behavior*. Physical knowledge, however complete, will be no longer sufficient, for in its terms no such event can be discriminated as "wrong."

In other words the processes just described (breaking sugars, storing energy, fissioning effectively) are all physical, and may be included in our purely physical knowledge. But at the same time they are physically insignificant; they are no different from billions of other molecular events in the primordial broth. To recognize them, we give them "theoretical significance." It is then we discover that the characteristics for which we study

85

them (metabolism, replication, etc.) are not explainable as such by physical knowledge—it "doesn't care" whether certain molecules metabolize (for instance) or not. To explicate the trains of events that interest us we need a new area of knowledge—knowledge of behavior—which is about such patterns. The new knowledge starts from an entirely fresh viewpoint. It treats the living pattern as wholly distinct from physical events, and describes occurrences within it in its own terms. It is knowledge that no physical understanding can yield.

It is clear that in one sense such a knowledge of behavior is arbitrarily derived. We hypothetical visitors from another planet might examine the primordial broth and decide to theorize upon any class of common molecular interactions. For instance we might be fascinated by the formation of sulfonic acids. We would go through the same motions—collect data, recognize patterns, and define correct and incorrect events—but the resulting knowledge would not be about life, about what we human beings call "behavior." Why then is knowledge of behavior special? The answer lies in the fact that we human beings are not "visitors from another planet": *we are products of behavior*. If we do not recognize behavior as a special order of events, among all the events that are equally significant in physical knowledge, we perish. We are the descendants of that "fermentation molecule," and over the eons we have learned to single out and understand the characteristic patterns exhibited by it and all its progeny, including ourselves.

This is a point of the most fundamental importance. In recognizing behavior the reality explored by a knower and the reality of the knower himself first coalesce. We study behavior because our studying itself *is* behavior. To do so we start by fashioning physical categories—metabolism, energy storage, replication, etc.—so we can separate the organic from the inorganic, the living from the "merely physical." But unlike the hypothetical extraterrestrial observers our choice of subject matter is not arbitrary; behavior is *inherently significant* to us because it includes knowledge itself.

We might say that behavior appeared on earth, then, the first time a living thing found it useful to recognize a behavioral pattern. We can imagine a more complex descendant of the "fermentation molecule" discovering (at first by chance) that it could live more effectively not by breaking up sugar molecules but by breaking up other living things. At the outset, perhaps, life could feed on life without the parasite recognizing other than simple physical facts about its prey, such as a molecular configuration or the presence of suitable receptor sites on which to seize. But as life became more complicated, as prey acquired defensive mechanisms or as parasites discovered that their tentative prey might equally well be a higher parasite, success would increasingly depend on discerning patterns in the environment that were not

86

physically explicable. At such a stage we must say that behavior was present because it was recognized.

The recognition of behavior is self-generating: that is, each organism that recognizes behavior in another organism alters its own behavior to create new patterns. Ultimately the totality of such patterns, all of which have been from the outset physically trivial, must be treated as a major part of reality: a new order. Studying this order is theoretically important because it contains a mass of material that can be understood in no other way. But it is also *vitally* important to behaving things, because without the resulting knowledge they cannot survive in the reality they have created.

It is common to treat life as a diverse collection of individual organisms; but this is not the way it developed. The primal "fermentation molecule" and all its progeny should more accurately be regarded as a single organism that has fragmented to achieve spatial distribution. This would be analogous to treating a gas as a volume rather than as a collection of molecules. From such a viewpoint the "fermentation organism" would be a very large individual, growing constantly and engaged in converting a sea of sugar into alcohol and carbon dioxide.

The growth of such an organism would proceed asexually (by budding or division, for instance), forming what biologists call a "clone." But in a changing environment the survival of life depends on its ability to adapt. The most significant instances of evolutionary adaptation occur when new species are formed; and clones do not, in general, form new species. Thus to our list of important "inventions" by life should be added sexual speciation by mutation and genetic recombination, for here lies the key to the amazing proliferation of life on earth. The term "species" is used variously by biologists, sometimes only to identify clusters of physical characteristics; but its most basic definition is that of a reproductive community, a collection of individuals among whom characteristics are genetically conserved.

Speciation gives life the potential for radical adaptation to changes in its environment, by generating wholly new living techniques. Each species conserves its adaptation to a particular "niche" in the environment, and usually perishes if that niche disappears; but life itself, the totality of species, survives. By contrast, an asexual clone may persist for millions of years but if its niche is destroyed it will leave no surviving form of life. Thus in terms of the evolution of life as a whole, speciation gives it a firmer and more flexible grip on the environment. Each species is an experiment in a particular way of living. The experiment tends to endure, in the sense that the species maintains a relatively stable approach to its environment, because its individual organisms reproduce only with each other and not with individu-

87

als from other species. At the same time the processes of mutation and genetic recombination that accompany sexual reproduction occasionally generate new species with different living techniques. To the extent these are viable, life forms a "clade"—a "tree" of species branching off from an original sexual community. When branches of the clade are extinguished by changes in the environment, others take their place.

A few pages ago I suggested we imagine ourselves visitors from another planet, observing the emergence of behavior in physical processes on earth. Let us now imagine returning in such a role at the time life is forming species. At that stage we would possess both knowledge of physical reality and knowledge of behavior to explain what we observe. The former would cover events on the molecular level; the latter would cover patterns such as metabolism, differentiation, and reproduction. At first speciation might not seem to be a significant pattern in life, just as behavior itself did not at first appear to differ from the mass of physical events. All we would see is certain groups of organisms preserving, through the transmission of genetic material, similar approaches to their environment; while random processes would occasionally produce new groups. Yet it would be significant to us to recognize that sometimes such groups were "wrong": they became extinct when the environment shifted beyond a certain range in which they could survive. I have already discussed the impossibility of explicating such wrongness on the basis of physical knowledge. Physics gives us no opportunity to frame concepts by which we could identify the molecular interactions that result in a species surviving, discriminating them from those that lead to its extinction. The same would now be true of our knowledge of behavior, however perfected it might be. We extraterrestrials could not formulate distinctions between correct and incorrect evolutionary events in purely behavioral terms, because our knowledge of behavior would be intrinsically unable to discriminate the processes of metabolism, differentiation and reproduction that led a species to either type of event. In order to conceive of such distinctions we would need to recognize the emergence of "descriptive patterns" in life; and these could be expressed only in terms of *ideals*.

Before considering further the role ideals take in the evolution of species it is important to grasp clearly where physical and behavioral theories fall short in explaining speciation. It is true that any species could be treated only as a breeding population, and hence could be characterized either by pointing out its physical constraints on reproduction outside the species (e.g. impossibility of fertilization) or by citing behavioral sanctions, such as mating cues. In this sense we could build a physical or behavioral characterization of speciation that would show why certain individuals reproduce only with certain other individuals, thus maintaining genetic lines. But such an effort would utterly fail to cover the "reasons" for separate species. Like pre-Darwinian biology, it would take the variety of life just as it is, without being able to further discriminate the suitability or unsuitability of genetically determined characteristics. For instance, why the amphibia developed a terrestrial adult phase in their life cycle would, in such an explanation, seem mysterious, since nothing in purely behavioral or physical terms would make it "better" than the equally successful life cycles of wholly aquatic animals. The emergence of such a technique (and hence the existence of the species itself) would seem mere happenstance in these terms. Individuals of each species would grow, metabolize, reproduce, and die in their varied ways, but we would have no way to discriminate their different "life techniques." However, once we analyze life in terms of ideals this mystery evaporates. The techniques evolved by various species reflect different *descriptions* of the environment; and whether or not they are successful depends on how "accurate" these descriptions are.

Ideals show up in physical life processes as speciation; their earliest behavioral manifestations are commonly called *instincts*. Such patterns are familiar. All living things, including man, are born with certain routines of behavior "built-in." Although they may be subsequently modified or embellished (as in the case of "imprinting") these instinctive patterns clearly represent something characteristic of the species, not of any one individual.

Among insects, instinctive behavior is usually dominant. The egg-laying procedure of the digger wasp is often cited as a classic example. At a certain point in her life, internal processes stimulate the wasp to dig a hole in the earth, then search for a grasshopper. She paralyzes the grasshopper, drags it by its antennae to the edge of the hole, releases it and checks the hole to see that it is clear, and finally drags the grasshopper into the hole. She then lays an egg on it (which eventually hatches into a grub that eats the grasshopper) and fills up the hole. The whole complex chain of behavior is accomplished with little or no "individual initiative." We can demonstrate this experimentally by breaking the chain. If we move the grasshopper while the wasp has left it to check the hole, she will move it back and then check the hole again; and she will do this over and over, not being able to complete the chain while any of its links are disturbed. If we break off the grasshopper's antennae she will not try to drag it by its feet instead, but will go off to find another grasshopper.

The behavior portrayed here might be characterized as follows. A certain species of wasp has determined (as a result of many millions of generations of evolution) that an effective technique for propagating its individuals

89

consists of laying, nourishing, and protecting its eggs in the manner described. Genetic material transmitted from wasp to wasp sets up in each one an elaborate mechanism of successively triggered stages, determining what that individual shall do at each point. Some decisions are left to the individual, such as where to dig the hole and where to look for a grasshopper. But most actions are rigidly set by the species, and further study might show that even some apparent individual options are highly controlled. It is as if the species has launched each individual with only a rudimentary on-board computer, the principal details of its voyage through life having been laid down in advance, in its very construction.

Let us consider another example. In a field of cattle a lightning bolt from a summer storm strikes a tree. One or two steers nearby react from fright, running and snorting. The others take up the reaction, so that presently the whole herd is stampeding across the field. We say that their behavior is "instinctive." What kind of knowledge would we need to explain it? First and parenthetically, as I mentioned before it would be futile to dredge physical knowledge for an understanding of the relation between atmospheric electrical discharges and muscular contractions in the legs of cattle. Such an understanding, even if feasible, would not illuminate the essential nature of this event. Knowledge of behavior would seem to offer more promise. We could relate each animal's perception of fear in his neighbors to the triggering of his own fear reaction and his desire to remain with the herd. We could show how the whole pattern of reactions is communicated from animal to animal and back, producing a mass of self-regenerating herd behavior long after the original stimulus has been forgotten. But such a set of explanations, although illuminating many areas of this occurrence, would leave one factor out: it would ignore the "foolishness" of the cattle's reaction. There was no "reason" for a stampede. The lightning bolt threatened at most one animal in the first place and the danger was totally past before any animal had time to react. The stampede, we must say, was an "overreaction." But it is not possible to define an "overreaction" in purely behavioral terms, because *every* reaction must be treated as the natural product of its stimuli. Put another way, no knowledge of pure behavior could distinguish between a "foolish" stampede over a lightning strike and a "prudent" stampede resulting from (say) an attack by predators; either must be understood as the outcome of its generating conditions (if it is to be understood at all) and hence could not be further qualified.

The principal pattern of the cattle stampede exhibits instinctive reflexes, like the egg-laying procedure of the digger wasp. It is behavior the species has "built in" to its individuals. Obviously cattle have a much greater capacity for learning, so the underlying instincts may become modified, repressed, or displaced more easily; but they are still there. From the viewpoint of the species they embody a determination that a good survival technique consists of moving as a herd, and moving with great energy if one or more individuals signals a strong fear reaction. The logical framework of this determination might be schematized thus:

1) When danger threatens the herd it must move away;
2) Sometimes danger is detected by only a few animals of the herd;
3) When danger is detected by an animal it will exhibit fear;
4) Therefore when a few animals exhibit fear the herd must move away.

This analysis reveals the "incorrectness" of the herd's behavior, for premise (1) is not valid. *Some* danger is effectively countered by herd movement, but not all. In the present case herd movement does nothing to protect it from lightning strikes, and may even be counter-productive by driving the animals from relative shelter to an exposed area where they are more likely to act as aerials. Since lightning has not been a significant environmental factor in the evolution of cattle, the species has not refined premise (1) to take this into consideration. Only we, with our more sophisticated knowledge, are able to detect the error. To do so, however, it is necessary for us to make something like the foregoing logical analysis, to connect the observed behavior with its underlying *generalizations* about the world.

At first it may seem strange to conceive of abstract processes manifesting themselves in instinctive behavior. There arises the implication of a "world-mind" calculating the reasons behind living patterns. But this would be a supposition based on *minima*, based on finding a unitary efficient cause for what we observe; in terms of *maxima* the picture is entirely natural. It is simply the case that when we try to grasp the complex reality of living things, certain patterns that we observe can be understood only by reference to the ideal order.

More specifically, we can make the following analysis. First, there is no inherent difficulty in our comprehending the patterns by which any individual organism survives and reproduces, all through an understanding of behavior. Second, the processes of mutation and genetic transmission of characteristics from organism to organism may all be explained in physical terms. These two processes—individual behavior and genetic mechanisms—combine in the actual evolution of species. Individuals who behave in such a way that they survive and reproduce pass on their characteristics genetically to new individuals: the whole pattern is one of adaptive response to the environment by different species. But the whole pattern (involving many individuals) cannot be understood either behaviorally or physically or by any combination of the two. There is a missing link—the

91

"rationale" of instincts—that is neither physical nor behavioral. It is not physical because it is manifested in living events that are inexplicable physically to begin with. It is not behavioral because it is a pattern *superimposed* upon behavior. In strictly behavioral terms the differences between instinctive patterns are trivial; yet it is important to distinguish them because we find some to be correct or "prudent" and others to be incorrect or "foolish." The only way we can understand such discriminations is by citing another type of reality, by referring to ideals. Thus, for instance, a cattle stampede is always "correct" in physical and behavioral terms, because within these terms we can formulate no alternative. It is only when we derive terms from ideals, setting up a logical rationale for this event, that we become fully able to comprehend it. Then we are no longer limited to understandings such as "the cattle stampeded because an atmospheric discharge led to muscular contractions" (a physical interpretation) or "the cattle stampeded because they were frightened" (a behavioral interpretation); instead we can make determinations such as "the cattle stampeded because their species had evolved that response to events fulfilling a certain description." The last explanation clearly comes closest of the three to expressing what we actually know about this happening.

The use of ideals in the basis of evolution is functionally similar to their use in theorizing. In theorizing, ideals contribute "logicality": by adopting them in categorization (as science does) we characterize reality as describable and predictable. Speciation also depends on treating reality as describable and predictable: describable in that a single genetically-coded pattern can reflect the essence of the various events to which an instinct is applied, and predictable in that the whole idea of instincts assumes that behavior which was successful in the past (because the individuals exhibiting it survived) will be equally effective at present. In a general sense, the constant creation of new species represents a series of ideal-based theories about reality. Species are scientific experiments conducted by life.

A characteristic of logicality is its separation of things by description. It forms reality into descriptive classes and insists that we preserve the boundaries between one class and another. This characteristic shows up in the basis of speciation. Each species differs from others primarily in the ways that it sorts reality into descriptive classes—things to be eaten, things to be avoided, things to mate with, etc. For instance, the digger wasp's "description" of a grasshopper differs radically from that used by (say) another grasshopper. Each species preserves its system of descriptions by means of the constraints of reproduction. Its instinctive living techniques are carried by its jealously guarded genetic equipment, and are not subject to indiscriminate mixing with other techniques. If individuals of different species could interbreed without constraint, all these carefully separated techniques would blend into a hopelessly "illogical" jumble of behavior, and none of the species would survive.

Thus speciation marks the appearance of ideal patterns on earth. It depends on the superimposition of ideals upon behavior, just as life itself depended on the superimposition of behavior upon physical events. The hypothetical "fermentation molecule" described earlier, living from energy obtained by breaking down sugars in the primordial broth and dividing repeatedly to form a growing clone, "merely behaved": we would have no difficulty understanding such life in purely behavioral terms. Even if there were a variety of such molecules, each behaving in a different pattern, behavioral knowledge would suffice. But as soon as true evolution appears—as soon as a clade of species is formed, each representing an experiment in living technique—then ideal explanations become necessary.

Morphologically, the distinction depends on life's ability to transmit successful characteristics to future organisms. The hypothetical "fermentation molecule" did not possess genetic coding; when it divided, the viable parts simply took up where the "parent" had left off. Without genetic coding, characteristics acquired by random changes in the molecule could survive only to the extent that the specific individual organism survived. In a genetically determined species, on the other hand, a single random mutation has the potential of being duplicated in billions of individuals for millions of years. The genetic machinery makes the difference: it contains a coding system—a set of effective symbolic specifications for behavior—by which identical instincts can be embedded in any number of separate organisms. The use of ideals is manifested whenever a single successful "experiment" is followed by incorporation of the result in the behavior of many different individuals.

The evolution of species may be said to exhibit "intelligence," cognate to the familiar process of individual deliberation. Life sets up a hypothesis about the environment in the form of a genetic variation in one of its organisms. If the variation has value, life "remembers" it by retaining it in genetically coded form; if not, it "forgets." In similar fashion we rational individuals conceive and test hypotheses about our world, remembering those that work and discarding those that don't.

In fact there is more than just similarity; individual intelligence is directly derived from the "intelligence" exhibited by species. In *The Sources of Value*, S. C. Pepper describes individual intelligence as filling a "gap" in instinctive reflex behavior:

93

A basic appetitive drive [in intelligent animals] may therefore be conceived as a broken-down chain reflex system, where a gap has opened up between the initial act and the terminal act… It may at first seem strange to think of our highly developed intelligent behavior as based upon a gap opening up within an instinctive chain reflex system. But once such gaps begin to appear in the evolutionary process, their biological advantage to organisms would become apparent on one condition: the provision of a technique of behavior, such as trial and error, which could be thrown into gear when a gap appeared, so that an organism could acquire by learning, and then maintain, a successful bridge over a gap whenever such a bridge had been found. Once this condition was met, intelligent modifiable behavior became possible.[25]

Much human behavior is of the intelligent sort found in these gaps; but Pepper points out that we can usually find the residue of an instinctive chain before and after our intelligent acts. Human eating behavior, for example, often starts with a set of instinctive "tensions" (e.g. stomach contractions) that arise automatically and are interpreted by our intelligent behavior as indicating a need for food. Identifying and securing food, preparing it, and bringing it to the mouth are primarily intelligent acts, although some reflexes may be present (such as instinctive revulsions at certain tastes and smells). When food is ready to be eaten instinctive salivation occurs, and once it is in the mouth a whole chain of instinctive acts ensues—biting, chewing, the muscular sequence of swallowing, peristaltic contractions in the esophagus, and the release of digestive enzymes in the stomach. Such behavior could be classed with the egg-laying sequence of the digger wasp, in that it has been evolved by the species as an effective routine for gaining a particular goal. In the simplest species, the equivalent of stomach contractions is linked reflex-ively, through a chain of instinctive food-seeking and food-capturing acts, to the equivalent of chewing and digestion. But in man most of the middle part of the process is left open, to be filled by each human being with behavior he has learned by himself. The species delegates the creation of these patterns to the individual.

In Section 2.2 I described the origin of theorizing as an interruption of common sense. This process is cognate to the one just described: we could say that theorizing fills gaps in human common sense, just as common sense fills gaps in chains of instinctive behavior. Theorizing, of course, is a pattern of individual intelligent behavior. From the viewpoint of problem solving, it arises when non-theoretical common sense is unable to cope with a situation, and ceases when the situation has been resolved and common sense is once more effective. Hence from the viewpoint of *evolution*, theorizing can be described as an individual behavior pattern that generates new material to fill the gaps in instinctive behavior chains. Most intelligent behavior is regulated by common sense; when that fails theorizing steps in, solving the immediate problem and generating new common sense as a by-product. Common sense constitutes the "archives" of remembered theorizing results. This keeps theorizing at the forefront of individual intelligence in man, leaving in its wake a body of common sense by which most of the gaps in species-determined instinctive behavior are filled.

It is easy to appreciate the "evolutionary value" of delegating some intelligence from species to individuals. The digger wasp occupies a narrow environmental niche: it depends (for instance) on the availability of certain grasshoppers to propagate. In a slightly modified environment the species would perish. Human beings, on the other hand, occupy a wide environmental niche—from the bottom of the oceans to the surface of the moon. We do not survive over this range by virtue of any physical traits or program of instinctive behavior; we survive by virtue of our individual intelligence.

Just as behavior emerged gradually out of physical events during the origin of life, so individual intelligence probably arose gradually out of instinctive behavior. Recent studies indicate that much instinctive behavior is modified by local conditions. Year-old chaffinches, for instance, learn complex songs that apparently identify their territory and can be classified in geographical dialects. Gulls, during the first few days of life, learn to take food from their parents' beaks; at first they respond indiscriminately to the general color, shape and motion of a beak, but soon sharpen this perception into a fairly accurate identification of the configuration peculiar to their species. At a certain early point in the life of goslings their instinctive behavior opens up just enough to become "imprinted" with the identifying characteristics of any properly responsive object, which they will henceforth treat as their mother. All such examples demonstrate limited individual learning inserted into a basic train of instincts. As such experiments were successful, life apparently tried increasingly greater reliance on individual intelligence.

Nevertheless, "lower" animals seldom exhibit lengthy spans of individually determined behavior. These organisms do not have the mechanisms—the "on-board computers"—that are required. In man, of course, such computers exist, and for that reason he is apparently unique among living things in the complexity and scope of his trains of individually intelligent acts. The use of man's computer, the human brain, constitutes what is traditionally called "intelligence"; but it is actually only the latest stage of a long evolutionary process. Traces of this process can be detected today in the physiology of human brains, as succesively developed "layers" of tissue. The oldest and most primitive layer—called by Paul MacLean the "Reptilian Complex''—directs the more elaborate aspects of human beings' dealings with physical reality.[26] The next layer, the limbic system, organizes each individual's emotional life. The final layer, the neocortex, performs the tasks of abstraction and reasoning; it gives human thought access to ideals. Note the characteristic historical sequence: physical, behavioral, ideal. It was the emergence of the neocortex, scarcely yesterday in the span of living evolution, that produced what is commonly called intelligence. A good general discussion of these aspects of brain physiology appears in Carl Sagan's *The Dragons of Eden*.[27]

In the foregoing description of evolution, life exhibits an increasing involvement with reality. The hypothetical original ''fermentation molecule'' was just behavior superimposed upon physical reality. At a later stage the competition among living things resulted in behavior responding to behavior, a technique that conferred survival advantages on the organisms adopting it. With the rise of speciation life became concerned with ideals; first as a means of transmitting living techniques over successive generations, then as the key to individual intelligence. In each phase of this history it is clear that knowledge of reality was vital to living things, and that later life forms evolved as a result of acquiring more knowledge than their ancestors. These facts, then, supply an antecedent reason behind the ''why'' of theorizing: it is pursued because it enlarges knowledge, and knowledge is sought because it is essential to the evolution of life. What we understand today are the parts of reality that it has been important for life to know in the past.

But why should life evolve, or even exist at all? I believe we can take the regress of explanations one step further before it becomes too general to be comprehensible. Life operates in specific ways, and the knowledge it has developed during its evolution is therefore specific and instrumental. Our present view of reality, complex and varied as it may seem to us, is a fundamentally parochial one: it is concerned with just those matters that affect living things directly. But this need not be so. The flexibility of man's intellectual apparatus permits him to explore areas of reality not directly tied to his living needs. Where these might lie is a subject I will eventually discuss in Section 6.3. The first step toward releasing ourselves into new areas of knowledge, however, is to measure the corridors of understanding to which we are presently confined. The most basic of these is shaped by life's fundamental position in physical reality. This forms the subject of the next section.

3.2 Energy

> The energies of our system will decay, the glory of
> the sun will be dimmed, and the earth, tideless and
> inert, will no longer tolerate the race which has for a
> moment disturbed its solitude. Man will go down into
> the pit, and all his thoughts will perish.
>
> A. J. BALFOUR

Scientists have been aware for some time that living physical organisms exhibit a fundamental difference from non-living material. Whereas in non-living physical reality change always results in an increasing amount of "disorder," in living things the opposite is true. "Disorder" can be characterized somewhat more precisely by using the concept of *entropy* introduced by Clausius in 1850. He proposed a "Second Law of Thermodynamics" in the form "heat cannot by itself pass from a colder to a hotter body," and pointed out that this means the universe as a whole is constantly losing its concentrations of energy as heat flows from hot spots to their surroundings. Entropy was defined as a measure of the "unavailable energy" in a physical system: that energy which cannot "do work" because it would have to flow into a hotter body. Later this idea was extended to cover physical phenomena of all kinds, so that by the end of the century Boltzmann was citing a "general principle of entropy" by which every process of change in a closed physical system (one that neither gained nor lost energy by interchange with the outside) resulted in an increase of *homogeneity* of all its internal parts.

But it soon became evident that any physical principle of this sort would have to be very carefully stated; for living organisms regularly managed to accumulate energy, build physical concentrations, and in general do all the things it seemed to prohibit. In Boltzmann's terms, living things *decreased* their entropy. This is why the principle had to be restricted to "closed systems": it was quickly pointed out that every decrease in entropy by an organism is accompanied by a greater increase in the entropy of its surroundings, as the organism radiates warmth, emits waste products, etc. If we place a live mouse with food and water in a large closed box, while it lives the entropy of its body will tend to decrease as it maintains its body heat and builds tissues. But because the system is closed the mouse will soon die. If we measure the entropy of the whole box from time to time we will find it steadily increasing, both while the mouse was alive and after it has died; in effect the mouse reduces its entropy at the expense of the rest of the box until it can do so no more, then joins the inexorable "homogenizing" process of the whole system. Thus the principle of entropy, if treated only as a statement about whole closed physical systems, can be asserted about both living and non-living reality.

But it is a poor "principle" that has to be so carefully hedged to preserve its validity. Ostwald, Weizäcker, and Schrödinger grappled with this problem and came to similar conclusions: life, by some means not yet understood, decreases its entropy in a systematic way. It does this at the expense of its environment and hence could be said, in Schrödinger's terms, to "feed on negative entropy":

> Every process, event, happening—call it what you will; in a word, everything that is going on in Nature means an increase of the entropy of the part of the world where it is going on. Thus a living organism continually increases its entropy—or, as you may say, produces positive entropy—and thus tends to approach the dangerous state of maximum entropy, which is death. It can only keep aloof from it, i.e. alive, by continually drawing from its environment negative entropy... What an organism feeds upon is negative entropy. Or, to put it less paradoxically, the essential thing in metabolism is that the organism succeeds in freeing itself from all the entropy it cannot help producing while alive.[28]

During this period when the concept of entropy was being applied as a differentiation between living and non-living physical events, it popped up in another context: as an indicator of the direction of time. With the possible exception of certain "weak interactions" among particles, all the basic mechanisms recognized by physics are "time-reversible": that is, there is no inherent reason they could not proceed in reverse order. If we were to make a motion picture of a variety of basic physical events and then run it backwards, there is nothing we could observe in viewing the backward version that would reveal a violation of physical "laws" or identify to us which was the forward version and which the reverse. Certainly on a gross scale we could distinguish the two: in the "backward" version burning candles would absorb smoke and grow longer instead of shorter, lead would "undecay" into radium, white dwarf stars would grow into red giants, and so on. But on the level of particle events, which are what basic physical laws are about, everything would appear normal. The difference is that the gross events include displays of entropy, a concept applicable only to large-scale arrangements of particles. This led Eddington, in a famous lecture (1925), to call entropy "time's arrow," asserting that the only way we can tell a later state of the physical world from an earlier one is by measuring their relative entropy. This view (with occasional reservations) is still held by most physicists.

When a single physical effect defines events in two seemingly different contexts, there is a strong presumption that the two contexts are really the same situation seen in two different ways. This principle was the key to general relativity: because mass measured inertially is always identical to mass measured gravitationally, Einstein postulated that acceleration and gravity are the same phenomenon seen from two viewpoints. A similar argument applies here. On the one hand changes of entropy are the effect by which we differentiate living and non-living physical events; on the other hand they are the effect by which we define physical time, i.e. earlier and later. Therefore we are justified in postulating that the organic-inorganic distinction and the process of temporal ordering reflect a single physical situation. How can we modify our understanding of each to make them comparable?

To answer this question in terms of current physical knowledge we must begin by understanding the "statistical" nature of thermodynamic principles. Because modern physical "laws," strictly speaking, are about particle events, they do not deal directly with configurations of many particles. To define and predict such configurations physicists apply the mathematical theory of permutations. The principles of "thermodynamics" (which include all assertions about entropy) then amount to statements about the expected permutations of particle states.

For example, imagine a sealed tube containing a gas under low pressure. Modern physics describes the contents of the tube as many billions of molecules travelling freely through space at a velocity determined by their temperature, recoiling elastically when they collide. Suppose we start with most of the molecules concentrated at one end of the tube. As we can easily visualize, over a short period of time the gas will "diffuse" throughout the tube until it is evenly distributed. Now physics does not attribute such diffusion to any immanent mechanism among the molecules themselves. Assuming that the system is adiabatic (does not exchange heat with the outside world) and that the molecules are very small relative to the average distance between them, each individual molecule may "fairly" take any position in the tube—each is a relatively "free agent." The fact that the molecules are mostly at one end of the tube does not create any decisive tendency in them individually to travel toward the empty end. But if we were to catalog all possible configurations of the totality of molecules in the tube, we would find that the overwhelming majority of the arrangements listed correspond to what we identify as "gas uniformly distributed." Only a tiny fraction of the possible configurations correspond to "gas mostly at one end." The molecular motions of the gas result in its constantly "trying out" all possible configurations in the tube; hence we observe diffusion simply because for every permutation we understand to be gas concentrated at one end there are billions we understand to be gas evenly spread. It is by virtue of this fact alone that at any given instant of observation we expect the gas to be diffused; and conversely there is nothing but the preponderance of permutations to prevent it from occasionally gathering at one end.

The same situation holds in throwing dice. The reason a pair of dice has a "tendency to come up 7" rather than (say) 12, is that there are six 7-permutations and only one 12-permutation. The individual cubes are like the physicists' particles, free to assume any position; but when we catalog their possible pair totals, 7 appears on the list six times as often as 12. If we catalog all possible totals of several throws, we find an increasingly greater proportion of ways to add up to 7 per throw. Thus if we were to throw a pair of dice a million times our expectation that their readings would total within a percent of 7,000,000 would be nearly absolute, corresponding to our expection that a gas will be found diffused in a tube, just because there are so many more ways to arrive at a total within that range than outside it.

The important fact to grasp here is that these predictions (and by extension the principles of thermodynamics in general) are functions not of physical events as defined by physics, but of our *system of observations*. In terms of particle positions the billions of configurations we lump together under the title of "evenly spread" are each as individual and distinctive as any configuration we call "concentration." But because there are so many more of them *under one identification* in the first case than in the second, we come to treat this case as a "tendency" of matter.

Consider the difference between basic physical "laws" and thermodynamic principles from the standpoint of theorizing as discussed in Section 2. Theories about particle events use ideal categories: in the tube of gas, molecules of uniform characteristics are said to travel in mathematically expressible trajectories until they collide with other molecules, when their trajectories change in mathematically describable ways. It is in such terms that we prepare the catalog of configurations of the molecules in the tube. But this viewpoint cannot yield any rationale for classifying such configurations (e.g. identifying some as "states of concentration" and others as "states of homogeneity") because *all* configurations are indistinguishable

100

in terms of particle events. Colloquially stated, the ideal particles moving according to ideal laws "don't care" whether they are arranged in one type of configuration or another; hence ideal-based theories that describe them are unable to make such distinctions. As a result, the concept of entropy is inexpressible in pure ideal-physical particle theorizing. On the other hand this concept is a natural product of theories in which physical reality is categorized *behaviorally*. Here certain physical states are distinguishable because they "behave" differently. When gas is concentrated at one end of a tube we treat the physical situation inside the tube as different because "work" can be "performed" while the gas is changing to a state of even distribution. This is what thermodynamics is about: the conversion of patterns of change in physical systems from one form to another. It treats such systems in a fundamentally behavioral way.

This explains why the "statistical" nature of thermodynamic principles has been such a thorn in the side of physics. Boltzmann was careful to point out that assertions such as the principle of entropy were not true in the same sense that (say) the law of acceleration is true. They describe what we may expect to happen, but only "to a high degree of probability." Nothing in ideal-based physical laws prohibits the gas in our tube from spontaneously gathering in one place, thereby apparently violating the principle of entropy for one instant. But for any time span over which such an event might endure there are billions of equal time spans during which the principle will be obeyed, and therefore the principle is "statistically true." Yet this is not the same as the way we understand the law of acceleration. If we apply a force to a mass we expect it to accelerate not "with a high degree of probability" but absolutely, in *every* case. Hence physicists have been worried that thermodynamic principles seem to have second-class status ontologically. But in terms of the present analysis we can appreciate this simply as a difference in "style" between ideally and behaviorally categorized viewpoints. Ideal categorization demands absolute compliance of its subject: an ideal-based law can be refuted by a single counter-example. Behavioral categorization demands only that we treat the subject in a usable way, making it relevant to our interests. This thermodynamics clearly does.

Now let us imagine that we have suspended a tiny and very light flag of gold leaf in the center of the hypothetical tube of gas. If we start with the gas molecules mostly at one end, as they diffuse into the rest of the tube the little flag will wave because of the net excess of gas molecules striking it on one side. In thermodynamic terms we have created a simple machine to convert the change of state inside the tube into mechanical motion—we have "made it do work." From another viewpoint what we have done is created a machine to *respond* to certain configurations out of all possible arrangements of gas molecules in the tube, namely those in which there is sufficient "concentration" to affect the flag. We could think of it as illustrating our behavioral theory. But this response is no longer merely a theoretical distinction; it is now an *actual physical event*. When certain configurations arise—those falling under a specific behavioral category—the presence of the gold leaf flag introduces an entirely new physical event (its motion) into the system, which would not otherwise have occurred. What had been a theoretical categorization has become a part of physical reality.

If we were expert craftsmen we might create other machines actuated by different configurations of gas in the tube. We might connect two flags by a tiny lever so that if gas concentrated in *either* end of the tube both would wave; or we might construct the link lever with a latching arrangement so that gas must concentrate in *both* ends before either flag waves; and so on. In all such cases the presence of the machine in the system changes its total characteristics, for what were previously "trivial" configurations of the gas (in the sense that its molecules would follow their trajectories regardless of whether they were in such configurations or not) have now become "significant," because only in those cases does the new physical event of flag motion occur.

The bodies of living organisms are like such gold-leaf flags, although enormously more complicated. But they do the same thing: they convert certain configurations of the environment into totally different events by means of responsive machines. They are able to do this under those circumstances where the principles of thermodynamics allow "work" to be done. In fact they can respond only to situations of low entropy, and therefore (in Schrödinger's words) seem to "feed upon negative entropy."

How does this relate to temporal ordering, the other manifestation of entropy? To understand the role of *time* in this situation, we must recognize a "difference of kind" between each responsive apparatus and its surroundings. Not "just any" mechanical structure in the tube of gas will respond to concentrations: the flags, for instance, must be thin and flat, their material must be rigid, they must be suitably hinged, the levers that transmit their motion must be connected to the right points, and so on. Similarly in living organisms only a narrow range of morphology is "viable." Previously I speculated on the steps that may have occurred in the evolution of organisms, from the first "fermentation molecule" to human intelligence; now I am considering the mechanics of that very first living thing, the least requirements life had to fulfill in order to exist at all. The most fundamental requirement for our model (and by analogy for the simplest form of life) is that there be a qualitative distinction between the responsive machine itself

102

and the environment that actuates it. Otherwise the concentrations it creates in order to be a responsive machine (i.e. its flags and levers) will themselves become candidates for response; instead of feeding upon the environment it will feed upon itself.

In the model just described (the flag in the tube of gas) there is such a distinction of kind between gas events and flag events. Physically the gas and the flag are not inherently different; but their thermodynamic behavior is distinct. The gas changes and moves, eventually assuming all its possible configurations in a random way. The flag conserves its structure and moves only under specific circumstances. To understand what is going on we find we must conceive of two entirely separate systems of events: first the nature and movements of the gas and second the pattern of movements of the flag. One is a system of events explainable in purely physical terms, the other a system requiring a behavioral explanation. Not only is this separation necessary for our understanding; *it is necessary for the existence of the responsive pattern itself*. In the case of living organisms, the way they separate their internally created responses from the external physical world forms their earliest and most fundamental treatment of reality. It is in fact their notion of "time."

Time can thus be visualized as a kind of separating procedure or "ordering algorithm" for making a clear distinction between physical reality and behavior. The totality of physical things and events to which life responds is called "past" and the totality of its behavioral responses is called "future." Temporal ordering shows up as the most basic algorithm of life: it is the means by which its thermodynamic processes are kept straight.

I am saying that the very earliest grasp of reality by living things consists of separating it into two realms, with nothing left over. The past contains all physical concentrations to which the organism might respond, which might cause its "flags to wave." It is the source of Schrödinger's "negative entropy." The future contains all the organism's responses to the past: its patterns of storing energy and constructing and improving its responsive machine. "Now," for the living organism, is the interface between these two realms.

This description of time is not at first easy to assimilate. Temporal ordering has such categorical force in our normal picture of reality that it is hard to turn around and look at it, to hold time itself in perspective. The best approach we can make involves using ideal categories, for ideals are eternal. Thus to understand how time appears in the actions of living organisms we must visualize a static "block" universe. Objects and events in such a universe are described by "world-lines," not in terms of change. In the block universe, physical reality for the organism consists of a spatial section orthogonal to a "time dimension." In one direction along this dimension stretches the past physical states of the organism, surrounded by all physical situations to which it is "now" able to respond; in the other direction stretches future physical states, including all events it is able to influence. Described ideally in this way, physical "past" and physical "future" are arbitrary distinctions, as is the selection of a "dimension" or vector along which they are strung. From life's viewpoint, however, this physical vector is carefully chosen (from all possible vectors in the block universe) to maximize its thermodynamic efficiency. In the "past" direction lie its *sources* of energy; in the "future" direction its *uses* of energy.

Hence life has adopted a physical time "dimension" in its basic grasp of reality, to orient the thermodynamic responses of organisms with respect to sources and applications of physical energy. Time is an environmental vector selected to achieve maximum separation of sources of energy from responses to these sources. The objective is that for every portion of the vector one end should be as close as possible to the richest concentrations of energy outside the organism and the other end as far as possible away from them. Thus ideally defined, this goal identifies the "best" vector, which (because life has evolved to maximize its thermodynamic responses) turns out to be the actual time vector we know. In our block universe description of physical reality, it is the *vector of propagation of radiant energy*.

We might naturally expect this, knowing that life has depended almost since its inception on energy radiated from the sun. At every stage of evolution, orienting the thermodynamic responses of living processes to-ward such an energy source—virtually the only energy source in the sun-earth thermodynamic system—would maximize life's success. We might visualize the propagation of radiant energy through space from sun to earth as a kind of four-dimensional thermodynamic "wind" that living things head into. By so heading they maximize the distinction between their upwind energy sources and their downwind energy utilizations.

The identification of life's "time vector" orientation with the block-universe direction of the propagation of radiant energy also follows from relativity theory. Starting in 1905, Einstein and others developed an alternative to Newtonian dynamics based on three assumptions: 1) It must be impossible in principle to detect the absolute continuous motion of any physical system; 2) Gravitation and inertia must refer to the same physical effect; and 3) The speed of propagation of radiant energy must be invariant, and independent of the motion of its source. Assumption (1) effectively got rid of the troublesome notions of absolute space and time, since it became impossible in principle to refer any physical observations to such entities. Assumption (2) satisfied a clear need to explain why measurements of inertial and gravitational mass were the same for all bodies. But assumption (3), that the propagation of radiant energy was absolute, seemed at first quite arbitrary. Why single out this particular phenomenon for special theoretical treatment, investing it with properties not shared by any other physical motions?

The reason is that in fact the propagation of radiation is a special, unique event from the viewpoint of living things. In physical theorizing using only ideal categories, we would not be able to justify distinguishing it in principle from other events. But assuming the invariance of the velocity of light recognizes an important relation between our *behavioral* observations and physical facts: namely that regardless of our physical situation we always adjust our system of observations to the vector of propagation of radiant energy. Doing this is not a conscious decision; rather it is built into the very way we conceive of space, time, matter, and energy. Relativity theory exposes the relationships implied by this evolved viewpoint.

Thus relativity embodies in a disciplined physical theory the primacy of radiant energy in our basic living world-view. It treats other physical entities (previously regarded as absolute) as functions of our inherited observational system. For instance the entities we call "mass" and "energy" are no longer regarded as fixed; they "interchange" around the propagation of light. Mass can better be treated as physical reality from a "space-like" viewpoint, while energy is the same reality from a "time-like" viewpoint. Parts of physical reality whose world-lines lie along our time vector appear to us as energy, whereas when their world-lines are differently oriented they appear more or less as masses.

If the velocity of radiant energy were infinite, Einstein's kinematics would not differ from Newton's. This is to say that if we could "idealize" its propagation vector by treating it as orthogonal to all spatial dimensions, then time and space would achieve the absolute character Newton intuitively gave them. But the actual orientation of this propagation vector in physical reality is an objective fact, and may not be idealized for our theorizing convenience. By recognizing that this is so we force our other idealized physical concepts—space, time, mass, energy—to follow it as theoretically interdependent notions.

Thus when we (as living organisms able to categorize our evolved viewpoint ideally) analyze physical reality, we find that temporal ordering has a specific physical embodiment: namely, the vector of propagation of radiant energy. We can now make a corresponding analysis of behavior, where we find a "parallel" vector: the chain of stimuli and responses that constitute the behavioral "history" of any living thing. Just as the propagation of light is a specific class of events selected from the totality of physical reality, so the stimulus-response chain is a particular subpattern within the totality of behavior. When we are conscious of it, it comprises our "inner experience" of the passage of time. The chain consists of a sequence of behavioral fragments, among which those that constitute "stimuli" or "bases of action" we call "past" and those that constitute "responses" or "commands for action" we call "future."

If behavior were always isolated from physical reality there would be no point in identifying a particular subpattern in it as a "stimulus-response chain." We sometimes experience such isolation in dreams, when our normal sense of temporal sequence tends to disintegrate. Similarly when physical reality is considered by itself the radiant energy propagation vector merits no special status. But in the behavioral-physical interchange that underlies all life these two vectors cooperate to form the ordering algorithm called "time." Each reinforces the other in our grasp of reality. More exactly, living things have evolved the stimulus-response chain in conformance to the radiant energy vector, in order to maximize their thermodynamic efficiency within the sun-earth environment. Organizing reality in a temporal order is a specific and fundamental activity of life: specific in that it selects, from all possible orderings, the one which makes it most effective in capturing and utilizing available energy; and fundamental in that it is the oldest evolved living technique of every cell, tissue, and biological process. It is here that entropy as an organic-inorganic differentiation and entropy as "time's arrow" meet. Entropy itself drops from the equation, and we are left with the insight that living things have established time ordering as a fundamental thermodynamic tool for dealing with their "niche" in the cosmos.

3.3 Understanding

> In completing one discovery we never fail to get an imperfect knowledge of others of which we could have no idea before, so that we cannot solve one doubt without creating several new ones. PRIESTLEY

The time ordering process just discussed is a fundamental algorithm that living things have evolved to secure their position in the sun-earth thermodynamic system. It is possible to trace the emergence of other such algorithms—spatial separation, for instance—in living development. When Kant proposed his scheme of categories to cover our inherent grasp of physical reality he was forced to call both time and space "intuitions," because he could not derive them logically; were he alive today he might be inspired to make an evolutionary analysis of their force instead. Similarly, the more sophisticated notion of measurable quantities can be shown to have evolved to facilitate life's increasing use of ideals. In all these cases, approaches to reality that are seemingly absolute and inescapable turn out, on analysis, to have been merely instrumental to a particular set of conditions in life's development.

Hence our most basic conceptualizations are essentially parochial, in the sense that they were selected to satisfy specific needs and might have been radically different if the needs had been different. The first step toward freeing our understanding from these specialized viewpoints consists of realizing what they are and why they are specialized. Yet the task is not easy, for they permeate every nook and cranny of our thought. Beside such algorithmic notions as time and space, our fundamental division of reality into physical, behavioral, and ideal "orders" colors all our understandings. This tripartite viewpoint forms a sort of underlying armature to which our myriad ideas about the world are molded.

The foregoing problem can be illustrated by an interesting example of a single idea (that of infinity) proliferating and taking on different forms as a result of our three-fold approach to reality. The modern mathematical theory of "transfinite cardinal numbers," introduced by Cantor, envisions a series of infinitely large numbers each of which embodies a "different order" of infinity from its predecessor. The first transfinite cardinal, the "power" of the integer set, denotes the totality of any *enumerable* collection. It can be shown to apply not only to the set of integers $\{1,2,3,...\}$ but also to many infinite sets that can be generated from them, such as the rational numbers. The second transfinite cardinal, the power of the "continuum," is best characterized as denoting the totality of points in any geometric domain, such as a line or a surface. It is non-denumerable—and hence has a higher "power"—because between *any* two such points there are infinitely many more points. The third transfinite cardinal is the power of the "functional manifold"; it can be visualized as denoting the totality of all possible *arrangements* (functions) of the points in a geometric continuum. It exhibits a "higher power" of infinity because it can be shown that there are infinitely many more ways of arranging an infinity of points than there are points themselves.

We can trace a direct association between these "different orders" of infinity envisioned by mathematicians and the orders of reality discussed here. The first transfinite cardinal, which measures any unending counting process, conceptualizes the result of unlimited *behavior*. It is described by showing the procedural steps by which the members of a collection can be totalled, comprising the familiar living process of enumeration. The second transfinite cardinal, however, surpasses any attempt to describe it as the measure of a behavioral procedure; in fact it applies to our understanding of *physical reality*. We think of physical things as "infinitely specific," i.e. as having more detail in them than we can possibly dig out by behavioral investigation. This is why they convey an "objective" quality to us. The notion of infinite specificity carries over into our geometricization of physical reality, so we automatically visualize "geometric space" as offering details stuffed among its details *ad infinitum*. Finally the third transfinite cardinal measures unlimited *ideals*. The "functional manifold" of all possible point arrangements is a purely ideal concept; it can neither be generated by any behavioral procedure nor embodied physically. We grasp its reality only by defining it.

In this example, an original naive idea—infinity—has become transformed by "interpreting" it in terms of different parts of our evolved grasp of reality. By extension, there should be other such interpretations which have not yet occurred to us because we have not yet evolved the necessary viewpoint.

Traditional theorizing has usually been based on the presupposition that

108

there is a degree of freedom between any theorizer and his subject, i.e. that it is not absolutely necessary to treat any particular subject in any particular way. We feel that our imagination can always frame other treatments, even if they do not appear to be valid. Yet in instances such as our evolved visualization of time we find a theoretical treatment of reality that is in some sense *necessary*; it has been by virtue of applying it that life has been able to exist at all. And even in such an imagination-centered discipline as mathematics we find difficulty in surmounting evolved barriers, for no transfinite cardinals other than the three mentioned have yet been described.

Does our present status as evolved reactive thinking machines of a special type, then, absolutely determine the ultimate limits of our possible knowledge? This is a question I will consider more fully in Section 6. Regardless of ultimate limits, however, it is clear that what we take to be limits are largely self-imposed restrictions. The methods for transcending them are already available, but have not hitherto been used in an organized way.

It seems to be firmly fixed in human consciousness that any expansion of understanding must take the form of a "search for truth." This seems such a natural idea that it is difficult at first to analyze it critically. If reality is not a fixed thing that we are capable of knowing truly as it is, then what point is there in trying to understand it at all? Many scientists claim that their researches are getting "closer and closer" to elucidating the ultimate nature of reality, and therefore their search for truth is justified. Even in the tangled world of particle physics this claim is now widely made for the newest level of micro-entities, the "quarks"; about them the physicist S. L. Glashow writes (1975):

> A solitary quark has never been observed, in spite of many attempts to isolate one. Nevertheless, there are excellent grounds for believing they do exist. More important, quarks may be the last in the long series of progressively finer structures. They seem to be truly elementary.[29]

It is difficult to fly in the face of such optimism, particularly when it is backed up by a mass of human work, analysis, and criticism. But there is also a certain amount of skepticism to be derived from realizing that at other times systems such as those of Aristotle and Aquinas (to name just two) were taken to be fully as definitive approaches to truth as modern physics. By what principle must we treat this new search for truth as more valid than theirs?

Several reasons for the superiority of the scientific approach are commonly cited: the overwhelming agreement on methods and results within the scientific community, the elegance of science's descriptive paradigms, the wealth of tangible scientific products ranging from electricity to atom bombs. But none of these arguments preclude the possibility that there are equally valuable routes to knowledge totally different from science. They all assume an epistemological position which might be called the "postulate of exclusivity." This asserts that for any given part of reality there can be only one correct theory. Therefore if we have a theory that satisfies many of the traditional criteria of correctness—such as common agreement, consistent presentation, and practical results—it must be "close" to the correct theory, and no wholly different viewpoint could possibly be correct or as nearly correct. It is this postulate of exclusivity that Kuhn questions when he asks "Does it really help to imagine that there is one full, objective, true account of nature and that the proper measure of scientific achievement is the extent to which it brings us closer to that goal?"[30] Even this pencil in my hand might be described quite differently, and equally validly, by an artist, a physicist, and a businessman. Why then should we assume single exclusive descriptions for "ultimate" reality?

The considerations cited in Section 2 provide good reasons for doubting the doctrine of exclusivity in theorizing. I argued there that theories are as much products of their categories as they are "reflections" of their subjects. We should be particularly wary of ascribing exclusive validity, or even any validity at all, to concepts of minima; they are artificialities that we create in order to correlate unlike parts of reality. Theories should be treated not as representations of reality with various degrees of "faithfulness," but rather as knowledge-generating tools, as instruments that make our understanding grow outside the theories themselves.

But even if we relegate theorizing to a wholly instrumental role (which would cast much of what passes for modern scientific knowledge into an epistemological limbo) there remains a similar problem with common sense. Time ordering, for instance, is part of my commonsense view of reality, yet it turns out to be a specific and parochial viewpoint. In general, human treatments of reality—both theoretical and commonsensical—have evolved to satisfy discrete needs, and hence do not necessarily provide any assurance that they "represent" reality as a whole to any particular degree of completeness or accuracy. Just as the digger wasp has evolved just enough knowledge of grasshoppers to be able to find one when she needs to lay her eggs, so we appear to have learned just enough about reality to be able to survive in it. We have not truly sought knowledge for its own sake.

What general method, then, leads to the broadest expansion of understanding? The method employed here might be called "*comparative theorizing*." It promotes the free interplay of separate parts of reality against one

110

another in order to illuminate the characteristics of each. For example, the way I exposed the behavioral factor in our concept of physical time was by using ideal categories, which describe physical time in a block universe as a vector of a certain type. Temporal sequencing is so embedded in our natural world-view that normally it might never occur to us to treat it as just one ordering algorithm out of a range of possibilities. But by developing an otherwise fairly complete physical representation without reference to time order we can grasp that it is a product of categorization, not an inherent part of the subject. We "compare" two theories—ideal physics and behavioral thermodynamics—to locate and expose the concept of physical time.

Consider another example. Language is a part of behavior which can be analyzed from several viewpoints, separated generally into schemes of physical categorization and schemes of ideal categorization. In the first case we proceed from lexicography, the assignment of specific meanings to specific language fragments, to the more general consideration of semantics, the study of relations between signs and designata. In the second case we proceed from examining the rules of grammar to theories of classical (Aristotelian) logic, then to the modern discipline of "syntactics," the study of the "formal" properties of signs. As scholarly pursuits, these two approaches to language have been vigorously promoted by somewhat opposing camps, each wishing it could reduce away the other approach in the interests of the "search for truth." For instance, Wittgenstein's semantical dictum that "every sentence has its own logic" opposes assertions by theorizers such as Tarski and Church that language is primarily a product of its formal properties. The most important outcome of these arguments, however, has been their mutual delineation of language behavior itself. Semantics alone is an empirical and somewhat fragmentary inquiry into "language games"; syntactics alone becomes a study of formal systems only remotely related to any actual speech or writing. But by spotlighting language from two directions, they act together to enrich our understanding of it.

A powerful tool for comparative theorizing is the creation of "artificial theories." Such theories temporarily ignore the "search for truth" because they are set up as tools for illuminating our understanding, not because they are thought to be valid in themselves. They are adopted for the deliberate purpose of introducing a change of viewpoint. For instance language theorists quite freely "set up" artificial languages as models of logical or semantical mechanisms, thereby deliberately creating an object of knowledge in order to clarify their methods and categories. When they discover properties that seem to inhere in such artificial languages independently of the rules by which they were created—such as Tarski's concept of "truth" in semantical systems—they are justified in supposing that they have in some sense uncovered an inherent property of actual languages.

One of the earliest uses of artificial theories was the mathematical technique of *reductio ad absurdum*. To show that the square root of two is not a fraction, the Pythagoreans set up a miniature theory in which it was and then showed that the theory led to a self-contradiction. This fulfilled the aim of comparative theorizing: it "cross-illuminated" our notion of numbers by introducing (in addition to the traditional physical categorizations of these ideals) the behavioral category of "contradiction" or "absurdity." The same technique is used today, in a more sophisticated form, to determine the "decidability" of mathematical problems. It is thus described by L. A. Steen:

> …the basis for most undecidability results is a delicate chain of reasoning in which one very carefully forces into existence a mathematical model with certain predetermined properties… Each undecidability proof requires construction of a model in which the proposition in question is true and another one in which it is false: the undecidability of the proposition follows from the existence of such models, for no general proof or refutation will be possible if the proposition is, in fact, true in some models while false in others.[31]

It is a remarkable method to "force into existence" a theoretical subject for the purpose of elucidating certain features of mathematical reality independent of that subject. It is in fact a procedure that becomes justifiable only when the "search for truth" has become subordinated to an enlargement of understanding.

The cognate method in studies of physical reality should appear in laboratory experimentation. Here one "forces into existence" the highly specialized conditions under which basic physical effects are observed. But in physical science the "search for truth" is usually dominant. Comparative theorizing emerges only as a last resort, at times of great confusion over data and their interpretations. As soon as an acceptable resolution appears on the horizon existing theories are usually adapted to receive it, in accordance with the "postulate of exclusivity": for it then seems that prior viewpoints had only strayed somewhat from the path toward the one true picture of reality, and can now be adjusted. A survey of actual procedures in the physical sciences shows that comparative theorizing is the exceptional, remedial technique, rather than a normal method for gaining knowledge.

When the postulate of exclusivity dominates theorizing, the comparative method advocated here tends to be rejected as "useless speculation." Why create artificial theories when what we need are "real" ones? My answer, of course, is that there is no such thing as a real theory. In practice, all speculations are like political revolutions: bothersome and wasteful until they succeed, after which they are endowed by hindsight with historical necessity. Thus what I am advocating, in these terms, is the deliberate adoption of speculation as a theorizing tool. For example, starting with the concept (discussed earlier) of time as an ordering algorithm based on the vector of propagation of radiant energy, we could ask what *other* such ordering algorithms might be devised to characterize physical reality. The result would be a series of artificial theories cognate to thermodynamics but covering entirely different facets of the physical world. If necessary to stimulate our conceptualizations in this process, we might imagine theorizing beings with different properties from ourselves—for instance, beings whose involvement with physical reality is not centered around radiant energy—and then ask what kinds of physical sciences such beings might create. These speculations could never be a direct "search for truth" because we would always be aware that they were based on an artificial, deliberately created theorizing situation. But at the same time they would never be mere "science fiction." They would illuminate from different angles the same physical reality we presently view primarily through the narrow window of traditional science. For all their artificiality, they would make an important contribution to understanding.

Human beings presently possess a basic set of tools for comparative theorizing: namely our commonsense understandings of the physical, behavioral, and ideal orders of reality. In theorizing (as analyzed here) we "cross-breed" these separate parts of reality in an artificial way: e.g. treat physical events as having ideal properties, behavior as apprehending physical things, and so on. If we were to theorize freely and eclectically, treating it as a purely instrumental procedure, we would use these tools to best advantage. Carried out as a deliberate program, such free comparative theorizing would amount to a full exploration of the *possibilities of knowledge*, as a consequence of which our understanding would achieve its greatest opportunity to grow. As long as theorizing is reduced to a rigid "search for truth," wherein theoretical approaches are not compared and minima are elevated from theoretical tools to ultimate objects of knowledge, understanding stagnates. In this case we simply fail to use the materials in our hands. It is only through the free interplay of theoretical viewpoints that we are able to deepen our grasp of reality itself.

One may ask: if this is the case, if comparative theorizing is a superior route to knowledge, why must it be advocated? Why does it not naturally take place? A first answer stems from the natural "inertia" of living things, human beings included. Knowledge is traditionally instrumental to other pursuits; when it has been acquired in a satisfactory form there remains little incentive to spend energy on its further development. Because it works indirectly, comparative theorizing seems unnecessarily laborious. For instance, conceiving and developing a physics in which radiant energy is a peripheral effect rather than a central ordering concept would be a major task; bringing it to the state where it could be meaningfully compared to traditional physics would entail a great deal of work undertaken with no immediate results. Furthermore at all times the theorizer would be criticized for wasting his time on "useless speculation" instead of joining his colleagues in the "search for truth."

Another reason for the rarity of comparative theorizing, however, cuts deeper into the human situation. "Behavioral energy" can be made available for comparative theorizing by the simple decisions of individual theorizers to do so. But as sociologists frequently point out, much of this "energy" is generated and controlled socially. Often the interchange between an individual theorizer and the society in which he is embedded is so "natural" that he never realizes how closely he is bound. Yet in the last analysis it is often society, not "truth," that determines whether a theory is accepted and followed, or rejected and ridiculed.

Thus no picture of the architecture of knowledge can be complete without examining its social determinants. Social patterns, of course, are patterns of behavior. So the succeeding sections of this book will be devoted to a broad consideration of human behavior, including its effects on knowledge. It turns out to take certain discrete organizational forms, in each of which specific kinds of theorizing are encouraged and other kinds are rejected. These orientations constitute the most powerful reason why comparative theorizing is rarely practiced, for each one survives in its society by virtue of setting certain limits on theorizing activity. By identifying and understanding them, however, we acquire the means to surmount them.

4. Organizations

Life, like a dome of many-colored glass,
Stains the white radiance of Eternity.
SHELLEY

There is a certain fashionableness about theorizing styles. Depending on the time and place, one way of viewing reality will usually be considered "proper" while another way will be considered "improper." For example, in industrialized countries today ideal-based science is "in"; behavioral-based animism is "out." The reverse is true on the island of Dobu. It is commonly assumed (by those living in industrialized societies) that the reason for this is that the Dobuans are less aware of the "true" nature of reality. In earlier sections of this book I have provided some reasons to doubt this claim: theories that make ideal categorizations of physical reality are no more "inherently better" than those which make behavioral categorizations, and in any event the latter are far more prevalent in everyday living. Nevertheless the claim is overwhelmingly promoted in our society, even by those for whom science is an arcane and largely unknown ritual. The forces that cause it to be "in" and other styles of theorizing to be "out" are powerful and pervasive.

In fact these forces emanate from the fabric of society itself. In the present instance, something happened in Europe during the sixteenth and seventeenth centuries that changed our whole approach toward understanding reality. Matters that used to be thought important became much less so, and matters that used to be ignored became new concerns. Thinkers worried less about the nature of the Trinity and more about the nature of combustion; less about the divine right of kings and more about the principles of common law; and so on. We should be suspicious of any claim that this shift was due to a sudden new realization of where "absolute truth" was to be found. Instead, it is more illuminating to apply to whole social changes such as this the same kind of analysis I have just applied to theorizing.

115

When the differences between two general modes of dealing with reality are discussed (such as the differences between modern science and animism) the word "organization" tends to crop up. A modern scientist will say that science is well organized, animism is not. If we then demonstrate that animism often has an elaborate organization of its own (for instance the discipline of alchemy discussed earlier), the reply may be that between the two organizations that of science is "better," that of animism "inferior." Finally, if we show that animism is in fact a more universally used and more practical approach to reality—and that it has maintained a fairly consistent scheme of categories over the centuries while science has gyrated wildly from one set of conceptualizations to another—then the only supportable conclusion left is that it has a "different" organization. At this stage we have tacitly abandoned the "absolute truth" criterion of theorizing and are treating it simply as a variety of behavior. We say that behavior (including theorizing) can be organized in various ways. Once we agree to treat it from this purely comparative viewpoint—even though it is behavior trying to grasp reality—we cease making invidious distinctions and concentrate only on its style or pattern of organization.

Understanding behavior as a whole comparatively helps comparative theorizing. The necessary freedom to choose and contrast categories at will depends on a corresponding freedom from absolute discriminations within behavior. At the same time the general behavior patterns compared must be sufficiently coherent to serve as practical objects of knowledge. The objects we identify as "organizations" tend to satisfy these criteria; hence it is an appropriate term to denote behavior maxima in general. For this reason my succeeding discussions will be about organizations—not only as disciplines within which knowledge is gathered, but as general patterns of human life.

In Section 1.1 I examined our most primitive grasp of reality, which divides it into physical, behavioral, and ideal "orders." It is clear that the behavior which does this is in some sense fundamental to everything else we do. Therefore I will call these three basic modes of knowledge "primary organizations," for it is on them that the rest of human behavior is founded. These primary organizations constitute the most general ways we approach reality, and the largest maxima discernible in our behavior.

From the primary organizations we build a set of more limited patterns, which I will call "secondary organizations." Examples of these have already been given, in the "theorizing styles" described earlier. The simplest way we can bring two primary organizations together is by using one as a basis or "setting" for operations on the other. In the case of theorizing, the setting provides a group of categories that discriminate among parts of a different primary organization—our commonsense grasp of the theory's subject. The secondary organization consists of the behavior that relates primary organizations in this way.

So in my terminology human individuals and societies develop secondary organizations of behavior to "fit" the three primary organizations of their grasp of reality into new and more integrated patterns. The ways that they do this appear as "styles" of human behavior, including (as a special case) styles of theorizing. There are three primary organizations, which taken two at a time yield six ordered pairs; thus there are six secondary organizations.

Among these we can find six basic styles of theorizing, most of which have already been mentioned: physical reality categorized by behavior, behavior categorized by ideals, and so forth. But this analysis now transcends the narrow subject of theorizing itself; and in fact the concept of secondary organizations is generally applicable to *all* human behavior patterns, not just those which generate new knowledge. As it turns out, the manifestations of secondary organizations most easily visualized are their embodiments in general social behavior. Groups behave according to readily identifiable "styles," which reflect group-adopted secondary organizations of human life. These group styles tend to sanction their "approved" theorizing approaches; but the nature of their behavior is more easily grasped in the group context than in the narrower context of theorizing. So a first step toward understanding secondary organizations is to recognize them in group behavior. For this purpose I have adopted the following sociologically-oriented names:

Primary Organization as "Setting"	Primary Organization as "Subject"	Secondary Organization
Physical Reality	Behavior	COMMUNALISM
Behavior	Physical Reality	AUTHORITARIANISM
Behavior	Ideals	INTELLECTION
Ideals	Behavior	ORTHODOXY
Ideals	Physical Reality	LEGALISM
Physical Reality	Ideals	COLLECTIVISM

Some of these group manifestations of secondary organizations are readily understood as generalizations or extrapolations of particular kinds of theorizing behavior I discussed earlier. For instance, legalism could be treated as the social extension of ideal-based science, wherein ideal statutes are developed to govern the actions of people much as ideal laws are supposed to govern the actions of nature; or conversely, science could be treated as a product of social legalism, wherein an approach found effective in regulating human groups is taken to also regulate nature. In other cases the connection between group behavior and theorizing behavior may not at first be apparent. But in all instances the connection is there, and by analyzing it we uncover some of the more subtle effects of knowledge and social form upon each other.

It may be helpful to visualize the relationships among three primary organizations and six secondary organizations of human social behavior by means of the following diagram. Shapes at the corners represent the primary organizations by which our behavior grasps the orders of reality; arrows represent the secondary organizations. Each arrow has its tail toward the primary organization that provides the ''setting'' or group categorial supply for the behavior named; its point is toward the primary organization that constitutes the ''subject'' or field of operation for group action.

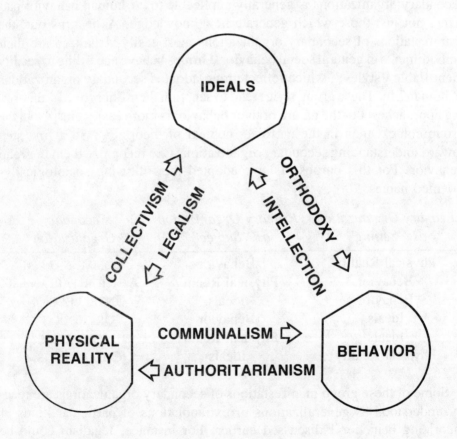

4.1 Secondary Organizations

> There were never in the world two opinions alike, no more than two hairs or two grains; the most universal quality is diversity.
>
> MONTAIGNE

Human primary organizations (our understandings of physical reality, behavior, and ideals) have already been discussed at length and should need no further treatment here. The way they enter into the formation of theories has also been examined in some detail. In one sense the secondary organizations to be described now might be thought of as *generalizations* of theories—whole modes of human behavior concerned with such matters as social interaction and individual personality, as well as with the acquisition of knowledge. By giving them sociological names I have already emphasized their broader scope.

Nevertheless all manifestations of any given secondary organization in human behavior—social, personal, theoretical, or whatever—are *connected*, in the same sense that the parts of any primary organization are. They can be understood in the same basic way, just as can two physical events or two mathematical abstractions. The secondary organizations cohere as fundamental "styles" of behavior, regardless of any other distinctions we may make. Thus in the following discussion I will explore each one in a variety of contexts, including some of its occurrences in the operations of groups, in the personality traits of individual human beings, and in the formation of human knowledge. Although these are usually treated as disparate areas of behavior, their commonness of secondary organizations explains why human life in general tends to become coordinated into a limited range of discrete behavior "styles."

COMMUNALISM. A communal secondary organization appears in human life whenever some part of physical reality becomes the basis ("setting") for exploring or manipulating some part of behavior. The physical situation is

119

"given" in this case, and forms the starting point for human effort. A behavioral situation is the focus of this organization: as a result of its manifestation some part of behavior is modified, developed, or understood where it had not been before.

Sociologically, a typical instance of communalism occurs any time two or more persons cooperate in solving a physical problem. Ten men, wishing to take shelter in a cave, find the entrance blocked by a large stone. No one man can move it, but the ten working together can easily roll it away. Here physical reality has provided the setting—the hostile environment that makes it desirable to enter the cave, the cave itself, and the stone in the doorway. Ten individuals, behaving at random, might eventually conspire to push the stone in the same direction at the same time, but it is unlikely. What is needed is a modification of each individual's separate behavior so it will aid that of the others, so that a true group will emerge to deal with the physical problem. In other words, *cooperation* is needed. When such cooperation appears—when in fact the behavior patterns of two or more individuals are modified to meet a common physical problem—it is clear that something new has been created: a communal organization of behavior.

Animals other than man exhibit communalism. Most birds, for instance, exhibit some sort of communal organization when rearing their young. Here again the setting is physical—the need to nourish infant birds, the fact that they must stay put until old enough to fly, the dangers from predators and the elements—and the solution is behavioral. The parents cooperate, often with risk and sacrifice for each one individually, until the physical setting has been resolved by the fledglings leaving the nest. Bird behavior while rearing young is quite different from that at other times, largely because of the emergence of this secondary communal organization. The significance of recognizing the difference (calling it "communalism") is that the same basic pattern occurs in many different contexts. In each case our attention is aroused by a peculiarity of behavior, which we are then able to understand by identifying the physical situation: we categorize the behavior physically as "nourishing," "protecting," etc.

Once we know where to look, we find communalism in many everyday human social activities. Driving in traffic, serving dinner, dancing—in each case a group of people modifies the behavior of each member to conform to a physical setting by creating among themselves a *new* pattern of behavior, a new secondary organization.

Just as with other animals, human child rearing is an important example of social communalism. Parent-child cooperation is also a principal point of entry for communalism into individual personality patterns; we can appreciate this by considering it from the infant's viewpoint. To a neonate, certain physical situations are "given." These include its own physiological needs, such potentially harmful situations as becoming cold, the mother's breast as a source of nourishment, the cry as a means of signalling, etc. At the outset the infant is powerless to alter any of these physical factors by himself; they must be taken as ineluctable categories for its initial organization of responses, while the responses themselves must be directed toward another area. In fact they are directed toward behavior, first that of the infant and then that of its mother. It is only through mother-child cooperation that the neonate's survival is ultimately possible. Thus its early responsive organization takes as its "subject matter," as its area of learning and manipulation, the behavioral interplay between it and its mother; and it takes a portion of physical reality, that centered around its requirements for physical survival, as the "given" setting this organization must satisfy. What behavior gains the breast? What new behavior then produces the milk? What to do when I am cold? Questions such as these fill the neonate's first struggles with individual learning, which rapidly pass beyond the instinctive set of reflexes with which it was born.

If we were to call the human infant a "theorist," we would say that it is studying behavior by means of categories drawn from physical reality, and hence is a tyro empiricist, as I shall discuss shortly. But "theorizing" is too limited a term to describe the vital task in which it is engaged; it builds a secondary organization in its behavior not just to expand its understanding, but to survive.

The infant's behavior in developing its communal responses within the parent-child group (what might be called more generally its "role" in this communal group) is characteristically cooperative. Of course the same holds for the mother. Each develops behavior patterns toward members of the group (in this case, toward each other) that make it possible for the group as a whole to achieve some physical goal (in this case, the survival and growth of the child). The physical goal can be achieved only by members acting in concert—neither can do it alone; and concert can be achieved only by mutual regulation of behavior, by mutual cooperation. When the mother presents her breast and the infant suckles, both have organized their group behavior to satisfy the physiologically given process of infant nourishment.

This example is a group of two, but the same organization can arise in groups of any size. Occasionally whole societies develop a predominately communal organization. One immediately thinks of "communes"—small bands of individuals cooperating to maintain a common physical setting—which become popular from time to time. While these may approximate pure communalism, they are more often mixed with other secondary organizations: orthodoxy in the case of religious communes and collectivism in the case of economically productive communes. Instances of truly communal societies are usually found only in reports of anthropologists. For reasons I will discuss in Section 5.1, pure communalism is not an enduring form of behavior for whole societies; nevertheless under optimum conditions it may occur.

A well-known example was described by Margaret Mead in 1935. The Arapesh people of the Sepik river area in northeastern New Guinea live in an isolated and difficult land, protected from outside contacts by "mountains so infertile that no neighbor envies them their possession, so inhospitable that no army could invade them and find food enough to survive, so precipitous that life among them can never be anything except difficult and exacting.[32] This provides the setting for their social organization, a setting composed almost exclusively of severe physical problems. The Arapesh respond to this setting by adopting a nearly total dedication to cooperation. They tend each other's gardens, build each other's houses, share the results of hunting, and help care for each other's children. Institutions that would reflect secondary organizations other than communalism—such as political units, private property, competition, and even lines of authority within family clans—are largely absent. Mead's account of the Arapesh in *Sex and Temperament in Three Primitive Societies* provides interesting details of what life in a truly communal society can be like.

I mentioned earlier that the human infant could be regarded as a theorist. He is in fact developing the most basic communalistic theory, that of perception itself. We notice parts of our behavior—sensations, images, pictures—that are best understood in terms of physical categories. All redness sensations are grouped under the physical heading "red"; various images of a book are associated because they are taken to refer to the same physical book; and so on. That perception is a theory at all is often over-looked (except by philosophers): but it is easy to see that it is from the opportunity for error. Perceptions may be mistaken as a result of illusions, hypnosis, disease, etc. When this happens it is necessary to theorize further, i.e. find new categories to cover the aberrant experiences. Perception is doubtless the most fundamental and most essential of human theories.

This style of theorizing falls under the general philosophical head of "empiricism." It examines human behavior from the standpoint of physical categorization and attempts to derive therefrom a grasp of physical reality. The English empiricists—Locke, Berkeley, and Hume—examined this process with great care, exposing many of the assumptions implicit in it. The more careful they were, the more evident it became that in empirical theories the categories and the subject matter came from two different kinds of reality. The best justification they could find for asserting the existence of a physical world (other than Berkeley's dependence on God) was that it supplied the most convenient categorial scheme for explaining our own perception behavior. Thus arose the "skepticism" of Hume, who concluded that because physical reality, behavior, and ideals are all independent of one another, and because among them only behavior is "known directly," therefore only behavior can be asserted to exist.

The secondary organization "communalism" thus occurs in a variety of human activities, including such areas as rearing infants, communal societies, and the theory of perception. It might at first appear that these are unrelated behavior patterns. But on careful examination their connection becomes clear: first, because in all cases the same pattern of behavior modification from a physical setting holds, and second, because we can actually trace the steps of development from one to another through such situations as the growth of a newborn child. As a result, it is possible to appreciate how this organization constitutes one of the fundamental threads from which human behavior is woven.

AUTHORITARIANISM. When the positions occupied by physical reality and behavior in communalism are reversed—when behavior provides the setting for exploring and manipulating physical things—the result is a different secondary organization, which I call "authoritarianism."

This is a familiar concept in sociology. It is applied to groups where the will of a leader (king, chief, dictator) becomes the basis for physical acts by individual members. Certain traditions are also said to work by "authority" when they carry no logical rationale: that is, when they are simply accepted as part of the common behavioral basis of a people and cited when decisions about physical actions are to be made. The physical subject areas of authoritarianism are as diverse as the interests of any group: who does which jobs, how goods are to be allocated, what individual actions are demanded or permitted or proscribed, even how individuals are to be punished when the authority is transgressed. The key to this secondary organization (and what separates it from the secondary organization I call "legalism") is that the basis for its dictates is a pattern of behavior, not a set of ideals. It springs from a group's agreement to accept the behavior of a chief, an oligarchy, or a traditional pattern as the basis for sorting out and regulating physical actions.

Authoritarianism is a common organization in human families, particularly in the subgroups containing young children. Once they pass the stage where they are wholly dependent on mother-child communalism to satisfy their physical needs, children acquire an organization where they receive prescribed patterns of behavior from their parents and in return are permitted individual manipulation of physical reality. Parents, too, tend to treat these

123

prescribed patterns of behavior as intrinsic to the parent-child group even though they have the power to hold them in perspective, which the child does not. In other words, authoritarianism arises in the family group through a common agreement that certain behavior patterns are "given," and its members (particularly the children) must deal with physical things in conformity with this behavioral setting.

Studies by Piaget of children's attitudes toward the rules of games illustrate authoritarianism from their viewpoint. For several years after infancy children normally treat game behavior as utterly fixed: "...rules are regarded as sacred and untouchable, emanating from adults and lasting forever. Every suggested alteration strikes the child as a transgression."[33] Despite this attitude, children are actually observed to play somewhat carelessly, randomly altering the physical configurations of their games. What is happening is that the child is learning the physical skill of playing (in this case, marbles) within a setting of behavior it regards as ineluctable. When asked to perform the physical game the child exhibits a range of trial-and-error learning; when asked to report the behavioral rule pattern it treats it as given by unquestionable authority.

Any closely supervised work group tends to exhibit authoritarianism. When a group achieves its goals through mere cooperation, of course, it is communal. But to the extent that its success depends on the members following behavioral directions, it is authoritarian. Perhaps the purest example is a slave gang or prison work detail. Here the behavioral setting is clear and explicit; it is often discipline just for the sake of discipline, and each individual act is governed by the rigid organization of the group. From the slave or prisoner's viewpoint he follows an authoritarian organization of the simplest sort: he does just what he is told to do with the materials in front of him.

On a larger scale, several functions of highly-regulated societies tend to be carried out by authoritarian groups. These may range from armed forces and police squads down to school traffic patrols. Usually these groups display other secondary organizations as well, for pure authoritarianism on a large scale seems despotic. The group may be guided by a book of abstract policy in addition to the established canons of behavior. But the principal organization emerges in the actions of each group member: he performs physical acts in accordance with a group-sanctioned pattern of behavior. If there can be no appeal from the behavioral pattern, then it is pure authoritarianism; if the prescribed behavior can be modified by reference to ideals, then it is authoritarianism mixed with legalism; and so on.

Authoritarian theorizing is animism, discussed earlier. In animistic theories, behavior provides the categorial setting for knowledge of physical

124

reality. Physical events are held to occur by virtue of a system of behavioral dictates, much as Piaget's children regarded games as governed by adult-established rules. In Section 2.1 I contrasted animism with legalistic science, where categories are derived from ideals. This difference is cognate to that between authoritarian and legalistic social organizations. In fact there is some historical evidence that as animism matures (as a theorizing style) in a society it tends to introduce authoritarian group regulation. Such maturing of animism takes the form of "deism," where systems of behavioral categories coalesce into the hypostatized personalities of gods, or ultimately a God. If understanding physical events depends on familiarity with a pattern of behavior, is it not natural to suppose that the behavior all emanates from one or more man-like beings? The development of this idea runs parallel to the political transition from tradition-orientation to kingship, and tends to offer it justification. "Divine right" becomes the first basis of royal rule. Thus men pass from regarding physical things as behaving, to regarding them as obeying the gods' behavior; and they pass from regulating their physical acts in society by a traditional scheme of behavior, to conforming them to the will of a king.

INTELLECTION. "Intellection" is my name for the secondary organization in human life that takes behavior for its setting and turns its attention to ideals. Its connotations are familiar: the formation of abstract ideas, the discovery of "principles," the grasp of generalities instead of sensations of specific objects. In such activities the setting is thought behavior, the ability of human minds to conceptualize. The subjects of intellection are ideals—not physical objects, not the behavior of other people, but pure abstractions.

Socially, intellection is promoted by writers, lecturers, academicians and "thinkers": this book, for instance, is primarily a product of intellection. Among smaller groups, a good place to observe intellection in a relatively pure form is in the classroom or seminar. Here the behavioral setting exceeds the thought processes of any one individual; the group *as a whole* agrees to join in a pattern of behavior designed to facilitate their mutual exploration of ideals. This pattern usually includes attempts to minimize physical distractions, an agreement to "stick to a subject," a scheme of terminology (i.e. common language behavior), etc. Such "classroom discipline" is important, for it establishes much of the behavioral basis without which this secondary organization could not exist. Group intellection of this type ("education") is vital to industrialized societies, as can be seen from the fact that their members typically devote a significant part of their lives to it.

In many primitive societies, intellectual education is applied in a concentrated form by means of initiation ceremonies. Such societies cannot spend

125

the energy required to indoctrinate youths for years (as we do) nor do they have that much ideal material to communicate. What they have to teach—typically the tribal institutions, its semi-abstract "secret" knowledge, and the value systems of manhood and womanhood—is inculcated by creating a setting in which behavior is rigidly disciplined. Thus primitive adolescents, when they are ready for their "schooling," are commonly sequestered in special houses and subjected to fasting, fear, and subjugation. This behavioral setting generates an intellectual secondary organization in which they absorb the tribal ideals relatively efficiently, emerging fully taught for the rest of their lives.

At one stage in European history intellection went "underground," surviving only in behavioral settings where it could withstand the political authoritarianism of the day. These settings were the monastic institutions that flourished between the dissolution of the Roman Empire and the rise of Protestantism. Although most of them also functioned as agents for the orthodoxy of Catholicism, they comprised (at least at the beginning) the only effective sources of abstract learning in Europe. They preserved and communicated much previous knowledge about ideals. Characteristically, they combined a regime of fixed behavior patterns (the "monastic life") with encouraging individual insights into ideals. An historically minded anthropologist might call this period of monasticism the "rite of passage" for modern Europe.

In formal theorizing, intellection first appears as the study of logic. Ideals are sorted out by using such behavioral criteria as implication, negation, and contradiction. Following the early insights of Aristotle, the development of workable systems of logical "notation" by Boole, Peano, Russell and others provided a new language (a new system of agreed behavior) with which to categorize ideals. This behavioral setting is distinct from the physical setting for mathematical notation because it is *dynamic*: it refers to notions such as implication (the concept that one set of ideals "leads to" another) rather than to static ideas such as quantity and equality. Logic is often called the "principles of thought."

One outgrowth of logic in this century has been a school of philosophy sometimes called "contextualism." Contextualism attempts to redefine the traditionally static concepts of classical philosophy by categorizing them behaviorally. An example is "pragmatism," which asks of abstractions: what do they do? what are they good for? Pragmatic theorizing examines the "behavior" of ideals as we employ them; it does not accept absolutes, but treats all generalizations as problematic, experimental, evolving. This philosophy (developed mainly by John Dewey and William James) tends to produce very elastic conceptualizations. Since it regards evolving behavior as categorizing ideals, it always reserves the right to form abstract descriptions of any new thing in an entirely new way.

From the viewpoint of contextualism, physical reality has only derivative importance, because it is represented in neither its categories nor its subject area. The contextualistic theorizer is trying to grasp the descriptive in terms of the operational; physical entities—which don't fit in—are most conveniently reduced to "phenomena" (in the sense propounded by Husserl and others), and hence become behavioral effects. Modern contextualists are more concerned with means than with ends, more with the methodology of knowledge than with its ultimate objects. Thus they tend to concentrate on exposing previous epistemological dogmas and presuppositions. Their theories become increasingly critical of others. This effect is in fact typical of intellection as a secondary organization of behavior: its search for new ideals constantly inspires it to redefine old concepts.

ORTHODOXY. In this secondary organization, ideals form the "given" setting and effort is directed toward categorizing or regulating behavior. Perhaps the plainest examples of social orthodoxy are established religions. A group ordains a set of ideals which are to be taken as categorical and not open to question; the members develop and adjust their behavior patterns on the basis of these received ideals.

Although they are both associated with religion, *orthodoxy* (the regulation of behavior from an ideal setting) must be distinguished from *deism* (the regulation of physical acts from a behavioral setting). Deism, previously mentioned as a form of authoritarianism, hypostatizes a God or gods whose commands run the physical world. Orthodoxy replaces the concept of a behaving, willful God with that of an ideal "divine order," and shifts its area of operation from controlling physical events to regulating human conduct. This change, from worshipping an authoritarian God of commands and retributions to obeying abstract orthodox principles through conscience, is illustrated in Judaeo-Christian religious history. The God of Moses was almost entirely authoritarian; the "divine guidance" of modern Protestant sects is almost entirely orthodox. Compare the opening line of the Pentateuch—"In the beginning, God created the heaven and the earth"— with the opening of the New Testament: "In the beginning was the Word." Because they spring from different secondary organizations of behavior, these attitudes easily exist independently: for instance, authoritarian deism without orthodoxy is found in primitive "nature god" cults, and orthodoxy without deism in such belief systems as Confucianism.

Somewhat less obvious examples of orthodoxy are found in human "social classes." Sometimes these sub-groups in complex societies have a common basis in physical reality, e.g. in their relationship to land or means of production. But their basic coherence is more often a product of a system of agreed values or principles. By their group acceptance of such ideals—applying them individually to their everyday behavior—such classes tend to pull away from the rest of society and appear as distinct sociological entities. They can best be identified by uncovering the ideal systems that their members regard as "given" for various instances of social behavior.

Much has been written about the reasons for the stratification of modern societies into classes. Marx attributed it largely to physical factors—property, coercion, and physiological needs. But for most social groups, their grasp of ideals forms a more potent separator than their physical circumstances. Class orthodoxy overrides material position. This creates a problem for schemes of class redistribution; a person's economic or legal status can be changed by fiat, but he cannot be made to shift from one form of orthodoxy to another without a difficult period of relearning ideals. Well-meaning social programs that seek to push individuals from one class to another tend to overlook their understandings of ideals, which form the actual bases for class membership.

People frequently associate their class membership with a particular set of moral or ethical theories. This style of theorizing is typical of orthodoxy. In each instance there is a presupposed set of ideal categories, more or less internally consistent, which is used to distinguish one pattern of behavior from another. The product of such theorizing is usually a series of judgments that such-and-such kind of behavior is bad and should be avoided or prevented, while such-and-such kind of behavior is good and should be promoted. An enormous variety of such moral theories are extant, so that it seems that for any conceivable bit of behavior there must be a scheme somewhere in which it is held to be good, and another in which it is held to be bad.

On a more general level, several influential philosophical systems have arisen in the orthodox secondary organization under the head of "organicism" or "objective idealism." Such systems take an ideal basis (such as the Hegelian *Geist* or Schelling's "absolute reason") to be "given" absolutely, and try to explain behavior in terms of it. The whole world is treated as evolving, but evolving in accordance with an ideal plan. Actual events are all more or less imperfect "realizations" of the Absolute, which is the master design of all that can ever be. These theories tend to display a mystical cast because they start from an abstraction that is treated as necessary and inescapable. A question always arises as to how the Absolute is to be known; the answer is either piecemeal, through the unfolding of events in accordance with it or (more mystically) through "direct apprehension." Moreover, because they are primarily about behavior (rather than physical reality) they tend to be expressed in terms of values; their pronouncements sound increasingly moralistic, and seem more like a set of biases than a theory about the world.

LEGALISM. A typical instance of social legalism is any system of legislatures, laws, courts, enforcement officials, and law-abiding citizens. As with orthodoxy, the group adopts a set of ideal principles, which are taken by its members as fundamental and not to be questioned: these are the "principles of justice." But unlike orthodoxy, the legalistic secondary organization tries to regulate *physical* events rather than behavior. No legal system can control pure behavior (separate from physical manifestations), because the enforcement officials cannot detect it. Thus laws banning "impure thoughts" or "unworthy motives" are technically alien to legalism, although such sanctions are common in orthodoxy.

At first it may be hard to realize that "pure law" is concerned only with distinguishing physical acts, not behavior. Is it not anti-social behavior that is proscribed and punished? But a careful examination of the "theory of the law" shows that it always tries to stick to tangible physical facts. When actual legal procedures depart from this policy they get into trouble. A properly drawn indictment, for instance, states that the accused performed certain physical acts at a certain time and place, such acts being proscribed by law. Where such behavioral factors as intent, motivation, or state of mind are brought up, a burden falls on the prosecution to show by physical evidence (statements, actions, circumstances, or the like) that these behavioral factors must have been present. In some cases physical evidence becomes converted by law into a substitute for intent, as when possession of a weapon or illegal drug "establishes" intent to use it.

Much "civilized" social life is organized legalistically. Beside laws imposing physical punishments for physical transgressions, there are legal systems that define wealth, property, and political power. A monetary system, for instance, starts with a prescribed abstraction—monetary value—and uses it to measure many of the physical objects handled by citizens. Working within such a system, the individual accepts the idea that financial worth applies to objects; he then manipulates the objects to modify or exchange this worth as if it were a more tangible property like weight or color. In a mature monetary system worth may be attributed to all sorts of physically insignificant objects, such as the magnetic pattern on a bank's ledger tape. The power of the legalistic organization is such that those adopting it will accept this physical trifle as actually possessing the abstract financial properties assigned to it. Similarly, physical objects and land are associated with physical human beings in the legalistic relation of "prop-

129

erty." A society assumes the ideal concept of "property rights" as a basis for determining what things "belong" to what people. An accessory process is the granting of ideal qualities to physical "legal instruments," such as deeds and securities.

The democratic political election procedure arises from a sophisticated form of legalism. That major political decisions should be determined by tallying ballots, and that each mature human body in the society should be allowed to mark just one such ballot, are by no means "self-evident" doctrines. In fact they smack of mathematical elegance at the expense of practicality. Yet wars have been fought to preserve or export this procedure. It is based on two abstract principles: that numerical surplus of votes should determine the course to be followed, and that the proper units of voting are human individuals. Once these principles are adopted by the group, shifts of political power can be accomplished by an essentially mathematical process.

The concept of social law suggests the concept of natural law. Legalism generates "mechanistic" theories, covering the whole range of physical science. In each such theory certain ideal categories are adopted by the "scientific community," whose members pry into reality using those terms. The secondary organization of legalism posits that every physical fact conforms completely to a set of ideal descriptions; therefore once we possess the proper ideal tools—a complete mathematics, for example—we will be able to find out all that can be known and predicted about physical reality.

In view of this it is not surprising that some of the most ardent supporters of mechanistic theorizing have been mathematicians. For instance, Laplace:

> In the midst of the infinite variety of phenomena which succeed one another continuously in the heavens and on the earth, one is led to recognize the small number of general laws which matter follows in its movements. Everything in nature obeys them; everything is derived from them as necessarily as the return of the seasons; and the curve described by the dust particle which the winds seem to carry by chance, is ruled in as certain a manner as the orbits of the planets.[34]

In other words physical reality is a gigantic machine driven by a few ideal principles. Mathematicians are the most adept at handling such principles, so it seems natural to them to suppose that the apparent confusion of physical events can be straightened out once we know how to relate them to the precisely ordered world of numbers and functions.

COLLECTIVISM. The last of the six possible secondary organizations of human behavior is one in which ideals are understood and classified in physical terms. In communalism the physical setting was used for operations on behavior; now the same effort is directed toward ideals.

In industrialized societies, group collectivism often shows up as "socialism." A physical situation—the availability of land, a store of goods, the existence of productive facilities, etc.—forms the setting; on this basis the group selects ideal values or institutional principles appropriate to the given physical situation. Thus social collectivism generates ideal guiding principles on the basis of physical (typically agricultural or industrial) facilities. When pursued independently of legalistic considerations, this secondary organization tends to concentrate on defining equitable ways for distributing goods, and often recasts the traditional legal concepts of money, property, and individual rights. In such "pure" socialism the availability of physical facilities is assumed categorically, as the basis for adopting group ideals. This is the reason why socialistic economies are typically less productive than legalistic "laissez-faire" ones.

In modern corporations the topmost policy level often operates collectivistically. Although externally the corporation is a creature of legalism, internally it tends to create its own organization. At the policy level, its assets as a whole constitute the physical basis from which its employees do their work. Among these employees, the policy-makers are particularly charged to determine what ideals (principles, goals, guidelines, etc.) are appropriate to best exploit the assets. Their policies usually become embodied in numbers: 5% of engineering costs for research, so many dollars for advertising, and so on. They are developing abstract formulas from a background of physical fact.

Such policy-making (social and corporate) is cognate to scientific "induction." Both spring from a collectivistic secondary organization in human behavior. Induction is the selection of ideal formulas to "fit" a given set of physical facts; its complement is "deduction," the legalistic exploration of physical events on the basis of a given set of ideals. When scientists mention "theorizing" they often mean only induction, the opposite activity being "experimentation" or "collecting data." It is characteristic of induction that it tends to treat data as "fixed," for it is from this platform that explanatory schemes are built. The job of the collectivistic theorizer is to describe and explain physical facts, not to "verify" them.

The philosophical school that includes collectivistic theorizing is sometimes called "formism." Ideals, categorized physically, appear to be "forms" of reality. In his famous allegory, Plato likened physical reality to the shadows on the wall of a cave, cast by perfect ideals that existed in the sunlight at its mouth. Ideals so conceived are entities such as "redness" and "chair-ness"—that is, ideals in the role of descriptions of physical things. Because it starts from our physical common sense, this viewpoint can exert a powerful force in our thinking. Consider the following modern exposition, from Pepper's *World Hypotheses*:

> Here we have together before us the two exactly similar sheets of yellow paper. Let us concentrate our attention on just one of the respects in which the two sheets are similar, their color. We note that the yellow on one sheet is *identical* with the yellow on the other. If there is any question of this, let somebody interchange the two sheets. Since we cannot tell which one was the original right-hand sheet, we must admit that the two sheets have an identical color. There are, moreover, *two* manifestations of the color. We also see that clearly. But we see equally clearly that the color, the yellow, is the identical yellow in both manifestations. There is *one* quality, yellow, in *two* particular manifestations. We see these conditions directly before our eyes, and there is nothing more obvious or certain in the world.[35]

Thus starting from our understanding of a part of physical reality (the two pieces of paper) we proceed directly to the apprehension of an ideal—yellow or yellowness—which we are forced to conclude does not reside in the reality before us because there is one ideal and two pieces of paper. Since the ideal can appear in this and any number of other instances of physical existence, without ever being a part of just one of them, it must have a separate reality. Moreover since we could annihilate all yellow things and then later create more, the yellow ideal must be immutable and eternal. This is the conclusion of formism.

In the hands of philosophers, formism sometimes becomes arcane; but it is far from being a mere intellectual exercise. It is the justification, as I mentioned, for the notion of "laws of nature." We observe two apples fall. About these two events we discern a third entity, the general process of falling, which is part of neither. After observing various objects falling under various conditions we imagine a "law" of falling, such as a "law of gravity." We express this law in ideal terms, e.g. "$F = G\dfrac{m_1 m_2}{d^2}$." We believe that the law has an eternal subsistence all its own: it would continue to hold during times when nothing happened to be falling. This is strictly analogous to finding one yellowness in two pieces of paper. Similarly in everyday discourse we refer to ideals such as "justice" and "beauty"; if pressed to explain what we mean we will be eventually forced to say, just as the characters in Plato's *Dialogues* did over two millenia ago, that we refer to entities which are independent of any specific just act or beautiful object. In other words we are all formists much of the time.

SECONDARY ORGANIZATIONS IN GENERAL. Just as the primary organizations in human life (our commonsense grasps of physical reality, behavior, and ideals) constitute our most basic understandings of reality, so the secondary organizations constitute our most basic approaches to social, individual, and theoretical situations. They are the "styles" in which human beings conduct their lives. But they are threads in a complex pattern: although we can see that secondary organizations are distinct and independent when we analyze them, in actual human life they seldom occur pure and alone. A good way to sort them out (as well as delineate them in our understanding) is to examine some of their characteristic contrasts. These appear mainly where the same subject area is being approached from two different settings.

For example, we can theorize about *physical reality* either from a behavioral setting or from an ideal setting, as I discussed in Section 2.1. Behavioral categories yield an animistic viewpoint characteristic of "primitive" people and of everyday technology in general; ideal categories yield mechanistic theories such as modern physics. The first attitude stems from an *authoritarian* secondary organization; the other from a *legalistic* one. Both attitudes are widely held and consistently practiced, the animistic one more commonly than the mechanistic. Both generate valuable theories.

The cognate contrast in social life is sometimes characterized as "rule by men" versus "rule by law." In the case of social authoritarianism, the men who rule include not only specific individuals (kings, chiefs, dictators) but also the more general tradition-makers of the past and the diffuse but powerful behavioral consensus of the present. "The way our ancestors did it" and "the way it is usually done" express authoritarianism, even though they refer to no specific individual authority. Rule by law, on the other hand, is based on a coherent set of abstractions which endure beyond the lives of any men and can be analyzed in their own right. Students of "the law" speak of the beauty of its underlying logic, the balanced fitting of rights and obligations, of wrongs and remedies. Those who "love the law" abhor the arbitrary, willful decisions of dictators, however benevolent; while those who live by tradition and personal loyalty hate the impersonal logic of "legal technicalities." And just as animism predominates over science on a world-wide basis, so rule by men predominates over rule by law.

Theories about *behavior* arise from either a physical or an ideal setting. In the first case, *communalism*, physical categorization produces empirical theories about our own perceptions. At a more formal level it also generates empirical theories about the behavior of others, creating disciplines such as sociology, psychology, and anthropology. In the second case, *orthodoxy*, ideal categorization also leads to theories about the behavior of ourselves and others, but with a moralistic tone. It is sometimes said that the first approach is "descriptive," the second "normative." Physical categorization of behavior takes it just as it occurs, whereas ideal categorization displays an inherent tendency to be critical, to replace observations of "what is" with judgments about "what should be."

A similar opposition appears in group attitudes toward the social behavior of their members. Communalism versus orthodoxy manifests itself as "tolerance" versus "discrimination" or "classlessness" versus "class-consciousness." In a truly communalistic group, behavior is treated objectively—in physical terms—with relatively little regard to the difference between "good" and "bad." In an orthodox group, on the other hand, even minor facets of behavior are given meanings which may elevate or condemn the individual. This ultimately leads to the generalized discriminations of social classes. In Victorian society, for instance, such bits of behavior as speech and table manners were differentiated by a fairly rigid system of abstract principles.

Finally, theories about *ideals* may be categorized either physically or behaviorally. When fully developed, physical categorization of ideals leads to theories of mathematics while behavioral categorization leads to theories of logic. Mathematical concepts such as number and shape are suggested by the physical things we observe, and seem to be the abstractions "most appropriate" to them; logical concepts such as negation and implication are similarly suggested by the ways we think.

On the more general level discussed by philosophers, physical categorization of ideals produces Platonic formism, which envisions a world of perfect forms that the commonsense physical world "participates in." This has not only been a dominant strain in Western philosophizing, but also the underpinning for the scientific commitment to discover abstract "laws of nature." Behavioral categorization of ideals, by contrast, leads to "contextualistic" philosophies such as pragmatism. Instead of seeking ultimate "laws," these approaches ask only that our scientific descriptions be useful and related to human interests.

The foregoing are a few examples of how secondary organizations of behavior stamp human life with its distinct and identifiable "styles." Sometimes they can be recognized by style alone. But the ultimate test of how human behavior is organized is to ask "toward what primary organization is it directed?" and "from what primary organization does it get its categorial setting?" Once we recognize the primary organizations clearly, answering these questions tells us to what secondary organization any pattern of behavior belongs.

Why is it important to distinguish one secondary organization from another? The reasons are basically the same as with the primary organizations, as with our need to separate our understandings of physical reality, behavior, and ideals.

An obvious reason is because they are "objects of knowledge," just as the primary organizations are. We do in fact treat secondary organizations separately in our grasp of reality, and any world-view that did not take this into account would be incomplete. Assigning a particular pattern of human life (say, religion) to behavior goes part way toward locating it in our overall knowledge; but it does not distinguish it from other behavioral maxima. For instance it does not distinguish religion from law, which is also a part of behavior but belongs to a different secondary organization. These secondary distinctions are real and important to us: religion and law exhibit fundamental differences of approach which it is possible for us to discover and understand. We cannot simply ignore such matters.

But the reasons for distinguishing secondary organizations go a step deeper. Our interest in understanding them is inherently non-trivial because they form a major part of our "civilized" existence. Just as living things have evolved their basic existences in terms of primary organizations (i.e. have developed physical organisms, behavioral patterns, and ideal life techniques, as I discussed in Section 3.1), so human beings have evolved a significant part of their existences in terms of secondary organizations. They live and think and react as communal parents, as orthodox class members, as "legal persons," and so forth. Parts of every human being *are* these entities. It is of course less vital for a human being to exist as a "legal person" (for instance) than as a physical person. This is one reason why the former is "secondary" to the latter. But in a modern society, a person who does not grasp legalism will hardly last longer than a person who does not grasp physical reality. If he does not understand that he and his fellow human beings in the society have adopted a set of ideals to regulate their physical actions, he will at the very least soon land in jail (or in a mental hospital). It is in this sense that being a "legal person" is almost as important a part of his existence as being a physical person. Just as life has developed itself through evolution, and thereby places on each living thing a burden of grasping that development, so human beings and their groups have developed "social beings," on whom fall a parallel burden. The secondary organizations of behavior described here are the most basic parts of this new "human reality," and hence are vital subjects for our understanding.

Finally, we need to distinguish secondary organizations in order to expand our knowledge by elucidating certain kinds of error, for the same reasons I discussed in Section 2.2. For instance, a man driving his own car and a man driving a stolen car are indistinguishable in any purely physical, behavioral, or ideal knowledge. There is no way to explain the difference by reference to

135

primary organizations. Understanding the secondary organization of legalism, however, yields the concept of legal ownership with which it is possible to make the distinction. In one case it associates with the physical man and the physical car the ideal relation of ownership; in the other case it assigns the different ideal characteristic of legal conversion. These distinctions, which might sound "merely theoretical," become the basis for very tangible events: stopping the car, arresting the man, etc. It is out of such distinctions, wherein the concept of error is crucial, that the fabric of civilized life is woven. Yet we cannot make them without at least a tacit grasp of secondary organizations. The hypothetical "visitor from another planet," observing civilization in action, would be utterly unable to fathom what was happening without such an understanding.

4.2 Tertiary Organizations

> A philosopher of imposing stature doesn't think in a vacuum. Even his most abstract ideas are, to some extent, conditioned by what is or is not known in the time when he lives.
>
> WHITEHEAD

Secondary organizations of human behavior often support one another. In the total pattern of human life they not only seldom occur alone, they occur in characteristic clusters. For example, when theorizers draw up a parallel "fit" between physical reality and ideals (as modern science does), they typically alternate between collectivistic induction and legalistic deduction. In the collectivistic phase, physical data suggest ideal formulas to "cover" them; in the legalistic phase, the formulas suggest further explorations in physical reality. By such mutual inspiration, collectivism and legalism form a combined theorizing approach that is more powerful (and more commonly used) than either approach alone.

It is appropriate to call such combinations "tertiary organizations." Just as secondary organizations arise through interactions among the primary organizations, so these arise through interactions among the secondaries. A tertiary organization shows up in human life any time there is a prevalent behavior pattern that moves fairly freely among two or more secondary organizations. The resulting "styles" tend to be somewhat more general than those displayed by the secondaries alone; nevertheless they are distinctive and important to understand. Tertiary organizations are vital facets of human behavior, and hence significant objects of knowledge.

There are 15 ways to form pairs of the six secondary organizations, and 20 ways to form triples. Most of these possibilities are not actually prevalent in human life, and hence are of minor interest: on examination we find that the secondary organizations on which they are based embody contrary approaches to the primary organizations, and thus do not support each other comfortably. However, there are three pairs and two triples among these possibilities which are commonly found, and which also have been treated extensively by psychologists and sociologists. They are important human behavior patterns. The three pairs are the "complementary doubles" *communalism and authoritarianism, intellection and orthodoxy*, and *legalism and collectivism*. The two triples are the "cycles" *communalism to intellection to legalism* and *collectivism to orthodoxy to authoritarianism*. The relationships within these clusters of secondary organizations can easily be visualized by referring to the diagram on page 118.

COMMUNALISM AND AUTHORITARIANISM. Communalism deals with behavior from a physical basis; authoritarianism deals with physical reality from a behavioral basis. Each phase provides the organizational setting for the other. Together they combine to form a whole tertiary organization which is one of the prevalent patterns in human life.

In discussing these two phases earlier, I mentioned their importance in human families: communalism is the approach by which infants are reared and authoritarianism is the approach by which they are trained. As a tertiary organization, they merge into what might be called "family life." Physical conditions are the setting for communalistic modifications of behavior, resulting in cooperation to achieve family goals; behavior is the setting for authoritarian regulation of physical acts by family members, producing effective results from a mixed group of children and adults. Although most typical of families, this organization appears in any relatively small group of people with common physical goals or problems requiring efficient group effort: tribes and clans, military units, labor details, exploring parties, etc. To the extent that they "behave like families" such groups display this tertiary organization.

As a way of life, communalism-authoritarianism predominates among "primitive" people, who spend most of their time either maintaining lines of communal cooperation with one another or obeying the authoritarian dictates of leaders or traditions. But it is also a common pattern in the everyday life of members of "advanced" societies. Any human being whose behavior lacked this fundamental organization would soon become lonely and ineffective.

In theorizing, the two phases of this tertiary organization first appear as notions of perception and animism. Perception, the most basic communalistic theory, generates an understanding of our behavior in physical terms— e.g. this sensation comes from that object, this thought is about that event. Animism, the converse authoritarian theory, generates an understanding of physical things in behavioral terms, by the ways they "act": one object moves, another object burns, and so on. As they merge into the tertiary organization the result is a concept of *causation*. In perception, physical things seem to "force" their qualities upon us; animism suggests that physical things must do the same to each other. Together they encourage us to interpret the world in terms of causes and effects, as a combined physical and behaving whole.

Causation could be thought of as a basic world-view without any grasp of ideals. Things push one another, A results in B which leads to C, but nothing endures in the process, no principles are realized. It might as well happen entirely differently. Hume analyzed causation from a logical standpoint and concluded it was quite unreasonable. Yet it is a deeply felt approach to understanding reality. This is because it embodies in theorizing the same basic tertiary organization that is so common to everyday human life.

INTELLECTION AND ORTHODOXY. Intellection explores ideals from a behavioral basis; orthodoxy turns around and uses those ideals to discriminate and regulate behavior. When they merge into a tertiary organization, the combination forms the basic pattern of "spiritual" or "ethical" life.

How the two phases merge can be seen graphically in the genesis of churches. An individual—a prophet—exploring abstract principles comes up with a set of ideals that can be categorized behaviorally, that seem to have relevance to human life. If he is successful (most are not) these ideals will be picked up and promulgated by a group of followers, who establish a church. For the prophet, the ideals were principally the outcome of his intellection; for the followers, however, they become principally the basis of an orthodoxy. The prophet sought knowledge; the followers seek to regulate behavior, to make men better. But for the church to survive these two approaches must blend into a single coherent process. Intellection alone is schizmatic and leads to the church's disintegration; orthodoxy alone is dogmatic and leads to its overthrow. It takes a constant interplay between the two to satisfy human "spiritual" needs. Thus in a successful church each new communicant is exposed to a comprehensive education in the ideal articles of faith, by a process of intellection; while at the same time these articles are consistently promulgated as an absolute setting for the definition and regulation of the behavior of the faithful. When this is done properly, the communicant never doubts that the system of ideals and the patterns of human behavior naturally correspond.

Many industrialized societies today have started to abandon such churches, replacing them with an intellection-orthodoxy tertiary organization built around class membership. Here intellection appears in school education, and orthodoxy in the maintenance of social class "norms." Students in these societies, like the communicants of a church, undergo a long process of learning the ideals that will largely determine to which social class they belong. At the same time the class members try to ensure that the education being given inculcates the orthodox behavior they take to be necessary for social life. The combined organization shows up as a major pattern in human behavior similar to that produced by churches, but now more "ethical" than spiritual.

On an everyday level, theorizing within this tertiary organization appears as "ethics" or "morality." Prevailing human behavior suggests a set of ideals by which it may be categorized; the categories then become the basis for calling behavior "good" or "evil," "moral" or "immoral." Such theorizing contributes heavily to the "tone" displayed by actual societies. This tone also depends on the "balance" of the tertiary organization: when intellection predominates we say the society is "liberal" or "open," and when orthodoxy predominates we say it is "repressive" or "closed."

On a more esoteric level, particularly in churches, the same theorizing tends toward mysticism. Ethical ideals, treated separately at first, may be envisioned as interconnected in a grand abstract "Absolute," which is then taken to be directly accessible to human behavior. Here is how Evelyn Underhill describes the characteristic dual conception of the mystic:

> …he is able to perceive and react to reality under two modes. On the one hand he knows, and rests in, the eternal world of Pure Being, the 'Sea Pacific' of the Godhead, indubitably present to him in his ecstasies, attained by him in the union of love. On the other, he knows—and works in—that 'stormy sea,' the vital World of Becoming which is the expression of Its will... To the great mystic the 'problem of the Absolute' presents itself in terms of life, not in terms of dialectic. He solves it in terms of life: by a change or growth of consciousness which—thanks to his peculiar genius—enables him to apprehend that two-fold Vision of Reality which eludes the perceptive powers of other men.[36]

The "act of Divine Union" of the mystic brings together these two factors, the ideal and the behavioral. It amounts to a decision to treat categories interchangeably: ordinary behavior becomes regarded as part of a Divine system, and Divine ideals become regarded as perfect forms of behavior.

These ethical and spiritual patterns in human life tend to ignore physical reality. Because they arise by combining behavior with ideals, they do not include a grasp of physical states, and thus are encouraged to treat them as "gross" or something to be overcome. One of the first things taught by any church doctrine, moral system, or mystical discipline is that it embodies patterns outside any human physical existence.

LEGALISM AND COLLECTIVISM. Much of the "civilized" way of life followed by industrialized peoples stems from this tertiary organization.

Their political, legal, and economic patterns arise from an association between physical reality and ideals.

Recall the communal-authoritarian tertiary organization discussed above; it associates physical reality with behavior, producing social processes which are "family-like" and based on cooperation, tradition, and personal loyalty. When legalism and collectivism merge, they substitute for this behavioral association a reliance on immutable abstractions, on ideals. The collectivistic phase starts from a given physical basis—available goods and facilities such as land, livestock, tools, raw materials, etc.—and consists of a search for appropriate ideals to govern the use of such things. The outcome is a system of advanced social concepts and institutions: private property, transfer and inheritance, monetary units, and the whole edifice of the law. These ideals then become the basis for a legalistic regulation of physical transactions, through the establishment of courts and regulatory bodies.

Merged into a tertiary organization, the legalistic and collectivistic phases of this process display an intimate and continuous interplay. New ideal concepts and new physical transactions constantly generate each other. Thus when a new physical situation arises that is not covered by the society's currently adopted abstractions (such as the introduction of mass automobile transportation), a search for new principles ensues. We say that we need new laws, and legislators set about drafting them. Enforcing the laws then tends to modify the physical situation, bringing it more into line with the new ideals. On the other hand, sometimes the operation of this tertiary organization is stimulated by changes in adopted ideals. For example, when it became evident in America (in the 1950's) that certain laws affecting racial minorities were inconsistent with more general concepts of civil rights, a cycle of legislation and enforcement arose to produce a more workable fit between physical treatment and ideal values.

In legalistic-collectivistic theorizing, the cognate process builds up a body of "natural law" instead of man-made law. A physical situation—a mass of data or a newly observed physical effect—suggests the need to formulate a new "law of nature." The new law in turn suggests new researches into physical reality, often requiring the construction of novel machines or methods that would not otherwise have been conceived. These researches turn up fresh data and the cycle continues. Knowledge of physical effects and an armory of descriptive abstractions grow side by side. The whole process might be called "*framework theorizing*," for its system of abstractions constitutes a rigid framework that is treated as "underlying" the things of physical reality. Theorizing in this tertiary organization contrasts with the "causation theorizing" of communalism-authoritarianism, which envisions only dynamic chains of causal links.

141

COMPLEMENTARY PAIRS IN GENERAL. The three tertiary organizations just described—in each of which two primary organizations freely alternate their roles of providing an organizing setting and providing its subject—constitute major "ways of life" for human beings. By means of them people merge their understandings of reality into large-scale coherent behavior patterns. Each can be represented as a fusion of two secondary organizations; but each fulfills a role in human life that exceeds the power of either of its components. These tertiary organizations produce such characteristic social patterns as family ties, religion, class distinctions, and economic and legal behavior. In the area of theorizing, they generate broad concepts of causation, ethics, and the "framework" of physical law.

In effect, human beings have carried evolution one step further: they have combined the primary organizations evolved by life into new secondary and tertiary organizations, which contribute much of the complexity and "texture" found in human behavior. By creating these new organizations, man has discovered new ways of living.

I mentioned earlier that these higher organizations in human behavior might be regarded as "generalizations" of theorizing. As a corollary, it is important to recognize that all the conclusions about theorizing set forth in Section 2 are equally applicable to social behavior in human groups. Theorizing itself is only a microcosm of organizational processes that occur on many levels and in many contexts. Civil law, for instance, associates people's physical acts with ideal descriptions, just as physics associates natural events with ideal formulas. The procedure is the same, but it is carried out on a much larger scale.

Thus groups and societies, just like individual theorizers, explore the orders of reality by creating parallelisms among them; but instead of generating only knowledge they generate whole ways of life. Of particular interest is the fact that (just like theorizers) groups and societies posit *minima* to "pin" their parallelisms together. For example, an assumption that helps make "civilized" societies work is that of the existence of "obligations." Just as concepts of obligations are central to any theory explaining civil law, so the assumption that obligations *actually exist* is central to any civilized scheme of social regulation. In this larger context, physical actions by members of the society are assumed to be aligned with a system of abstractions ("the law") by which these actions are to be governed. Obligations are among the unanalyzable "fasteners" that justify this alignment. An obligation is an abstraction that is "fulfilled" by a physical action; conversely, the physical action is treated as having ideal (legal) properties.

Such "social minima" fill the same role as theoretical minima, and exhibit the same deficiencies. Thus (for example) whenever the accepted

142

social alignment between ideal law and physical actions "shifts," old obligations tend to be erased and new ones created, just as shifts in theoretical alignments change our inventory of theoretical minima. Obligations tend to proliferate, creating one another, as the alignment between ideals and physical reality matures with more sophisticated legal concepts that more finely discriminate physical actions. Finally, the behavior of a society becomes stultified whenever it treats minima (such as obligations) as absolute objectives, rather than as tools to realize larger social goals. These are examples of the ways in which the problems of theorizing are also the problems of human life in general.

Tertiary organizations are recognizable patterns of behavior in their own right, and identifying them as "combinations" of secondary organizations does not mean they are merely derivative. But it helps us analyze the process by which tertiary organizations respond to social and theoretical problems: when such problems arise the tertiary organization tends to reduce itself to one or another of its secondary 'components.''

As an illustration, consider any example of building a "framework theory"—say the construction of modern physics. Such theorizing consists of simultaneously exploring physical fact and ideal systems, in this case laboratory effects and mathematics. As new physical data are uncovered in the laboratory, new mathematical formulas are needed to describe them; conversely the search for new physical facts is often initiated by the discovery of a hitherto unrealized mathematical consequence of current theory. The development of mathematics to fit physical knowledge constitutes a collectivistic phase: it is the exploration of ideals from a physical basis. The corresponding legalistic phase is the exploration of physical effects on the basis of ideal (mathematical) concepts. As I mentioned in discussing the tertiary organization of legalism and collectivism, these phases are often called induction and deduction. In problem-free scientific work they tend to be used evenly and continuously, now one and now the other, to create a theoretical "fit" between physical reality and ideals. But note what happens when a problem arises. If it is a problem arising in the physical data—for instance an unforeseen effect not covered by current theory—the collectivistic phase emerges more strongly. Mathematical models are tinkered with, equations are modified, new descriptions are sought, until the parallelism of the ideal system with the newly expanded physical understanding is restored. Conversely, if a problem arises in the ideal scheme—say, a prediction based on mathematics which is currently unknown among the observed data—the legalistic phase emerges more strongly. New experiments are devised to discover or confirm the effect that is presently "only predicted by theory."

Thus theorizers select one of the two phases implicit in each of the tertiary organizations just discussed (i.e. one of its secondary organization "components"), depending on where they discern problems with the whole process. The principle of selection is that the phase used takes the problem area as its *setting*. In the example, collectivism is selected to solve problems with physical data because its setting is physical reality; legalism is selected to solve problems in the mathematical scheme because its setting is ideals.

This procedure is followed beyond theorizing, in all the appearances of these tertiary organizations in human life. For example, "primitive" groups are largely regulated through a communal-authoritarian organization, which establishes parallelisms between behavior and physical reality. When a physical problem arises (such as a natural disaster), communalism tends to dominate; when a behavioral problem arises (such as an internal rebellion), authoritarianism tends to dominate. The society emphasizes that phase of its overall tertiary organization where the problem area is taken as the "given" basis. In a church, organized between behavior and ideals, problems with the behavior of its members are resolved by increased intellection: the members are urged to explore the divine order by study and prayer. Problems with the church's ideals, such as the discovery of inconsistencies in its abstract canon, are met by a resort to orthodoxy: heresies are declared and members are punished for holding them. Such flexibility of approach accounts for much of the power of these tertiary organizations, for each is able to apply the most effective of two different organizational tools to the solution of its problems.

COLLECTIVISM-ORTHODOXY-AUTHORITARIANISM. This tertiary organization can be analyzed into a "cycle" of three secondary organizations, where the subject area of each one constitutes the basis for the next. Thus collectivism classifies ideals on the basis of physical fact; orthodoxy uses those ideals as the basis for regulating behavior; and authoritarianism takes the behavior as the basis for physical transactions, thereby closing the ring. The whole tertiary organization derives much of its coherence from this process of serial support among its component phases.

In large social groups this mode of organization is sometimes called "statism." It shows up as an overall tendency to form public institutions and establish group sanctions, rather than promote self-reliance and individual decision-making. Today, it is the principal organization by which human beings maintain effective groups beyond tribal size.

An example will illustrate how its three phases contribute to the whole. Suppose a relatively complex society is threatened by incursions from hostile neighbors. This physical situation provides categories for the development of a set of ideals, in the collectivistic phase. The ideals would typically consist of militaristic concepts: the desirability of "serving one's country," the idea of war as an honorable profession, etc. These ideals now become the basis for an orthodoxy, often creating a new social class—e.g. a warrior caste. The orthodox phase defines certain behavior patterns and imbues them with value: bravery, service, glory, and so on. Such behavior, finally, becomes the basis for the authoritarian phase, which dictates what physical acts are to be performed. Arms and fortifications are created, men are impressed into service, war is waged. Note that the original physical problem (hostile incursions) is now being solved physically, by military retaliation. But this solution has been reached by a somewhat roundabout tertiary organization of social behavior, involving significant modifications to all three primary understandings of reality.

The usefulness of this tertiary organization can be appreciated by considering a typical alternative. In the present example, another way of meeting the physical threat of hostile incursions would be to merge communalism and authoritarianism. Here the physical problem would lead to communal cooperation among the group members and adoption of a group behavior pattern; this would then become the basis for authoritarian dictates of individual physical acts. Thus the threat might be met by the group coalescing under a chief, investing him with the authority to lead a war party. Such a response is common in "primitive" societies. By contrast, the statist organization yields a more complicated solution; but it is one that will ultimately prove more effective, especially in large groups. Note that its first response to the physical problem is not behavioral, but ideal: instead of just forming ranks to take action, the group sets out to create an institution, a system of agreed ideals. The institution (not the physical problem) then becomes the setting for discriminating and regulating behavior. Only after this is accomplished is the group ready to take authoritarian action, to perform physical acts in the field designed to counter the original physical threat.

The increased effectiveness of the statist tertiary organization is also evident in smaller groups. A well-studied example is the growth of modern corporations out of simpler (usually authoritarian) businesses. Here the three implicit secondary phases (collectivism, orthodoxy, authoritarianism) are revealed by analyzing corporate behavior into three "layers" of management. In the top-most layer, policy-makers perform the collectivistic phase. They start from a predominately physical setting—the assets of the corporation—and strive to form a consistent set of general principles that will "govern" the exploitation of the assets. In the next layer, "middle managers" receive this set of ideals as a basis for defining specific patterns of behavior to conform to its abstractions. They select employees, write job descriptions, issue general instructions, and monitor "performance." Their job is an exercise in orthodoxy, wherein the ideals prescribed by the policy-makers are translated into behavior to be pursued by the workers. In the lowest layer, workers and their supervisors adopt an authoritarian organization, manipulating physical things in accordance with the prescribed behavioral regime. Job instructions created by the middle managers become, in their hands, a setting for the sequences of physical acts that comprise the "work" done by the corporation. This work, in turn, alters the assets of the corporation, presenting new physical situations to the policy-makers. Thus the "management cycle" forms a closed loop.

Statism exhibits two characteristics that are not present with simpler organizations (such as communalism-authoritarianism). First, the group adopting it acquires greater efficiency in solving chronic, long-term, or large-scale problems. In the example of military statism, it creates such things as permanent fortifications and a cadre of professional warriors, whereas with the simpler "war-party" organization the group just bands together, does the job, and then disperses. The second characteristic (related to the first) is that the creations of a statist organization—such as military establishments and corporations—are likely to acquire a "life of their own," enduring after the original problem for which they were created has disappeared. This is because each phase of the tertiary organization is instrumental to another phase, and none can be related directly to the problem. For instance, consider what happens when we question the validity of a military establishment. If we ask about the physical part—why are there troops, arms, and fortifications?—the answer will be that these are necessary to carry out the behavior of waging war. If we then ask "why wage war?" the answer will be that such behavior supports certain ideals: freedom, responsibility, perhaps also glory and destiny. If we finally ask where the ideals come from, the answer will be that they are appropriate to the society's physical situation: the value of its natural resources, its strategic geographical location, even the racial qualities of its members. Although the military establishment amounts to a physical response to a physical situation, it tends to be explained differently because of the intermediate behavioral and ideal factors in its generating organization. Such a roundabout explanation tends to shield it from criticism. The physical part is maintained for behavioral reasons, the behavior is pursued for ideal reasons, and the ideals are held for physical reasons. All these reasons may appear individually sound, even when their totality is absurd. Thus the same factors that make the statist organization more effective in dealing with large, long-term problems makes it endure after such problems have ceased to exist.

146

In effect, this cyclic "three-phase" organization produces an endless sequence of explanations. Physical reality is referred to behavior, behavior to ideals, and ideals to more physical reality. The process also shows up in theorizing, where the result might be called "general idealism." When developed into a complete philosophy, it offers a chain of three explanations. What are ideals? They are the perfect forms of worldly things. What are worldly things? They are the creation of a behaving world-spirit. What moves the world-spirit? Its destiny unfolds according to an ideal plan. Such a three-phase scheme lies behind much "Eastern" philosophy; in the European tradition it is most closely represented by Hegelianism. It tends to be more complex and harder to grasp than the two-phase approaches discussed earlier; but it also provides a greater richness of conception because it touches on all three orders of reality. It appears to cover more ground, in a consistent way, than the simpler philosophical schools.

COMMUNALISM-INTELLECTION-LEGALISM. This tertiary organization may be analyzed into the three secondary organizations omitted from the one just described. In terms of the diagram on page 118, the cycle of categorizations "goes in the other direction." Physical reality forms the basis for manipulating behavior, behavior is the setting for selecting ideals, and ideals are the basis for physical actions. There is the same process of serial support among the primary organizations, but they are taken in the opposite order.

Philosophically, this tertiary organization forms a clear contrast to the prior one: it is just as "materialistic" as the other was "idealistic." What is behavior? It is the manifestation of physical events in living organisms. What are physical events? They are the realizations of the ideal laws of nature. What are ideals? They are conceptions produced by human behavior. This is the common, secular, "down to earth" world-view that underlies much of modern knowledge. It evokes no world-spirit or ideal plan, but pins all its explanations on mundane, empirical scientific concepts. By embracing all three primary organizations in one cycle of explanations it appears to tie up loose ends more neatly than the corresponding philosophies of its secondary phases (empiricism, contextualism, mechanism). However it shares with the prior tertiary cycle a disquieting lack of absolutes. Everything is explained by something else, and the explanations never end. Because each of its three phases is supported by another phase, none of them seem to explain reality in its own right.

When this tertiary organization is adopted socially, the result is often called "individualism." Compared to the statist cycle discussed earlier, it tends to emphasize individual (rather than group) action toward physical reality. In the communalistic phase a physical situation leads to cooperation among group members—an agreement to share work. This cooperative behavior next becomes the basis for exploring and establishing group ideals. The ideals then become the setting for a system of laws governing members' actions toward the physical situation and one another. Because of the intervening stage of abstract legal formulation, individuals in the group are not directly subject to behavioral sanctions; they work within ideal guidelines, rather than obeying personal commands. The component of legalism in this organization—substituted for the authoritarian phase of statism—establishes "rule by law" instead of "rule by men."

It is worth noting that this "individualistic" tertiary organization is more successful in groups where the physical situation is more one of opportunities than one of dangers. It tends to be adopted by "frontier" societies, where individuals are encouraged to build or mine or plant; statism tends to be adopted by "threatened" societies, where individuals are encouraged to unite and defend. The difference in effectiveness seems to stem from the different approaches of individuals to physical situations. In the first case, each individual's responses are abstractly categorized (by a legal system), and he is left to work out the details; in the second case, these responses are behaviorally dictated. Individualism supports individual creativity, while statism emphasizes individual subservience.

A basic manifestation of the individualistic tertiary cycle in human life is *communication*. I have already mentioned the appearance of two of its phases in this role: the communal (empirical) categorization of verbal behavior physically, and the intellectual (contextualistic) exploration of ideals on a behavioral basis. As explained earlier, the first generates agreements about lexicography, the precise correspondences of words to things; the second produces notions of logic, the "rules of thought." The third phase—legalism—shows up as the "rules" of a specific language: the abstract guidelines adopted to regulate the actual sounds or marks made when using the language. The whole tertiary organization (in this application) could be summed up by saying that physical things categorize the bits of language behavior that we agree "mean" them; the language behavior then becomes the basis for adopting an ideal system of "usage"; and the ideal system regulates the actual generation of sounds or marks.

Among animals other than man, communication consists mainly of one kind of physical reality (sounds or actions) modeling another. By using this tertiary organization, man adds an intervening phase of ideal systematization, giving it the "logical" character peculiar to human language. This increases the range of subjects that can be communicated (to equal the range of things for which we can frame descriptions) by allowing us to model pure abstractions, such as generalizations and conditional predictions.

148

TERTIARY ORGANIZATIONS IN GENERAL. Tertiary organizations are the latest and broadest of human behavior patterns. The *primary* organizations—our grasp of the "orders of reality"—were first developed during the evolution of living things in general, and they come to mankind as innate capacities of human organisms. The *secondary* organizations were then built on them, forming new patterns characteristic of human culture. They allowed people to cooperate, form groups, educate one another, define good and evil, adopt laws, and create institutions. It was the richness of these secondary organizations that made human behavior distinct from that of any other form of life. Now *tertiary* organizations have appeared as larger patterns built upon the secondaries. They give us a set of problem-solving abilities both more powerful and more subtle than any repertoire of secondary responses. They allow human groups to understand, plan and act on a broad scale, focusing many areas of knowledge into meeting specific challenges. Amid the complexities of present-day civilization, they are the most effective living techniques we have.

The three complementary-pair tertiary organizations tend to co-exist in most modern societies, being adopted quite freely to meet different basic needs. Thus a blend of communalism and authoritarianism is favored for family life and small cooperative groups in general; combined intellection and orthodoxy appears in social classes, religious groups, and any place where ethical considerations are more important than cooperation; and the merger of legalism with collectivism is adopted for "public" matters— economic and political life, business, and the like. Adopting the "wrong" pair in a given social situation usually appears as an error, although often not a serious one. For example, a family organized along legalistic and collectivistic lines will be "cold" and unsympathetic, and will produce alienated children. Similarly, a legal system operating through communalism and authoritarianism, like the stereotypic backwoods sheriff's office, will tend to ignore general human rights. This is because vital primary organizations are being slighted: the legalistic family does not deal adequately with its members' behavior, and the backwoods sheriff's office is not committed to the ideals of justice.

Human theorizing approaches tend to mirror these applications of tertiary organizations to social life. "Causation theorizing," pursued between physical reality and behavior, is used in much of everyday life; it is the earliest and most unsophisticated source of knowledge. "Ethical theorizing," in which behavior is associated with ideals, supplies most of our consciousness of class and religious values, morals, and "right conduct." "Framework theorizing," constructing parallelisms between physical reality and ideals, generates much of our understanding of science and "civilized" life. As with their corresponding social manifestations, these theorizing approaches tend to be appropriate to different situations. In everyday dealings with physical objects we are causation theorists; in normal dealings with one another we are ethical theorists; and in our legal and economic dealings we adopt framework theorizing.

In human societies the choice between the two tertiary cycles—statism and individualism—is less fluid. Individuals tend to prefer one or the other for long periods, frequently for life. Societies tend to become caught up in one or the other, particularly in statism. As I noted earlier, statist patterns have a "self-protective" tendency to endure after their generating conditions have disappeared. Statism is the social organization that best solves group physical problems, while individualism is the organization that best exploits opportunities. Political revolutions typically take the form of sudden shifts from statist patterns (which have become weak because they no longer solve real problems) to individualistic patterns, and then back again. Such violent shifts in group attitudes are usually accompanied by corresponding shifts in the focus of group action—from solving problems to seizing opportunities, and back—which reflect the different capabilities of these tertiary cycles.

The theorizing attitudes derived from these cycles—general idealism and materialism—are even more enduring than their social counterparts. They are the most general attitudes a person may take toward reality, and hence seldom change. It is worth noting that the history of Western thought has seen only two major periods of dominant materialism—Greco-Roman times and the Renaissance to the present—while Eastern history shows none. Thus if our criteria were simply duration and dominance of attitude, we would have to conclude that statist idealism is the "natural" overall theorizing attitude of mankind.

Medieval Catholicism provides a familiar example of a full-blown idealistic tertiary organization dominating people's approach to knowledge. Two of the three secondary patterns into which this cycle may be analyzed were mentioned earlier: church orthodoxy, where behavior was discriminated on the basis of a system of ideals, and authoritarian deism, where a behaving God was assumed to control physical events. Closing the ring was a collectivistic phase in which Catholicism, much like a modern corporation, used its physical assets as a basis for promulgating its ideal concepts. But these phases were not promoted separately: they merged into a single tertiary pattern, a complete world-view, capable of answering any question. This is why it predominated for over a millenium. In the authoritarian phase, medieval Catholicism posited a supreme God, ruler of the world, who through a chain of deputies had delegated some of His authority to the heirarchy of the Church. His and their behavior, then, became the basis for the physical actions of the Church: performing rituals, building cathedrals and monasteries, holding land and treasure. In the collectivistic phase, this physical plant became the categorial support for defining Catholic ideals such as piety (adhering to Church rituals) and support (giving goods to the Church). Finally, in the orthodox phase the ideals became the basis for regulating the behavior of the Church's communicants. They were admonished to seek grace, avoid sin, confess and do penance, and otherwise modify their natural behavior to fit its ideal system. The whole tertiary pattern was rounded off in such a way that any question about a part of it could be answered by reference to another part. The physical establishment of the Church was explained because God had commanded it to be built; its ideal values were designed to support and glorify this construction; and man (whom God had created) was bound to adhere to the values. An endless cycle of explanations was offered.

The opposite tertiary cycle is materialism, best represented today by modern science. From the viewpoint of our present-day industrialized life-style, it may be hard to realize that it was scarcely 200 years ago that theorizers such as Laplace first clearly saw the possibility of constructing a complete scientific world-view, and less than 100 years that a sufficient body of explanations has existed to make such a view seem plausible. To make it work we have to treat physical reality as the manifestation of ideal laws, ideals as the products of human thought behavior, and behavior as the outcome of physical processes. The first task, explaining physical reality by reference to ideals, has enjoyed the most success: modern physics has reached a point where its claims for its mathematical description of the world are widely accepted, or at least there are few who can figure out how to criticize them. The second task, explaining ideals as products of behavior, seems simple but has proved troublesome. If ideals are no more than constructions of human thought, why is it that certain questions about them (such as unsolved mathematical problems) have hard, real answers that we are yet unable to discover? The last task, explaining behavior physically, still eludes science. Despite all its progress in molecular biology, science's description of life itself is confused and rudimentary; it does not yet amount to an explanation.

Thus materialism remains a recent, and not yet completely successful, alternative to idealism. Except in a few highly industrialized societies, it has not attained the dominance over thought that has been enjoyed by idealistic institutions such as Catholicism. Yet most readers of this book will find they are personally committed to it—largely because it is the individualistic

151

theorizing attitude, with which "freedom" is associated in many minds.

The reason for this association can be analyzed. The most primal process of life is an interplay between behavior and physical reality; this occupies the bulk of everyday human responses. In sophisticated societies a new factor, ideals, has entered with increasing force. The question is, how are ideals to be used in the total organization of human activity? If they are used to categorize behavior the result is ultimately statism and idealism, because to complete a total world-view the orthodoxy thereby adopted must be supplemented by authoritarianism and collectivism. On the other hand, if they are used to categorize physical reality the result is individualism and materialism: the total world-view now consists of a merger of this legalism with communalism and intellection. In the first case, using ideals to categorize behavior oppresses it with "other-worldly" sanctions and feels to us like a loss of freedom. In the second case, ideals are applied to physical reality and behavior is left free to pursue its original process of reacting to the physical world; this feels to us like a preservation of freedom. In this way, the most basic approach we take toward reality is colored by the use we make of ideals.

In the foregoing discussions, I have tried to locate knowledge within the larger context of human life in general, showing how it is inextricably bound up with group behavior. I have considered these relationships in their static states, as a series of "snapshots" of social and theorizing attitudes. Such analyses help us to understand, for any given instantaneous human situation, how the acquisition of knowledge may be partially or wholly determined by other attitudes toward life in general.

But it is clear that these attitudes display historical sequences; and in fact the serial patterns which we can discern explain much that would otherwise be obscure about the trends of human theorizing. They show us why knowledge develops the way it does, and give us one last tool with which to attack the artificial constraints that have grown up around human understanding.

5. History

The philosophies of one age have become the absur-
dities of the next, and the foolishness of yesterday has
become the wisdom of tomorrow.
                                              OSLER

The reader may have already noticed a pattern among the various organizations of human life: namely, that many of their manifestations seem to
follow one another *in a predetermined sequence*. This is in fact the case.
Natural dynamics operate among the ways we organize behavior, so that
history for us is largely a matter of following a predictable succession of such
organizations. Exposing the dynamic processes involved, and establishing
the sequences they generate, yield profound insights into the forces that
shape human knowledge.

In Section 3.1, I discussed the sequence in which primary organizations
appeared in the history of life: first physical reality, then behavior, and
finally ideals. This sequence emerges repeatedly in all phases of human
behavior, including that of human groups and human theorizers. Of particular interest is the fact that it forms the basis for natural sequences of the
secondary and tertiary organizations. For reasons to be discussed shortly,
secondary organizations tend to arise in human life in this order: *communalism, authoritarianism, intellection, orthodoxy, legalism, collectivism*. The natural starting point for this sequence is communalism, since it
represents an approach in which the oldest primary organization, physical
reality, provides the setting for working in the second oldest primary organization, behavior. The other secondary organizations then follow in the order
given. Understanding this fundamental historical process, and the reasons
for it, adds significantly to our grasp of human behavior.

Why a *sequence* of organizations in human life? Why don't we simply
choose the most appropriate organization for each segment of our behavior
from the totality of possibilities? As I argued in Section 3.3, this is the most
effective method for developing knowledge—the method I call "compara-

tive theorizing." If social development occurred in the same way, adopting the "best" secondary and tertiary organizations for each human situation, both knowledge and life would be greatly enhanced.

The problem is that human beings normally do not have the means to make absolutely free choices in their organizations of behavior. The supply of "behavioral energy" is always limited, and must be meted out to those activities which promise the easiest and earliest results. Recall the discussion of living responses to the thermodynamic environment, in Section 3.2. Although energy, strictly speaking, is a physical entity, its close association (in time ordering) with the living stimulus-response chain gives it a behavioral meaning as well. We can distinguish behavior patterns in terms of their "applications of energy," referring to the means by which responsiveness shows up in organisms. Thus we can say that "energy becomes available" for a given set of living actions, meaning that the organism is behaving so as to create a route through it from the available energy in its environment to the performance of these actions—just as the gold-leaf flag described in Section 3.2 created a route from the dissipation of certain molecular concentrations in a tube of gas to the physical action of a flag waving.

When describing such processes among living things, it is essential to remember that energy in this sense is always limited in amount. When an organism arranges itself so as to capture and employ energy for one type of behavior, it is usually at the expense of another type. Hence the *choice* of how energy is to be used becomes a paramount concern for life. In any given situation, the organizations of behavior that are currently dominant tend to lay the groundwork for energy to be channeled into specific new organizations. The living unit—society or individual—finds it relatively easy and natural to switch its energy utilization into certain new modes. On the other hand, it seems laborious and awkward to choose *other* organizations, for which a groundwork does not exist. More effort is required to achieve what seems to be the same result, and energy appears to be wasted in the process.

For this reason—because of natural limitations on the supply of "behavioral energy"—human affairs tend to follow a preset historical sequence. They are not free to adopt behavioral organizations at will. Some of the energy shifts that generate this sequence are described in the next section.

5.1 Dynamics

> There are seasons, in human affairs, of inward and outward revolution, when new depths seem to be broken up in the soul, when new wants are unfolded in multitudes, and a new and undefined good is thirsted for.
> CHANNING

A book of examples might be assembled to illustrate the natural sequential tendency of secondary and tertiary organizations in human life. There will be room here to cite only a few instances. But our understanding can probe deeper than a mere recital of "the way it is." Inherent processes drive human affairs forward from one organization to the next, and we can best comprehend the sequence by first examining these processes.

They appear as a set of *transitions* from one secondary organization to its successor. The natural sequence mentioned above—communalism, authoritarianism, intellection, orthodoxy, legalism, collectivism—is circular: that is, the last stage (collectivism) is naturally followed by a reborn form of the first stage (communalism). Hence there are six normal transitions by which human behavior forms an unending chain of secondary organizations.

FIRST TRANSITION: COMMUNALISM TO AUTHORITARIANISM. Communalism is the earliest of the secondary organizations. Life arises when behavior is superimposed upon physical reality; hence the first way it occurs to living things to combine the primary organizations that grasp these realities is by using the existing physical situation to categorize behavior. A basic instance of this, mentioned earlier, is the process of perception, whereby certain of our thoughts, images, and sensations are understood in terms of physical entities to which they "refer." Such an idea—that certain parts of behavior are "about" external physical things—is clearly fundamental to many other patterns in human life.

Communalistic theories such as perception help accelerate the development of behavior. But once behavior has matured into a complex pattern in its own right, a new mode of organization becomes possible: one in which behavior is the basis for physical operations. These two—the modification of behavior to fit physical situations and the modification of physical situations to satisfy behavioral goals—are the counterpoint of affect and effect, cognition and action, which constitute the earliest and most fundamental processes of life. They are the secondary organizations of communalism and authoritarianism.

The transition from the first to the second shows up clearly in social behavior. In a group, the earmark of communalism is cooperation. A physical situation (such as a challenge from the environment or a physical opportunity to be exploited) provides the setting; social individuals then cooperatively modify their behavior to meet the challenge or seize the opportunity. Cooperation multiplies the physical effectiveness of behavior: in my earlier example, ten men together could move a stone while ten separately could not. A communal organization is called for, because it is physical reality that sets the problem and behavior that provides the solution. The earmark of authoritarianism, on the other hand, is obedience. Here behavior sets the problem and physical acts provide the solution. Authoritarianism arises out of communalism when the focus of group problems shifts from the physical to the behavioral.

Perhaps authoritarianism first appears when a "division of labor" becomes necessary. In the instance just mentioned, ten men moving a stone does not particularly require an authoritarian organization. Either they get together and do it, or they don't. But consider a more complex task, say a hunting expedition that requires both beaters and spear-throwers. How is the group to determine which individuals take which jobs? There is no "invisible hand" immanent in communalism that will cause the individuals best suited for these different tasks to volunteer for them in the optimum ratio. Actual experience suggests that most of the group would want to be spear-throwers, while few would opt for the more menial, arduous, and hazardous job of flushing game out of its hiding places. Here then is a behavioral problem, one that can be understood only in terms of the wants and expectations of human beings. It forms the setting for the group's making a physical distinction among its members. We observe the physical distinction when in fact certain of them take sticks and disappear, shouting and beating, into the high grass, while others crouch with their spears in the clearing. Assuming some individuals would not ordinarily prefer the roles they are taking under this arrangement, how do we explain their compliance? It is because a new organization in their behavior has made them obedient—to the social pressure of the group, to a tradition (such as that young boys have always been beaters), or to the dictates of a chief. The original concept of communalism—if we don't work together the job won't get done—has been transcended by a new idea: getting the job done requires doing what you are told.

This new secondary organization of authoritarianism develops in human life as a result of a problem in the primary organization (behavior) that forms its setting. The communal organization arose because of a physical problem, such as the fact that game moves too elusively for individual lone hunters. The authoritarian pattern now arises to meet a behavioral problem: the separate wants of individuals do not always produce the best pattern of cooperation among them. It is to solve this new problem that the new secondary organization is formed.

The reasons for this transition can be analyzed in more detail. Human beings develop secondary organizations to enhance their grasp of the primary organizations. When a ''problem'' arises—a situation in one primary organization that consumes behavioral energy and cannot be resolved within that organization—human beings cast about in the other, different primary organizations for modifications that will resolve the problem and lower their total energy needs. This process constitutes the formation of a new secondary organization. In my earlier illustration, a group in which all members have a physical need to take shelter in a cave find the entrance blocked by a rock. In the immediate primary organization (physical reality) there is no way to gain the cave, because no individual is able to remove the rock. However if the group members cooperate (modify their *behavior* toward one another) they can enhance each member's physical environment by entering the cave. They cooperate and the cave becomes accessible. Almost magically, an operation on behavior has achieved a physical result, by virtue of the application of a secondary organization. This secondary organization (communalism) will continue to develop as long as there are group physical problems. But its development entails an increasing complexity of group behavior; eventually problems must emerge here, because the adoption of communalism has generated a hitherto unknown mass of social transactions. Member A is dissatisfied with his role in the group, or is envious of B's social position, or is stirring up trouble between C and D. Although some of these problems may be solvable within behavior alone, many will persist. They will become the basis for a search for a new secondary organization, one that attempts to resolve them by physical means. Such resolutions may be as gentle as pointing out to A his physical characteristics (e.g. his youth or ancestry) that by tradition preclude him from B's role; or they may be as severe as killing A or locking up his body so he won't get the group into further turmoil. In all cases, the result of developing the new secondary organization (authoritarianism) will be to solve behavioral problems that grew out of the original adoption of communalism.

157

In an earlier discussion (Section 4.1) I mentioned that pure communalism is rarely displayed by whole societies; usually it thrives only in small groups. The foregoing analysis explains why: communalism gives rise to social transactions that eventually require authoritarian control. Beyond a certain size, any group of human beings is bound to generate interpersonal behavior conflicts. Since these problems are not solvable within communalism itself, adoption of that organization on a large scale might be thought of as "unstable"—a state of society that evaporates quickly when its members acquire enough energy and behavioral complexity to interact with one another. A counterweight is the severity of the physical problems impinging on the group, which will tend to keep it communally organized. In the example of the Arapesh, cited earlier as an instance of social communalism, the persistent difficulty of their mountainous environment had outweighed their potential behavior problems within, so they had not yet been able to find enough energy to make the transition to authoritarianism.

SECOND TRANSITION: AUTHORITARIANISM TO INTELLECTION. The transition from communalism to authoritarianism just considered might be characterized as an enlargement of knowledge of behavior at the expense of knowledge of physical reality. Human beings' capacity for action in physical reality becomes relatively circumscribed (because it is directed by authoritarian dictates), while the richness of their behavioral interactions becomes relatively deepened. Energy that used to be directed toward physical work now becomes applied to participating in a social system. The group as a whole may persist in this direction for some time; but eventually certain members will find they have "surplus energy"—energy not absorbed by the existing communal or authoritarian organizations. In effect, they have learned as much about physical reality and behavior as the problems in their environment force them to know. Thus they find an outlet for their surplus energy by turning their attention to ideals.

At first, such individuals are those in relatively "protected" circumstances—those who, by good luck or through quirks in the prevailing social arrangements, are relatively free from problems and have "time on their hands." Their earliest explorations of ideals are not regulated by the group, because ideals are irrelevant to the interplay between physical reality and behavior that drives their society. They become the speculators and philosophers of their time. They make up stories, invent reasons for the way things are, and inquire into the true nature of gods, spirits, and divine forces. As their skills mature, they become identified as prophets, priests, and wise men. In the role of professional explorers and expounders of ideals, they fill much the same need in their societies as academicians do in ours.

158

The natural categorial setting for these ideal explorations is behavior, because behavior currently supplies categories for exploring physical reality. In other words, the obvious initial method for exploring ideals consists of replacing the subject (physical reality) of an existing secondary organization (authoritarianism) with a new subject (ideals).

The new secondary organization, intellection, may at first take the form of attempts to "rationalize" authoritarianism. The same behavioral categories that justified social regulation by traditions and chiefs now give ideal subjects the form of guiding myths and evidences of the divinity of kingship. But the process of logical abstraction is also developed, producing the skills of the orator and teller of fabulous tales. All this lays the foundation for religion.

In this way, intellection is spearheaded by individuals with the leisure to dream about ideals. Eventually their behavior becomes accepted and adopted by the group. But it is important to recognize that intellection does not flourish until the group's needs for communalism and authoritarianism are fairly met. To put it another way, behavioral energy does not become available for intellection until the demands on it from these prior secondary organizations are substantially less than the total group energy being generated. Hence the transition from authoritarianism to intellection will not occur in a group with serious physical problems in its environment, because energy will be spent instead on a communal search for cooperative patterns to overcome these problems. Nor will it occur in a group with intractable behavioral problems among its members, because the same energy will flow into forming an authoritarian organization to preserve the group. To the extent that a group has mastered its physical and behavioral situation, however, the energy it generates will become available for intellection, and it is into developing this new secondary organization that it will naturally flow. Once a group of human beings is adequately fed and sheltered, neither threatened by enemies nor by the elements, and once its members have accepted their social roles and agreed on a set of dictates for their actions, then whatever energy is left over becomes the driving force for the development of intellection.

From an individual viewpoint this transition entails "freedom" and a satisfying enlargement of understanding, for it evolves largely outside of group sanctions. Group needs are pursued through the existing interplay of communalism and authoritarianism, and it is principally individuals who explore the new world of ideals. Their enthusiastic cries of discovery have illuminated some of our most exciting periods of history. Yet much of what they find is ultimately adopted by the group, becoming the basis for the next transition.

THIRD TRANSITION: INTELLECTION TO ORTHODOXY. At first intellection stocks people's minds with a somewhat miscellaneous collection of ideals. Powers and values, spirits and magical potencies, heroes and myths become understood as inspiration flourishes. But as these entities gain social currency, it soon becomes apparent that some of the ideals discovered by intellection can be used for internal group control. In the same way that authoritarianism used traditions and commands to regulate people's physical actions, so the newly understood ideals can be used to regulate people's *behavior*. Hitherto the only basis for discriminating individual desires and plans had been their physical effect, in accordance with the group's communal organization. But now it becomes possible to set ideal criteria. Regardless of its physical effects, individual behavior may now be judged by "spiritual" standards, or by such abstract value categories as "just," "kind," "manly," etc. When this pattern in fact emerges—when the group starts adopting ideal categories to regulate behavior—a new secondary organization, orthodoxy, has appeared.

Orthodoxy receives its initial energy because it solves certain problems more effectively than authoritarianism. Trying to regulate group behavior by limiting physical acts, as authoritarianism does, is often inefficient. While it may prevail in the physical sphere, it leaves individuals free to expend energy on inner rebellions, unsatisfied desires, and so on. It does not touch their behavior directly; it coerces without convincing. But convincing the social individual that his very desires are wrong, by referring them to ideals through orthodoxy, controls behavior at the source. No energy flows into plotting against the authoritarian establishment, because such plots themselves become regulated. Thus at the beginning orthodoxy serves authoritarianism: traditions become holy, kings rule through divine right, and individuals refrain from "anti-social" acts—not just because their bodies might be caught and punished, but because they now understand that not only the acts *but the desires to perform the acts* are wrong.

This substitution resembles that of the first transition (communalism to authoritarianism). In the earlier case, certain social tasks (such as organizing a hunting party) were performed inefficiently under the prevailing communal organization; bringing in a new organization (authoritarianism) decreased the amount of energy required to achieve the desired results. Now the group's adoption of orthodoxy achieves a similar reduction in the energy needed to regulate individual activity. In the earlier case the task was physical and the solution behavioral; here the task is behavioral (regulate society) and the solution is ideal (establish values).

As intellection was a stage of discovery of ideals, so orthodoxy is a stage of consolidation and application. The transition from one to the other is largely a transition from individual involvement with ideals to group involvement. As such, it feels to many individuals in the group as a "loss of freedom." But orthodoxy becomes an important tool for solving problems among ideals. What happens is that intellection, as it spawns a hodge-podge of separate notions of ideals, creates a demand for consistent ideal systems. This whole area of knowledge becomes increasingly unsatisfactory, because there is no group agreement on how it is to be treated. Orthodoxy solves the problem by using the new ideals as a basis for regulating the behavior that understands them. This solves the problem of inconsistency, and firmly establishes ideals in human consciousness. Such mature religions as Christianity, Buddhism, Moslemism, Judaism, Confucianism, Taoism, etc., testify to the power of orthodoxy in this role.

FOURTH TRANSITION: ORTHODOXY TO LEGALISM. During the stage of intellection, individuals explored ideals and developed a variety of notions about them. During the stage of orthodoxy, groups adopted these notions, forming ideal systems to discriminate and regulate behavior. Through the present transition, these ideals are now applied to physical reality. Thus arises legalism in human life.

This transition resembles that from authoritarianism to intellection. In the earlier case, authoritarianism established the usefulness of behavioral categories, while the area of their application "swung" from physical reality to ideals. Now the success of ideals as orthodox categories has stimulated a "swing" of their application from behavior to physical reality. As before, the transition occurs only when there is enough "surplus" energy in the society to allow individuals to devote themselves to the new organization, for it seems at first to have no tangible value. For instance, the mathematical concepts thought up by the Pythagoreans were at first mere philosophers' playthings, new ways of describing the physical world that were of interest only to curious men of leisure.

Ultimately, of course, legalism establishes scientific concepts in human thought. The idea of "laws of nature" arises to replace the authoritarian notion of animistic causes. In social polity, the cognate idea of human law arises to replace the rule of one man over the actions of another. As was true earlier (during the swing from authoritarianism to intellection), the transition from orthodoxy to legalism feels like a time of increasing individual freedom and expanding knowledge. Absolute principles now replace traditional dictates, both in knowledge and in society, and areas of physical events and acts hitherto regarded as understood must now be re-examined from the new perspective. In Western societies, several factors contributed to the rise of legalistic commerce and industrialization: 1) absolute standards in law permitted long-term investments in capital goods (ships, mines, factories) without fear of arbitrary authoritarian confiscation; 2) a mobile labor force emerged, where membership was based more on abstract criteria (skill, knowledge), and less on behavioral factors such as patronage; and 3) such abstract rights as inventions, promotions, and investments became recognized as tangible property, creating incentives for individuals to create and market them. The new treatment of physical reality led to a sudden proliferation of physical goods.

In theorizing, legalism encourages scientific experimentation and the formulation of abstract descriptions. Physical things are now seen as having such abstract qualities as mass and energy; the concept of "mechanics" is born. In the regulation of society, legalism offers alternatives to both authoritarianism and orthodoxy. By replacing authoritarianism, it permits construction of a system of regulation that will subsist beyond the frailties of human will and shortness of human life. Society can count on its laws in ways that it can never count on a king. By replacing orthodoxy, legalism substitutes the regulation of physical acts for the discrimination of behavior; difficult and somewhat arbitrary inquiries into people's beliefs or motivations are replaced by objective inquiries into what people *did*. Society begins to depend less on guardians of morals and faith, and more on keepers of the peace.

FIFTH TRANSITION: LEGALISM TO COLLECTIVISM. Legalism encourages human beings to create new physical things. In science it stimulates the invention of new instruments and machines designed to investigate physical reality from an ideal viewpoint: calipers and cloud chambers, thermometers and cyclotrons. In society it facilitates such things as power and communication nets, factories and warehouses, indentures and negotiable instruments; these social creations depend on legalistic disciplines that define property, establish units of wealth, and support such "legal persons" as corporations. Once these physical things have been engendered, they become objects of knowledge in their own right. Much of "civilized" people's lives become centered around them, just as it had previously been centered around indigenous things like land, crops, and livestock. The new physical things now comprise the basis for a new secondary organization in human life, collectivism.

In theorizing, collectivism springs from the new physical effects uncovered by legalistic experimentation, using them as a setting for developing ideal explanatory systems. Refined observations of such things as motion, gravitation, and electromagnetism inspire new mathematical descriptions and abstract models. Even everyday objects join in this process: ordinary physi-

162

cal motions and surfaces, for instance, suggest the ideal explorations of analytic geometry, the calculus, and theory of functions.

Social collectivism takes for its setting the newly created goods of industrialization, using them as a basis for selecting and developing institutional ideals. Its earmark is *planning*. Thus the social transition from legalism to collectivism often appears as a transition from *laissez-faire* economics to group economic planning, from "capitalism" to "socialism." Under legalism, ideal rules were adopted as the basis for physical actions: individuals went forth as builders and entrepreneurs, creating the goods of industrialism. Now these goods, with all their attendant physical problems and opportunities, become the setting for a new appraisal of ideals, of society's value systems.

This change resembles the reversals mentioned earlier—communalism to authoritarianism, intellection to orthodoxy. Many feel it as a "loss of freedom." Under legalism, individuals were free to exploit their physical goods pretty much as they pleased, as long as they adhered to legal guidelines such as property rights: they could undercut competitors, corner commodities, monopolize utilities, despoil natural resources. But ultimately such practices lead to waste and human suffering. Society experiences famines and gluts in essential commodities due to market manipulations; predatory exploitation of workers and small businessmen; and a heedless plunder of the natural environment. The solution is to adopt new ideals (such as "fair practices" and "community goals") to regulate the uses of the goods of capitalism. To the entrepreneur this means a loss of freedom, an infringement of his right to build things and make money. To the socialist it is an essential transition, without which industrialism is wasteful and inhuman.

SIXTH TRANSITION: COLLECTIVISM TO COMMUNALISM. With the emergence of collectivism, human behavior has tried all possible ways of combining the three primary organizations of its natural knowledge into secondary organizations. Does this then terminate the development of the secondaries? The answer is no. A sixth transition occurs, from collectivism to communalism, by which the sequence starts over again. In fact there is never a break in the procession of secondary organizations; the sequence forms an endless circle, although at each repetition human beings tend to apply these patterns to new and different areas of the primary organizations.

As with the second and fourth transitions discussed above, the change from collectivism to communalism is a "swing" of understanding, wherein physical categories previously applied to ideals are now applied to behavior. Theorizers turn from seeking abstract formulas to investigating the nature of the human condition. There is a resurgence of empirical knowledge about behavior—often with a distinctly "unscientific" cast, because ideals are being abandoned in favor of a more "organic" understanding of the interactions between behavior and the physical world. Psychology flourishes as physics wanes.

In this transition society becomes more "humanistic." Legalism had encouraged the production of the goods of industrialization: factories, transportation, consumer products, etc. Collectivism used the existence of these things as the basis for exploring new ideals: values and institutions designed to curb capitalistic "abuses" and introduce "fair" schemes for the distribution of the goods. Eventually, however, human nature itself rebels against such ideal systems; while logical in conception they tend to fail in practice, because they cannot comprehend the independent adaptability of human behavior. The socialistic schemes become as rigid and "inhuman" as the capitalistic practices they were designed to correct, and are increasingly subverted by everyday human life. Hence the next step is to use the physical setting for a new exploration of behavior, to determine how people can actually cooperate in an industrial community.

This new communalism differs in outward appearance from the earlier "primitive" communalism by which people originally cooperated to solve physical problems: but organizationally it is the same. It seems different because the physical setting is now predominantly industrial and artificial, instead of the natural situation of "primitive" life. One manifestation of the underlying similarity of the two communalisms is a renewed concern with the physical environment as a basis for life (rather than as a basis for industrialism); conservation assumes a new importance.

From these descriptions it is evident that the principal movements occurring today in "advanced" societies are the fifth and sixth transitions: from legalism, through collectivism, to a new industrial communalism. Of course no society makes only one transition at a time, any more than it displays a single secondary organization. Among the complexities of human behavior, virtually every possible pattern can be found to some extent. But some always predominate, and the transitions among these "principal" secondary organizations usually appear as the characteristic focus of social change at any given time.

Many will rejoice that the main thrust at the forefront of human society today is toward industrial communalism, for this is one of those transitions that typically emphasize individual freedom and new horizons of understanding. Working out patterns of cooperative behavior from a setting of industrial goods will deepen our knowledge of human life as a whole. It will feel like a time of individual initiative and human fellowship, freed to some extent from abstract rigidities. However, such rejoicing must be tempered by the recognition that the *next* succeeding stage will be a new form of authoritarianism, brought about by intractable behavioral problems arising from the abandonment of ideal regulation. Human command will have to take over where law has atrophied. In the more "advanced" countries, this future transition is likely to occur during present lifetimes.

TRANSITIONS IN GENERAL. Thus human behavior not only builds secondary organizations upon its innate primary organizations, it builds them in a certain order. The sequence just examined—communalism, authoritarianism, intellection, orthodoxy, legalism, collectivism, and then communalism again—unfolds as a result of natural transitions, by which each secondary organization leads us into the one next in order. More formally, we can say that to the extent societies generate surplus energy, and to the extent we recognize certain typical organizations or ways of life in social behavior, the organizations will usually be adopted in the order specified. Legalistic industrialization, for instance, will usually follow religious orthodoxy, not precede it; royal authoritarianism will usually follow tribal communalism, not precede it; and so on.

This sequence is not arbitrary. We can appreciate its inner workings by analyzing it in terms of the primary organizations of physical reality, behavior, and ideals. The odd-numbered transitions described above (communalism to authoritarianism, intellection to orthodoxy, legalism to collectivism) all represent reversals of application of two primary organizations in building secondary patterns. The old subject of exploration or regulation becomes the new categorial setting, and the old setting is now explored or regulated on that basis. The odd-numbered transitions also carry behavior from the tertiary cycle of individualism to statism, feeling like a "loss of freedom." The even-numbered transitions described above (authoritarianism to intellection, orthodoxy to legalism, collectivism to communalism) are all "swings" of attention from one primary organization to another, using the third primary as a categorial basis for both. The old setting serves to explore or regulate a new subject. These transitions carry behavior from statism back to individualism, feeling like an access of freedom.

Tertiary organizations—patterns formed by the "merging" of secondary organizations—tend to appear and disappear during these transitions. In most societies, all secondary organizations are present to some extent; those that predominate at a given time tend to support others that make up the tertiaries. Thus a predominance of collectivism in a society will nurture orthodoxy and authoritarianism as well, producing the more complete tertiary "way of life" of statism; examples of this effect were described by W.

165

H. Whyte, Jr., in *The Organization Man*. On the other hand, a shift to the new "industrial" communalism will supplant this overall attitude with the tertiary cycle of individualism. Now legalism will be enlisted to break up the collectivistic institutions, and intellection to refute the bases of orthodoxy.

Many historical and anthropological examples could be cited to illustrate the scheme of transitions outlined above. But in addition to such empirical evidence, the sequence itself has an inherent rationale. Given only the existence of three primary organizations in human behavior, and the process of forming secondary organizations from them, it is possible to analyze the likelihood of transitions among the secondaries in absolute terms. Thus to a recital of "how it is" we can add an explanation of "why it is."

Let us denote the three primary organizations by x, y, and z, and the secondary organizations built on them by expressions of the form "x categorizes y." Without assigning values to x, y, and z, let us call the first stage of a transition "x categorizes y." There are five possible second stages that might result from the transition:

(1) y categorizes x
(2) x categorizes z
(3) y categorizes z
(4) z categorizes x
(5) z categorizes y.

These define five possible "transition types," which can be ranked in order of likelihood just on the basis of our understanding of the process of forming secondary organizations. The order is in fact the one given above, and the reasons for it are as follows.

(1): "X categorizes y" is most likely to be followed by "y categorizes x" because the transition from one to the other does not require introducing a new primary organization. The two stages have a natural affinity, because together they form the x-y "complementary pair" tertiary organization. As we form the "parallelism" between two primary organizations that is the basis for every secondary, it is easy for us to give them the alternate roles of subject and category source.

(2): The next most likely case is that "x categorizes y" will be followed by "x categorizes z." Although this involves the introduction of a new primary organization z, it does so in the least disruptive way among the four remaining possibilities: it just enlarges the subject field covered by familiar categories. By making this transition we simply assume that what was sauce for the goose y is now a suitable sauce for the gander z. However it is not as easy a transition as (1), because it requires fitting existing categories to an entirely independent order of reality. It cannot be derived from any prior theoretical parallelism. Hence this transition becomes possible only when current explanations in x terms become rich and varied enough to suggest applications to z.

(3): In going from "x categorizes y" to "y categorizes z" we start to form one of the tertiary "cycles" described earlier (Section 4.2). This transition is less likely than (2) because it is now the current subject area (rather than category area) that must supply new categories. We must not only categorize a whole new order of reality, we must fashion those categories from material presently understood only as a subject area. Yet it is more likely than either of the remaining two possible transitions because it fashions its new categories out of existing knowledge, instead of being forced to draw on the unknown primary organization z.

(4): In the cyclic tertiary organizations, x categorizes y, y categorizes z, and z categorizes x. These three secondary organizations support each other in an endless chain. Type (3) transitions, just discussed, move from the first link to the second; a type (4) transition would move from the first to the third, from "x categorizes y" to "z categorizes x." The effect would be to categorize our categories. But this would defeat their purpose, which is to provide a stable platform for explorations in another order of reality. When a tertiary cycle forms, it is more natural for it to proceed by a series of type (3) transitions, two of which will have the effect of a type (4).

(5): The transition from "x categorizes y" to "z categorizes y" is least likely of all. Because they occur in different primary organizations, the x categories and the z categories will be totally unlike. Switching from one to the other will require us to change our understanding of y to a radical degree. Since y is already thought to be explained (in x terms), there can be no advantage in spontaneously deciding to explain it in terms entirely different. Such a change of viewpoint, if it occurs at all, is likely only through a chain of type (1) and type (2) transitions, from which the new categorial scheme will build up its justification.

By analyzing the transitions needed to form the natural sequence of secondary organizations (communalism, authoritarianism, intellection, orthodoxy, legalism, collectivism), it is easy to see that it proceeds by alternate type (1) and type (2) transitions. In fact at every stage it executes the most likely transitions available, and hence is the most likely sequence.

Since this sequence is endless (because collectivism is followed again by communalism), it has six possible starting points. Yet we naturally regard communalism as its first stage. The reason for this depends on the way we, as observers, first identify the existence of secondary organizations. In understanding living things we first identify their units physically: for instance, a

167

society as a group of physical organisms in a common physical location. We then study their behavior. Thus our understanding of human life tends to start with communalism, because it is in this organization that behavior is distinguished in physical terms. This is an appropriate attitude, since physical reality and behavior are the oldest and next-oldest primary organizations; but it is not valid in any absolute sense. We could equally well first understand societies by examining their common ideals. However, this is not the traditional view, so history for us starts with communalism. From there the other secondary organizations follow in the order cited.

REASONS FOR CHANGE. Why do transitions from one secondary organization to another happen at all? When human beings have achieved a successful organization of behavior, what impels them to change their basic approach, adopting a different organization?

An examination of actual social changes suggests two reasons: the power of specific secondary organizations to solve specific types of problems, and their more general role as absorbers of surplus behavioral energy. In the first case, problem solving, a need for one of two specific secondary organizations emerges when a problem arises in one of the primary organizations. The two desirable secondaries are the ones that use the primary as their category source. Thus physical problems will encourage a society to establish either a form of communalism (which seeks cooperative behavior responsive to the physical setting), or a form of collectivism (which will explore ideals for a set of abstract guidelines). Similarly, behavioral problems will encourage the establishment of either intellection or authoritarianism; and problems among ideals will call for either legalism or orthodoxy. Any human group that is not totally static will encounter different such problems at different times. This alone will tend to cause shifts in the secondary organizations of its behavior. By applying the hierarchy of transition types just discussed, it is generally possible to predict (on the basis of currently predominate secondary organizations) which new organizations are likely to be adopted to meet any particular problem.

Consider an example. Industrialized societies organize their social behavior predominately between *ideals* and physical reality, i.e. in legalistic and collectivistic modes. "Primitive" societies, however, are organized predominately between *behavior* and physical reality, in communal and authoritarian modes. Imagine that the same physical problem—such as a crop failure leading to a food shortage—arises in both societies. The industrialized society will typically respond with a form of collectivism: it will adopt such institutional ideals as the concepts of agricultural price supports or tax incentives to farmers. In this way it will modify its agreed group ideals

168

to include new factors which will tend to solve the problem, in accordance with its predominate theories of government. In contrast, the "primitive" society is more likely to respond to the physical problem of a food shortage by communalism, by modifying its agreed pattern of group behavior. New traditions may be adopted, which encourage more or better planting and hunting. Conflicts within the group may be subordinated to mutual help in securing food. Again, a secondary organization that promises a solution (under the society's predominate theories) will be adopted, but one that is quite different from that in an industrialized society.

In terms of the transition types just discussed, the most likely responses to emerging problems in a society will be those that require only type (1) transitions from existing secondary organizations. The predicted responses in the foregoing example were of this type. For each society to adopt the other's solution would require type (4) or type (5) transitions, which are much less likely. Thus from the prevailing viewpoint of a "primitive" society, solving a food shortage by formulating ideal principles would seem an unbearably remote and indirect procedure. Until a group has gathered considerable experience guiding their lives by abstractions, such entities do not seem to be useful in solving physical problems. Conversely, from the prevailing viewpoint of an industrialized society solving a food shortage by purely communalistic means would seem naive and ineffective. Merely seeking group cooperation would be a "weak" response, one that would fail among the complexities of self-interest in a modern society. Collectivism would appear to provide a powerful general solution, which could be adopted and enforced within existing group legal institutions.

Beside solving problems, secondary organizations also serve to absorb "surplus" human energy. One of the ways life improves itself is by investing unneeded energy in new ways of doing things, ways that apparently have no immediate utility. As societies become highly successful in following a given secondary organization, they tend to "outgrow" it; their energy seeks other outlets. Thus even when no specific problem calls for a change, individuals in a society may seek new modes of organization just because energy is available to try different approaches. This generates instances of change that seem to originate spontaneously, appearing to represent a simple organic development of attitudes.

Such growth inspired by surplus energy shows up in theorizing. In fact, according to Kuhn (*The Structure of Scientific Revolutions*) it may be more common than change resulting from the need to solve problems. He points out that new theories ("paradigms"), despite their claims, seldom actually solve problems better than the old. Instead, they are often supported at first just by the promise of opening up a new approach to reality:

But paradigm debates are not really about relative problem-solving ability, though for good reasons they are usually couched in those terms. Instead, the issue is which paradigm should in the future guide research on problems many of which neither competitor can yet claim to resolve completely. A decision between alternate ways of practicing science is called for, and in the circumstances that decision must be based less on past achievement than on future promise.[37]

The considerations which evoke change of this kind in theorizing are those that arise spontaneously, within a body of knowledge, by the free application of a new organization to an existing understanding of reality. Such developments typically take place when theorizers have the extra energy available to speculate, even in the face of initial failures by the new approach to aid in problem solving.

5.2 Individuals

> It is the lone worker who makes the first advance in a subject: the details may be worked out by a team, but the prime idea is due to the enterprise, thought and perception of an individual.
> ALEXANDER FLEMING

Knowledge is first acquired by individuals. In the preceding discussions, I have outlined some of the purely social processes that tend to shape human knowledge, particularly the sequential formation of secondary and tertiary organizations in group behavior. These processes impinge upon individual theorizers in two principal ways. First, prevailing social attitudes—the organizations that are most powerful in group behavior—exercise direct control over the support of theorizing activities and the dissemination of new knowledge, as well as providing sanctions against theorizing approaches that are seen to threaten the social process. In every place and time, including our own, certain theories have always been branded "dangerous." This is the ancient phenomenon of censorship, one that can be overcome once we recognize its existence and trace its roots to the particular social organizations predominating at the time.

A second effect of social organizations upon individual theorizing, however, is more subtle. Individuals grow up in societies, and each one carries within him a pattern of personal organizations largely borrowed from, and hence determined by, his social surroundings. In other words, the process of individual learning is far from neutral and generalized; it consists of adopting highly specialized attitudes toward reality, many of which are so deeply implanted that it never occurs to the individual that there might be any others. Yet if the method of "comparative theorizing" outlined in Section 3.3 is ever to flourish, human theorizers must be freed from these parochial viewpoints. In modern societies, all six possible secondary organizations are available; hence to explore the three orders of reality it is not necessary to devise new organizations, but only to employ more freely the organizations which already exist. This individuals can learn to do. In my analysis so far, I have discussed the first requirement: recognizing how organizations arise and change in societies, and what pressures they bring to bear on specific theorizing approaches. The second requirement is to recognize how these pressures manifest themselves within individuals. This subject (to be examined now) provides a foundation for making the individual adjustments necessary to compensate for them.

Human individuals are born with their primary organizations well started. Evolution has endowed them with an innate ability to grasp physical reality, behavior, and ideals. Of course during his lifetime the human being will greatly extend his understanding of these three orders of reality; but the basic approach is there from the outset. Secondary and tertiary organizations, however, are mostly built during a lifetime. The impetus and guidance for this process of behavior development come largely from the groups to which an individual belongs.

The starting point for building higher organizations of behavior is the parent-child communal group. Learning starts from a physical situation that must be dealt with for the infant to survive. Thus the mother and neonate immediately establish a group in which biologically required physical acts form a prescribed setting for the mutual exploration of cooperative behavior. The mother learns how to satisfy the needs of the child, while the child learns how to behave in various physical situations. The infant begins life with a learning process where its discoveries about behavior are automatically categorized in terms of its physical needs. Before it has acquired any freedom of choice or capacity for perspective, the human child is forced to adopt a communal secondary organization, becoming an empirical theorist.

Before long, however, the child's new grasp of behavior gained through this first learning process becomes extensive enough to constitute the setting for a new secondary organization, authoritarianism. Behavior patterns which were explored in communalism now become prescribed by adult authority. Among these patterns, for instance, are the behavior of approval and disapproval in others: these are now adopted as categories for governing the child's physical acts in the family group. Physical reality becomes divided into toys and untouchables, permitted acts and "no-no's." This is a typical reversal of setting and subject, a type (1) transition as discussed above. It is often suggested that this change (from communalism to authoritarianism) is first deeply implanted in the child's personality at the time of toilet training, when what had been a necessary and accepted physical act in the purely communal group now emerges as a discriminated physical act in the authoritarian family group. The cooperative behavioral interchanges with parents, which the child learned in order to satisfy the needs of his physiological processes, are now turned around to constitute a categorial setting from which the child is expected to discriminate and regulate those same processes.

Of course each child shifts back and forth between communal and authoritarian organizations of its behavior, exhibiting the tertiary complementary pairing described in Section 4.2. At no specific age does he "switch" from communalism to authoritarianism. Every new pattern of behavior learned communally is a candidate for inclusion in the authoritarian categories by which physical acts are distinguished; and each new physical discovery may be tried out on parents to elicit a behavioral reaction. But over the general course of early childhood, the organizational emphasis shifts more and more into authoritarianism, away from the pure communalism of the neonate.

In industrialized societies, a new secondary organization begins to dominate the average child's life about age four or five. He discovers there is a "logic behind" behavior, that parental dictates are not monolithic and unquestionable. Piaget has documented this transition in detail. The child develops intellection: he uses language and other behavior as a setting from which to explore ideals. Authoritarianism recedes as his attention "swings" from physical reality to ideals. Typical of childhood intellection are the "why?" stage of questioning and the period psychologists call "latency."

The onset of "latency" is thus a symptom of an overall shift in the young human individual's dominant field of learning, from physical reality to ideals. The apparent sexual dormancy is part of a more general withdrawal from the physical in order to grasp the ideal; it is cognate to the period of monasticism in European history and the (much briefer) "rites of passage" in tribal life. Language behavior constitutes the key to sorting out values and abstractions. Typically the child's interests outside the home enlarge, for society in general is the principal repository of ideal information. Classroom schooling also plays a decisive role as the child's repertoire of ideal knowledge grows.

As soon as ideals coalesce into some sort of system for the child, he starts using them as a categorial setting for discriminating behavior, by developing the secondary organization of orthodoxy. Behavior that was previously simply permitted or punished becomes "nice," "naughty," and so forth on ideal grounds. The young individual receives ready-built value systems (which he can now understand and absorb in their own terms) from peers, school, parents, church, and the communication media. Often these value systems are taken uncritically, so that the child becomes a bigot in many areas. Simultaneously his understanding of behavior deepens; he com-

173

prehends it in a new way, by fitting its many varieties into the new ideal systems.

Again, the average child shifts constantly between intellection and orthodoxy, developing the tertiary pair organization that will eventually comprise his "spiritual" life. Each newly understood ideal becomes a key to the orthodox treatment of some area of behavior; and each newly understood pattern of behavior exemplifies some set of ideals. But gradually the emphasis on intellection declines and the emphasis on orthodoxy, often manifested as conformism, grows. Yet there is no dramatic switch from one to the other. Of course the earlier communal and authoritarian organizations continue to operate in the individual's life, but no longer as the principal focus of learning.

In industrialized societies, an overall tendency toward orthodoxy continues to dominate the average child's learning up to the time of puberty. At this stage, the adolescent has become accustomed to using ideal categories. But now his physical growth—his increasing ability to manipulate the tangible things of adult society—turns his attention back to physical reality. The "latency" period is terminated by new biologically generated demands and opportunities. He applies the ideals he now understands to distinguishing physical objects and acts, becoming a legalist. His attitude eventually becomes quite different from what it was in the early authoritarian family group: he seeks ideal reasons for his actions toward physical things, rather than just receiving behavioral dictates. This change is often regarded by parents as "rebellion." He also begins to grasp some of the abstract categories behind legal institutions, such as property rights and monetary value. His comprehension of the physical reality of industrialization deepens.

Lastly the adolescent, as he enters adulthood, begins to shift his focus of learning toward collectivistic organizations. The physical reality he now understands as a legalist categorizes his ideal systems. He gradually aligns his values toward industrialization, and his physical capacities and expectations of property become the basis on which he defines his role—both as producer and consumer—in modern society. Having now learned and participated in all the secondary organizations that contribute to group life, he is treated as an adult.

It is of course characteristic that the same sequence of secondary organizations (communalism, authoritarianism, intellection, orthodoxy, legalism, collectivism) typical of social development appears in individual learning as well. Societies and individuals both build secondary organizations of their behavior, and hence are both subject to the dynamic processes outlined in Section 5.1.

In particular, the sequence of individual learning approaches just discussed can be understood as a succession of problem-solving maneuvers, whereby the growing individual tries to resolve difficulties arising in each stage by adopting the next one. Thus at the beginning of individual life, the neonate discovers that modifications of its behavior tend to resolve physical problems. He does not recognize that this is by virtue of the communal organization inherent in the mother-child group; he simply learns that it is so, and therefore adopts a communal organization in his own life. This expands the complexity of his behavior, which if unregulated eventually leads to failures of the family group to achieve physical goals. Hence behavior problems provide the next basis for building an individual secondary organization; by a type (1) transition, the child's principal focus of learning changes from communalism to authoritarianism.

As the problem-solving child acquires a firm grasp of communalism and authoritarianism, the whole tertiary pair organization they form appears increasingly mysterious. Certain patterns of cooperative behavior solve physical problems, while certain physical acts elicit behavioral responses from parents; but from this there emerges no inherent, primary connection between physical reality and behavior. The correspondences seem arbitrary and ad hoc. The discovery of ideals, however, promises the child a general solution to this mystery. Behind parental behavior lie "principles" and "values" which, if understood, would surely reveal why some physical acts are permitted and others forbidden. Thus the child uses family behavior as a basis for exploring ideals, adopting the new secondary organization of intellection by means of a type (2) transition. Through intellection he expects to discover secrets of the operation of his group that escape analysis in terms of communalism and authoritarianism.

And so it goes. Inconsistencies among newly discovered ideals are resolved by adopting orthodoxy. The limitations of intellection and orthodoxy in organizing physical responses inspire a swing to legalism. And the need to define a system of practical ideals for the conduct of adult life leads to collectivism. At each stage of this process the human individual is drawn forward to a new secondary organization by implicit promises to resolve problems not presently solvable.

Another effect can be discerned in the interplay between the growing individual and his group. The individual is pulled into each new secondary organization by its potential to solve his problems; but once he adopts it, the group tends to operate in such a way as to *exclude* his return to previous

175

secondary organizations. The group encourages him to move into a new approach toward knowledge, then shuts the door behind him.

For example, as a child moves from mother-child communalism to the authoritarian family organization it encounters a new interpretation of interpersonal physical contact, namely that it is discouraged. The close physical intimacy that was essential to neonatal survival is now proscribed by the next succeeding secondary organization. The child finds himself partly shut out of communalism by his adoption of authoritarianism, a situation that engenders the "Oedipus complex" and incest taboos. Two factors are characteristic here. First, it is *physical* contact that is barred; cooperative *behavior* is still permitted—in fact, encouraged—but the physical core that originally provided the basis on which it was learned is cut away, so that the same physical acts may now be discriminated by the new organization. Second, the prohibition is dictatorially given, as an inherent part of the setting which must be accepted if one is to adopt an authoritarian approach. It is a group attitude toward reality, imposed on the individual as a condition of his learning. If the group does not teach authoritarianism, then the individual's adoption of communalism will never be impaired. An example would be the communal Arapesh, mentioned in Section 4.1; they were reported to lack an incest taboo. This is in line with their general social distaste for authoritarianism, and indicates that the group did not try to drive its individuals out of communalism.

Why do societies impose such proscriptions on their individuals? To answer this, we must appreciate the overall power of secondary organizations in human life. In a basic sense societies *are* secondary organizations, for without these uniquely "higher" patterns in their behavior we would not be able to identify any human groups as "social." Hence from a group viewpoint it is essential that secondary organizations flourish. But they can do so only to the extent that individuals adopt them. Thus an effect of "self-preservation" evolves within each group secondary organization: it incorporates specific patterns designed to prevent individuals from easily discarding it. Once an individual has begun to adopt a new secondary organization, it is simple enough for him to slip back to the stage he just left; to forestall this, the new organization includes inherent patterns that tend to color the individual's new knowledge in such a way that the old approach becomes less and less accessible to him.

Another such exclusionary effect in individual learning (in industrialized societies) occurs at the onset of latency. At this stage the child is moving from family authoritarianism to the new organization of intellection. He is exploring ideals on the basis of behavior. Intellection now tends to shut out authoritarianism: the child finds it increasingly difficult to analyze abstractly

176

the "principles" behind family dictates, although he is free to explore other ideals. In effect, his original family behavior code becomes inaccessible to logic. It becomes that part of human behavior Freud called the "superego," a sort of parental conscience which typically resists integration with the rest of individual behavior because it is forever shut out from normal intellectualization.

After the instilling of incest taboos and the encapsulation of the superego, further exclusions of one secondary organization by the next become less firmly entrenched in individual behavior, because they are now accessible to the integrating function of intellection. They may be analyzed rationally, and overcome when it is recognized that they are "illogical." Thus when an individual moves from intellection to orthodoxy, he often learns that parts of the language behavior by which he originally explored ideals are now forbidden. They are "dirty words," representing "bad thoughts." Such words and thoughts, which threaten to undermine the ideal foundations of the orthodoxy, must be abjured as an inherent part of its adoption. When the individual moves from orthodoxy to legalism, he learns that it is improper to introduce religious or class distinctions—"prejudices"—into social behavior. By adopting the legalistic organization of modern industrialism, he agrees to suppress those of his orthodox patterns that might constitute an easy retreat from such legal concepts as equality and impartiality. Finally, when the individual moves from legalism to collectivism he learns to reject the "robber baron" aspects of capitalism. Exploitation and vested interests become "undesirable" goals. Such exclusionary beliefs are particularly visible in socialist countries. All the foregoing processes can be more or less overcome by analyzing and exposing their patterns logically, through intellection; it is the earlier processes (incest proscriptions and superego dictates) that become "lost" in behavior inaccessible to idealization.

In these ways, then, individuals and societies conspire to erect the architecture of secondary organizations in human behavior which we know as "civilization." As a result, human beings pass substantially beyond the primary organizations with which they were endowed by evolution; much of what they know pertains to things the human species has itself created.

But in the course of becoming "civilized," human beings have developed a broad repertoire of artificialities by which knowledge is limited and distorted. In the preceding sections, I have tried to expose a few of these artificialities to analysis. Once we recognize the forces that impinge—unnecessarily—on the development of knowledge, it becomes possible for us to compensate for them. This is a prerequisite for the effective practice of "comparative theorizing." We become able to establish a measure of control over our explorations of reality, instead of being shoved hither and thither by parochial preconceptions and group dictates. Each time we recognize and discard a pattern of enforced ignorance, we approach that much closer to a full realization of the possibilities of knowledge.

6. Conclusions

> ...to myself I seem to have been only like a boy
> playing on the seashore, and diverting myself in now
> and then finding a smoother pebble or a prettier shell
> than ordinary, whilst the great ocean of truth lay all
> undiscovered before me.
>
> NEWTON

The discussions of this book proceeded from an examination of how knowledge is generated to a more general consideration of human societies and individual learning, because it is on this broader stage that the actual development of knowledge is played. I noted at the end of Section 3.3 that if gathering knowledge were the "pure" activity it often purports to be, we should simply adopt the neutral process of "comparative theorizing" as its best form. However, it is clear at this stage that the acquisition of knowledge is inextricably mixed up with social change—is, in fact, but a particular facet of the larger organizations which dominate civilized human life—and so must be treated primarily as an adjunct to other behavior. It is seldom, if ever, undertaken for its own sake. As a consequence, the neutrality of viewpoint needed for comparative theorizing is hardly ever attained.

This does not mean that knowledge can never be freed from the rituals, presuppositions, and artificialities under which it labors. In this book I have suggested several ways we could further that end. But the job is nowhere near as easy as it might appear on the surface. First we must identify clearly the constraints that have crept over human understanding during our evolution as living things and our development of "civilized" social groups. Then we must estimate (as fully as possible) what further constraints on our understanding may emanate from the nature of reality itself. Recognizing our present artificial constraints will help us transcend them, creating as nearly as feasible a "neutral" method of acquiring knowledge; recognizing the real constraints that remain will then help us determine where to explore most effectively.

The first task—identifying the extrinsic constraints on knowledge that we have acquired by our evolution, history, and ways of living—has been the subject of this work so far. These constraints turn out to be extensive and subtle: often the most "certain" facets of our knowledge can be shown, on analysis, to embody misconceptions and parochial viewpoints. Section 6.1 contains a summary of my preceding arguments in this area. In Section 6.2, I will attempt to develop some illustrative models of reality that are designed to escape these constraints, models which are to some extent more neutral than traditional ontological schemes. Section 6.3, finally, contains some speculations based on these considerations, indicating what next stage the development of human knowledge might take. They are not intended to constitute an epistemology, or even a program for explorations; they are only offered in a preliminary sense, as suggestions for deciding in what directions such explorations might fruitfully proceed. Taken together, these succeeding three sections comprise the conclusions I have reached.

6.1 Summary

I have taken all knowledge to be my province.
FRANCIS BACON

The starting point is a distinction between *maxima* and *minima*. Maxima are the units of reality "swallowed whole"—the objects of everyday life, the thoughts and sensations naturally found in experience, the generalizations we normally make when dealing with the world. In any area of human understanding, maxima are what we find before we embark on critical theorizing. Minima, on the other hand, are products of analysis. We question the maxima of naive understanding, digging and dissecting, trying to find out what is "really" there. We create sciences and academic disciplines, some for the sole purpose of refining our knowledge from that of maxima to that of minima.

The peculiar result of such activity is that our new understanding of reality (couched now in minima instead of maxima) is always different, and usually so radically different it is hard to believe it is an understanding of the same things. One who had never encountered the refinements of science would be excused for supposing that they must simply clarify our original ideas of maxima, not replace them wholesale with utterly new ideas. In fact the earliest manifestations of this process, such as the systematizations of Aristotle, mostly did just that: they grouped together known facts in a more comprehensible form, with few attempts to redraw them. But human knowledge is said to have "progressed beyond" Aristotle. Most scientists today would say that when he wasn't being trivial he was wrong. Science now "knows" that reality is far more complex than Aristotle ever imagined, and is made up of elementary units that would have astonished him. Thus has science forced us to alter our natural view of the world.

The question naturally arises: of what value is this new world-view, the one built of minima? The answer seems to be that it has some value as an

additional (or accessory) body of knowledge, but not as an exclusive understanding of reality. We note first that the bulk of it is unknown to most of the
world's inhabitants. Any anthropologist will attest that the majority of
humanity finds the "basic truths" of science laughable. Next we note that in
their practical application, concepts of maxima are used by everybody (even
scientists) most of the time. Finally we note that if we were forced to choose
between understanding a world of maxima or one of minima, the former
would have to win. While it might be true that without ideas of minima we
could not design an atomic bomb, or even a radio, it is quite clear that
without ideas of maxima we could not survive at all. This is why so many
people can get along without knowing about minima, but nobody can get
along without knowing about maxima.

But even in the role of accessory knowledge—useful but not essential—
science still claims *exclusivity*. While perhaps admitting that we are not
absolutely forced to build their kind of world-view, scientists claim that once
we analyze reality at all we will be driven to adopt a depiction filled with
minima. Maxima cannot be used directly in analyzing reality because they
are too unwieldy, too individual, too inchoate. They do not "lend themselves" to orderly knowledge. Thus the ultimate argument for minima is that
they are the only choice, if we are to generate any understanding of reality
beyond its "surface appearances." This argument I reject, and ask: what
happens when we treat *maxima* as the basic units of reality, making a serious
attempt to build from them a total world-view?

Just as a discipline based on minima must divide and reduce, seeking ever
smaller and more basic units, so a world-view built of maxima must spread
outward, seeking to put the objects of common experience into larger and
larger contexts. Maximal knowledge must be based on the most comprehensive possible units of understanding. In pursuing this program, however, we
discover a remarkable thing: there are at least *three* such units, not one.
Starting from one point of everyday reality and expanding our understanding
outward we arrive at a very large whole that I call *"physical reality"*;
starting from another such point we arrive at an entirely different whole that I
call *"behavior"*; and starting from a third point we arrive at yet another
whole that I call *"ideals."* We sometimes find parts of these very large
wholes associated together: my example is a physical book containing a
record of Plato's behavior (his writing) on the subject of the five ideal regular
polyhedra. But this does not mean that there is one thing existing simultaneously in the three wholes. On careful examination, we find that the physical
book lying on my desk is one maximum; the Platonic composition is another,
different maximum; and the geometric ideals it discusses are yet other

maxima. In fact these entities are so generically different that we must say they belong to separate *orders of reality*.

The generic separations between physical reality, behavior, and ideals reflect more than just a technical inability to fuse these maxima in thought; in some fundamental way they are built into the very way we grasp reality. When we start from a given part of any one order of reality we can readily conceive of its connections to other entities in the same order, until we have wholly mapped that kind of reality; but between the orders lie conceptual barriers of the strongest sort. They are inherently unlike kinds of things. The barriers between them are most evident when we deal just in maxima; with minima—the realities conceived by analysis—they are far from clear. In fact we find that minima are quite regularly characterized in such a way that they seem to lie simultaneously in two orders of reality. A good example is the physicist's particle: it is physical because it is the basic unit of physical reality, but it is also ideal because it exhibits many properties that are essentially mathematical—perfect identity between one particle and another, immutability, and total describability. Thus building a world-view from maxima leads immediately to a conflict with world-views based on minima. In the first case there are absolute separations between certain areas of reality; in the second case these separations are bridged.

This leads to a consideration of theorizing, for it is by this human activity that concepts of minima are generated. The basic process of theorizing consists of establishing "parallelisms" between the orders of reality that we apprehend as maxima. Modern physics provides a clear example: its history exhibits a growing conviction that physical reality and ideals are somehow alignable. Mathematical formulas seem to be descriptions of physical events, and physical events seem to "conform" to mathematical formulas. Here also the role of minima is clear: they constitute bridges at critical points, entities that are conceived of as both physical and mathematical, which tend to establish the parallelism and give it justification. This process occurs not just in physics (between physical reality and ideals) but generally in all theoretical disciplines, and among all three orders of reality.

Because there are *three* orders of reality, when theorizing establishes parallelisms between them in pairs it follows that there is always a choice of pairings available. For any given order, there are two other orders, either of which may be selected to parallel it. Such choices are in fact commonly made, and when we examine the results we find that quite different "styles" of theorizing ensue. Returning to the example of a parallelism between physical reality and ideals (physics), if we choose instead to associate physical reality with behavior the result is what may be broadly called "animism." Among scientists this style of theorizing is derided; but when we examine it dispassionately, in its various applications, we find that it is not only widely practiced but is in general a more useful way of understanding reality than physics. Thus it is impossible to judge that one style is intrinsically "better" than another unless we adopt an arbitrary criterion for "betterness"—such as "universality of descriptions" in the case of physics, or "applicability to everyday life" in the case of animism.

An examination of actual theories suggests the reason for their different "styles." Theories use *categories* to characterize their subjects, and these categories are normally drawn from another order of reality. A typical instance is the science of chemistry. Modern theories of chemistry employ *ideal* categories: "element," "bond," "valence," etc. These give its treatment of the subject a flavor of being precise, predictable, and describable in abstract formulas. By contrast, its precursor—alchemy—employed *behavioral* categories, such as "seed," "womb," "nourishment," etc. This approach had the flavor of being dynamic, familiar, and useful. In each case, the categories provided a coherent scheme by which the reality being studied was gathered together; but by taking these schemes from different orders of reality, chemists and alchemists wound up with wholly different gatherings and different theoretical styles.

The primary function of theorizing now comes more sharply into focus. When we simply explore maxima, it is as if we are categorizing each order of reality in its own terms; the result is what I call "common sense." By taking categories from a *different* order we become able to "question" common sense. More specifically, we become able to frame a concept of error—an idea of alternatives that are correct or incorrect, valid or not valid, better or worse. We acquire a powerful new exploratory tool, because we can now make distinctions among maxima that would not otherwise occur to us. This exploratory capacity depends entirely on our recognizing the separation of reality into independent orders: to the extent that we allow this separation to become blurred in our understanding, so much does our concept of error become also blurred, and its force in the acquisition of knowledge become diminished.

The foregoing analysis thus yields the following general schema for theorizing. First we draw parallelisms between two independent orders of reality, maxima from one order providing the subject matter and maxima from the other providing the categories. Because the orders are utterly separate and dissimilar, however, such parallelisms would normally seem inherently erroneous—we would be "describing apples in orange terms." To get around this problem, we hypostatize minima: theoretical devices which, because they are treated as lying simultaneously in two orders of

184

reality, "pin" together the parallelism at certain critical points. Put another way, concepts of minima "destroy" or "bury" (in small regions of our theory) the error we would normally detect between dissimilar ways of understanding reality. These points are then used to justify our parallelisms. They become centers for developing "new knowledge" within the subject matter of our theory. One consequence of this procedure is that when our theoretical parallelisms "slide" (due to our discovering new maxima among subject or categories), there tends to be a wholesale replacement of minima; this is what happens during "revolutions" in scientific knowledge. Another consequence is that as long as the parallelisms hold, concepts of minima tend to generate one another, as we find more and more points at which the two orders of reality might be pinned together. An instance of this effect is the proliferation of particle concepts in physics.

Section 2.4 contains a short detour to consider the theorizing style called "structuralism." One source of this approach has been the realization that behavior is in fact an independent order of reality, deserving theoretical treatment in its own terms. But the most interesting basis for structuralism is the idea of forming a new class of categories drawn from all three kinds of reality—categories that are physical, behavioral, and ideal all at once. Such an integrated methodology has cropped up before: e.g. in physicists' field theorizing and parts of practical engineering. It has an undeniable power, and tends to overcome some of the problems of other methods. But it does not constitute any absolute improvement, for it does not directly address the difficulties discussed above. "Structures" themselves become new minima, the only difference being that they are "three-way fasteners" instead of the more traditional "two-way fasteners." They still amount to theoretical artificialities, hypostatized solely for the purpose of justifying our associations of maxima from different orders of reality.

As so far described, theorizing appears to be a peculiar and somewhat roundabout activity. It is natural to inquire why it developed the way it did. To answer this we must place theorizing within the total context of human life, to appreciate it as an effective procedure for expanding human knowledge. The necessity for knowledge, however, is not obvious. To understand the role of knowledge in human behavior we must trace back (as best we can) the larger process by which life itself evolved; it turns out that each major step of this process required a new kind of knowledge from living things.

The best guess from present evidence is that life arose in physical reality when certain reactions on the primordial earth produced what might be described as a "fermentation molecule." Such a molecule would twist and

185

break sugar molecules, releasing carbon dioxide and concentrating energy. Later, it is supposed, more complex molecules and groups of molecules evolved the processes of photosynthesis, differentiation, cellulation, growth regulation, and replication. For the present analysis it is not necessary to define precisely the nature or sequence of these events. What I am looking for here is the first appearance of *behavior* on earth. Taking the hypothetical role of an extraterrestrial observer, I ask at what stage it would be proper to assert that behavior was present. The answer, in terms of the previous discussion of theorizing, is that it would appear as soon as we could judge that a particular pattern of events was "correct" or "incorrect" with respect to its physical surroundings. This would be an instance of the theoretical generation of a concept of error, which I showed earlier is the foundation of theorizing and a direct result of the separation of the orders of reality. Clearly if we are truly "visitors from another planet," having no preconception of earthly events, this observation of behavior must be somewhat arbitrary. But not so with the earthly living things themselves. For *them*, recognizing behavior as an order of reality distinct from the physical is a vital necessity; in this context, being able to discriminate error is basic to survival. In other words, the procedure for identifying what we know as behavior is the same for earthly living things as it would be for a hypothetical extrinsic observer; but the former performs this procedure in order to exist at all, while for the latter it would be just "pure theorizing." In this way, knowledge and existence meet for living things.

By a similar analysis, it is possible to identify the first appearance of *ideals* in life: they emerge in the genetic process. Evolutionary speciation is the method by which living things develop generalized "life techniques." Through patterns of "instinct," individuals of each species constantly experiment with a specific set of routines that constitute that species' approach to the rest of reality. When we try to distinguish the approach followed by one species from that followed by another—particularly, when we try to judge that one approach is more or less "correct" with respect to a given physical or behavioral situation than another—we can do so only by understanding ideals. One could say that each life technique is based on a set of generalizations, or abstract descriptions, about reality. For each species, using these ideals is a vital (not just theoretical) task.

From this standpoint it could be said that species exercise "intelligence" toward their environment. One of the more interesting techniques that life has evolved is that of delegating part of this intelligence to *individuals*. This appears first as a supplement to instinctual patterns; the chain of behavior pre-programmed by the species breaks off at some point, whereupon the individual is "on its own" until it picks up the chain again at another point.

186

In human beings, of course, these gaps in instinctive patterns are very large, so that the bulk of human life displays individual intelligence.

Thus the orders of reality and our knowledge of the orders of reality are like two sides of the same coin. Physical reality, behavior, and ideals (in that sequence) appeared in our corner of the cosmos both as objects of knowledge and as the reality of knowing beings. Each stage of understanding was also a stage of creation.

But because the way we view reality is so much bound up with the part of reality we *are*, it is meaningful to carry our explanations back another step, asking what it is about reality that caused life to be the way it is and no other. The answer is found principally in the specific physical arrangement of the sun-earth thermodynamic system. This determined not only the basic form of life (and hence the forms of reality it understands), but also several specific factors that influence the exact ways we grasp reality.

Appreciating this involves examining the role of what physicists call "energy" in life. For some time it has been known that life somehow reverses the natural tendency for energy to become less concentrated and more evenly spread. One of the curiosities of physics has been that "purely physical" processes always result in an increase of entropy—they distribute energy more evenly—while living processes decrease entropy, at least within organisms themselves. Another curiosity has been the role of entropy as "time's arrow." The direction of time ordering normally does not appear in descriptions of unitary physical events, and can be defined only by reference to entropic changes. These two observations can be combined in terms of the fundamental living interplay between behavior and physical reality. Thus time can be understood as an ordering algorithm by which living things separate their physical energy sources (past) from their applications of energy (future), while distinguishing behavioral stimuli from responses. The "orientation" of the time vector within timeless physical reality corresponds to the propagation of radiant energy, for this is the axis along which actual organisms have evolved the most efficient separation of energy sources from uses. By a similar analysis it is possible to derive equally primitive concepts about the world (such as quantity and spatial separation) from other utilitarian life techniques. Thus the peculiarities of life's niche in the sun-earth thermodynamic system has shaped much of its viewpoint. It has funneled our knowledge into specific channels, and has filled it with concepts (such as time) which are so embedded in our grasp of reality that it is hard to realize they are actually specialized understandings.

From all these considerations it becomes increasingly evident that human knowledge is limited in many ways. We are the slaves of our own environment and evolution, having developed parochial world-views just adequate to our immediate needs. But once we realize this it becomes possible to examine neutrally the basic question: what are the possibilities of knowledge? To what extent can we overcome our inherited limits?

The answer to this question is half methodological, half sociological. The methodological half-answer follows directly from the preceding discussions: once we understand the mechanics of traditional theorizing it becomes possible to modify it to achieve the results we desire. Present constraints on the possibilities of knowledge are largely self-imposed, as a result of treating as absolute and unanalyzable matters that are in fact relative and analyzable. A way to surmount such constraints is the method I call "comparative theorizing." It rejects the "postulate of exclusivity" by which traditional disciplines of knowledge have justified their "search for truth," and substitutes therefor a kind of creative speculation. By comparative theorizing, we establish the same fruitful parallelisms among the orders of reality that illuminate traditional methods; but unlike the prior approaches, we do not come to rest with the hypostatization of minima, nor do we assume that whichever parallelism happens to be current is the only, or even the best, way to explore reality.

The sociological factors constraining knowledge are less easy to resolve. Human theorizing consumes behavioral energy, and comparative theorizing consumes more than traditional theorizing. The energy required, although supplied by individuals, is largely controlled by societies. Freeing this factor in the development of knowledge thus requires that we know more about human behavior in general.

For purposes of analysis, I use the term "organization." At the most basic level, then, our grasp of the orders of reality—physical, behavioral, and ideal—constitute *primary organizations* of human behavior. Upon them are built *secondary organizations*, which constitute much of the characteristic patterns of human life. They emerge when the primary organizations are taken two at a time, one providing a "setting" or organizing basis from which the other is explored or manipulated. The process of forming secondary organizations could be regarded as a "generalization" of the theorizing process discussed earlier.

The three primary organizations yield six possible secondaries. For ease of identification, I give them sociological names: communalism, authoritarianism, intellection, orthodoxy, legalism, and collectivism. Each represents a unique way of behaving. As a part of shaping social events, each generates a particular "style" of theorizing, and therefore a particular approach to reality. Each produces a specific variety of knowledge.

Tertiary organizations result when secondary organizations merge, forming more comprehensive "ways of life." Five of these are of significant interest: three that may be analyzed into complementary pairs of secondaries (in which each provides the setting for the other), and two that may be analyzed into endless "cycles" of three secondaries, each providing a setting for the next. The complementary pairs organize general areas of social behavior: everyday family life, spiritual and social class life, and "civilized" life in industrialized societies. The two cycles organize the most general level of social and theoretical orientation: statism and idealism on the one hand, individualism and materialism on the other.

Modern societies normally display all these secondary and tertiary organizations, but tend to emphasize certain ones at various times. Identifying the predominating organizations in a society has intrinsic interest because it illuminates much that would otherwise be obscure in human behavior. For present purposes, it also reveals the sociological determinants of knowledge, for these organizations engender the theorizing "styles" discussed earlier. People dedicated to a particular organization in their social and individual life will apply that organization to the acquisition of knowledge as well. In any given situation there will be a variety of basic approaches to reality available to the theorizer, each manifesting a specific secondary or tertiary organization of behavior. Which he adopts will depend largely on the overall hierarchy of these organizations in his general way of life. Thus (for instance) one reason modern science depends more on ideal categories in theorizing than on behavioral categories is because it flourishes in industrialized societies where legalism is considered a better way of life than authoritarianism. In this way social factors enter into our world-view, influencing the ways we acquire knowledge.

One insight resulting from this examination of human behavior is that the secondary organizations succeed one another in a roughly predictable sequence. A natural dynamics operates among them, so that each one tends to lay the groundwork (in a group or society) for the adoption of the one next on the list. These dynamic processes are easy to understand, and once understood allow us to analyze in a new way many of the broad movements of human history. In particular, it becomes possible to appreciate why our grasp of reality evolves the way it does. Human beings are impelled from one viewpoint to the next—not because "absolute truth" lies at the end of the road, but because at each step the inherent nature of the way we theorize promises us new knowledge if we just go a little further. Yet the steps never end; the sequence is circular. When we have run through all possible organizations for acquiring knowledge we smoothly and imperceptibly "advance" to the first organization and start running through them again. By then our commonsense grasp of maxima has expanded enough that it is not evident we are redoing a previous style of theorizing.

Human *individuals* learn their attitudes toward knowledge from the groups they are in. As groups build secondary and tertiary organizations, they also develop routines by which individual behavior is shaped. Secondary organizations become "self-protective": they draw individuals into their patterns, and then try to prevent them from shifting to other patterns. Thus the attitudes within each individual personality become reflections of the organizations by which his society solves its problems, and in many subtle ways he absorbs and clings to a set of biases and presuppositions about reality.

In short, human knowledge is shaped and manipulated by several extrinsic factors, among which "ultimate truth" plays virtually no role. Our understandings depend on the methods we choose when theorizing; upon limitations and viewpoints acquired during our evolution as living organisms; and upon the ways societies operate. Unlocking the doors of knowledge now devolves into a matter of deliberately overcoming all these factors. Recognizing what they are and which ways they impel us is obviously the first step. By so doing we can free ourselves from inherited presuppositions and imposed obligations, and adopt the method of "comparative theorizing." The preceding pages have been devoted to laying a foundation for such liberation, by exposing some of the artificialities which burden present knowledge.

6.2 Reality

During the act of knowledge itself, the objective and subjective are so instantly united, that we cannot determine to which of the two the priority belongs.

COLERIDGE

The first goal of knowledge should be freedom from preconceptions. But suppose we were to achieve this freedom, what then? Is reality such that we might eventually attain a perfect knowledge of it, or is it such that our understanding will evolve forever? Once we are able to hold the extrinsic factors impinging on human knowing in such perspective that they can be nullified, we will have attained the greatest possible capacity to comprehend the world. But we will still be bound by the nature of reality itself. Buried under the mass of shortcuts, presuppositions, and artificial controls that deform our knowledge is some form of bedrock existence that it is trying to grasp. How *understandable* is this thing? The perspectives I have developed so far are only a beginning, but in these terms it is possible to attempt a few generalizations about reality itself.

Earlier I described certain large patterns of behavior—the primary organizations—which, because they are so fundamental to all understanding, should by implication be regarded as referring to the basic units of reality. These entities (physical reality, behavior, and ideals) are so embedded in the foundations of knowledge that they seem to be in some sense prior to it. The secondary and tertiary organizations that engender such concepts as ethics and causation are similarly so embedded in the way we live that we cannot exist as human beings without them. Surely, then, these entities are prime candidates to denote some kind of reality independent of the vagaries of human theorizing.

Yet it is clearly difficult to extrapolate beyond simple assertions about our present understanding, to argue the reality of things *independent* of any specific knowledge. This is the "egocentric predicament" so beloved of philosophers. In Section 2, I developed a rationale for separating the primary

191

organizations that hinged on the notion of *error*: we must hold these entities to be independent because otherwise our world-view could not frame the distinction between "correct" and "incorrect." In Section 3, I took a somewhat different tack, examining the reasons for our need to understand reality in such terms at all. It turns out that life has evolved in such a way as to make these distinctions part of its *survival*. If our knowledge were not forced into certain forms, we would not exist to know anything. Thus we must grasp the orders of reality the way we do not only for the world to make sense to us, but also for us to be part of the world.

The two arguments just cited amount to applying two separate styles of theorizing to reality itself, to the most general possible subject of knowledge. When I argue that we must treat reality in a certain way in order to frame concepts of error in our understanding of it, I am applying an *ideal* category. I am saying that it must have a certain fundamental rationality, the very least manifestation of which is that (to the extent we understand it at all) our understanding will be capable of incorporating the logical dichotomy of true versus false. Reality must display the basic characteristic of logicalness. On the other hand, when I argue that we must treat reality in a certain way because otherwise we could not function as living organisms, I am applying a *behavioral* category. I am saying that it represents the matrix in which we (as behaving beings) developed, and hence is always related to ourselves. It must display the basic characteristic of being relevant to life.

Escaping from the "egocentric predicament" may now be treated as requiring that we apply a *physical* category to reality. Actually the task is even simpler, for as soon as we apply *any* non-behavioral category to a subject of our understanding we are assuming its reality independent of our thought behavior. By doing so to reality itself, we are acknowledging that there exist some entities which are not our thoughts. It is only to the extent that we find ourselves forced to understand something solely in terms of our perception of it that we are trapped in behavior, in the "egocentric predicament." Thus by treating reality as having a basic logicalness—by recognizing that our understanding of it *requires* certain divisions and that these divisions manifest an ideal property, namely the definition of error—we are already grasping a part of it independently of our thoughts. We are saying that it forces upon our thought behavior a characteristic that cannot be explicated in behavioral terms.

But we can deepen this assertion by categorizing reality physically, by recognizing its inherent *objectivity*. That this is at least possible is suggested by the symmetry of the whole depiction of understanding I have presented here. Subjects of knowledge become equally and freely sources of categories for knowledge; so to the extent we can conceive of a possible physical order of reality, we are immediately able to convert our understanding of it into a physical categorization for all of reality. In fact such a categorization is already contained in the basic process of understanding: it lies in the inherent separation of knowledge from its subject. The notion of objectivity itself, which is basic to knowledge, thus amounts to a physical characterization of reality in general.

Let us consider two heuristic models of reality to illustrate how it might be possible to characterize it, independently of any specific knowledge we might have of it, from the standpoint just outlined. By "model" I do not mean an accurate depiction in terms of something else, which would obviously be impossible for reality as a whole; rather I mean a simplified metaphor, an "as-if" substitute which can be easily visualized.

The first such might be called the "tapestry model." Imagine reality as a very large, very complex tapestry woven from multi-colored threads. In it we are able to trace a variety of designs, which link up into larger and larger pictures. These designs are the maxima of commonsense understanding. There are, however, three constraints on our ability to recognize a design and assert that it exists—in other words, on our capacity to know something about reality. First, the design must actually be there: this is the physical or "objectivity" requirement. Second, we must have acquired the ability to recognize the design, out of the whole mass of threads before us. If (for instance) the design is a fragment of Arabic writing and we have never learned Arabic, it will appear to us to be disconnected loops and dots, not a design. This is the behavioral or "relevancy" requirement. Finally, the design must be sufficiently clear and separate from other designs that we can delineate it uniquely; it may not be inextricably mixed up with other patterns, but must be a separable thing by itself. This is the ideal or "logicalness" requirement. Once these conditions are satisfied—once we have found a design that is in the tapestry and that we can recognize and separate uniquely—we can assert that we know some part of reality.

A second heuristic model might be called the "dimensional model." Imagine that reality consists of many solid blocks of complex shape distributed within a room. To illustrate the present state of human understanding we need only imagine that the blocks and the room are three-dimensional; but for a more general model of reality they would have to be conceived of as having an unknown (larger) number of dimensions. There are small windows cut in the boundaries of the room, so that we can observe one dimension of the collection of blocks from each window. Thus in our present three-dimensional version of the model there might be one window each in the north wall, the east wall, and the ceiling. We have cut these windows in order to be able to look into the room and see its contents; but there are three conditions to be satisfied before we can know anything about the arrangement and shapes of the blocks in the room. First, our knowledge must be derived from actually observing blocks: it must be "objective." Second, the blocks must be observed through one of the windows we have cut, for we do not have any other way of looking at them; this establishes their relevancy to our observations. Finally, the window through which we are looking must view just one unique dimension of the room; we cannot imagine looking through two windows at the same time, because even if such an act were possible we would be unable to distinguish the objects or see their shapes. Looking through one window at a time makes our observations "logical." Thus we move from window to window, seeing a different view each time. We know some part of reality each time we observe some of the blocks in the room from one and only one window.

In the tapestry model, the number of orders of reality is represented by the number of very large interconnected designs we recognize; in the dimensional model, it is represented by the number of dimensions. In both cases this number is left undecided, and in fact there is no inherent reason why it should be limited to three. As we discover new major patterns, or cut new windows, our reckoning of the orders of reality will increase correspondingly.

These two models are not intended to represent ontological theories. They are just graphic illustrations to help us grasp certain characteristics of reality itself, in the same vein as a physics lecturer's description of a gas as a collection of billiard balls. They help us understand. The basic characteristics of reality that they illustrate, which follow from various discussions in this book, can now be outlined.

First, reality is much larger and more varied than can be grasped by any specific knowledge we have of it. In terms of the models, the tapestry contains more designs and the room more objects and dimensions than those we know at any given stage. How many more, of course, we do not know. But there is no natural limit—either in the characterization of reality developed here or in the models illustrating it—to the number of orders of reality we can know and the number of primary organizations our behavior might display. In the next section I will consider some possibilities for future development in this area. Furthermore, within each order of reality there is no natural limit to the number of different facts we could know. There is no natural justification for imagining any restriction in the number and extent of designs in the tapestry, or the size of the room and the number of blocks in it.

Second, our ability to know is inherently changeable, even though it may

194

deal with the same reality. Tomorrow we may discover an entirely new way to look at things—a new design in the tapestry or a new dimension in the room—and thereby decisively expand our understanding. Again, there is no inherent limit to this process. Moreover, no future discovery need negate any present knowledge. In Section 3.3 I criticized the "postulate of exclusivity" that tries to limit us to a single "correct" description of reality. Such a restriction finds no place either in the argument presented here or in the models that illustrate it. Knowledge is an expanding and evolving thing, a process without culmination or termination.

Third, however, none of the foregoing means that knowledge is arbitrary. There are two good reasons why we cannot cook up "just any" picture of reality and call it knowledge. Firstly, we must be objective: we must describe patterns that are really in the tapestry and blocks that are really in the room. And secondly, we must satisfy the difficult condition of uniqueness: any new characterization must be such that it yields a definition of error. We must trace a clear and discrete pattern in the tapestry, or view the contents of the room in only one way.

By this route, then, the preceding arguments lead to a general characterization of reality that is itself objective, relevant, and logical. *Any* such characterization must have these qualities. Because we find three orders in reality, we must apply them to our understanding in the form of three overall categories before we can grasp reality as a whole. Put another way, they characterize reality because they are the three most general characteristics that reality itself forces upon our understanding.

The models just described need amending in one respect—namely to show that we, the observers, are *inside* them. We do not look at the tapestry from a superior location, but as one of the patterns of threads; and we are one of the objects inside the multi-dimensional room, whose windows could better be described as mirrors that allow us to see ourselves and other objects from a single perspective. The fundamental characteristics of reality just discussed are also fundamental characteristics of ourselves. Life, the knower, is wholly contained within the reality it tries to know.

Thus there is no intrinsic discontinuity between ourselves and what philosophers call "external reality." We understand reality to be objective, because we are a part of it and know that we ourselves are objective. Similarly, we understand that reality is comprehensible—i.e. relevant to our behavior—simply because we have been created within reality. This is not the same as claiming we could ever comprehend all of it at one time. In fact, just the opposite; as evolving things we wish to reserve the right to comprehend new reality in the future. It just means that we cannot identify

195

anything as ''real'' while asserting that we could never know it. Because we are *in* the world, the world for us must be whatever it is we are in; it must be relevant to every characterization we might make of it, present or future.

Finally, we understand reality to be in some basic sense logical because of the *way* life evolved. As described in Section 3.1, ideals appeared in living reality first in speciation and then in individual intelligence. The key to both the genetic transmission of characteristics and individual thought processes is life's ability to make logical separations and define error. Error is significant to us as an indicator that our ideas (or living techniques) are sufficiently distinct that they ''make a difference.'' But life would never have learned to use ideals in this way if they did not in fact characterize reality. Thus reality must contain inherent logical separations; it must be capable of being sorted out into ''orders,'' one of which is of course the ideal order itself.

In any overall characterization of reality, knowledge and existence must meet. The classical philosophical positions of objectivity and subjectivity must merge into a single world-view before it can be called complete— before it can be called a view of reality itself. The preceding considerations indicate how this comes about. On the one hand, the philosophical *objectivist* can understand the orders of reality in their own terms, as a natural configuration of the world. He can also trace the development of life in this setting, seeing how living organisms have evolved an increasing complexity of involvement with the orders of reality by following an explicit sequence of events driven by specific dynamics. All this will lead him to a characterization of reality itself in concrete and objective terms, for which the models outlined earlier provide heuristic visualizations. Life and all its manifestations (including thought) can be understood as parts of the objective whole.

On the other hand, the philosophical *subjectivist* can understand how we, as living things, maintain certain ways of looking at the world, which I call ''organizations.'' Of the primary organizations, he can understand physical reality because it categorizes our most basic perceptions. He can understand behavior, because it is the form in which thoughts themselves occur. And he can understand ideals because the basic processes of thinking cannot take place without logical separations. In this way the subjectivist can describe all the characteristics of reality as techniques by which our understanding operates, and hence suppose that reality itself is merely a projection of that understanding.

But as each position—the objectivist's and the subjectivist's—is developed, it must ultimately lead to the other. As the objectivist explores reality in his terms he will eventually come across human beings; as a part of this reality he will discover human behavior, and within human behavior he will find the thought patterns of the subjectivist. Going in the other direction, the subjectivist will explore the organizations that constitute the ways human beings understand reality. Among these he cannot ignore physical reality and ideals, for they provide categories without which thought behavior cannot function. Yet the very fact of such categorization will carry him into the reality of the objectivist, for it represents a necessity to recognize real entities outside behavior. Thus the original apparent disagreement between the two positions—arguing whether understanding operates the way it does because reality provides certain pathways for it, or whether we attribute certain characteristics to reality because our understanding operates the way it does—evaporates when both sides discover that understanding is a *part* of reality. By including both positions in a more general viewpoint we become able to resolve a host of traditional philosophical problems: objectivism versus subjectivism, the "mind-body" problem, and the conflict over the "priority" of knowledge against existence.

My approach to these dualisms is cognate, at a higher level of generalization, to the method used by Kurt Gödel (1931) to resolve certain difficulties in describing very general properties of natural number systems.[38] To make his celebrated "incompleteness theorem" possible, Gödel constructed a scheme for encoding statements about mathematics into long numbers, which themselves could then be manipulated mathematically. This technique allowed him to prove a series of remarkable propositions about axiomatic number systems "internally," without having to frame a separate meta-theory in which to express them. The traditional dualism between statements *in* a number theory and statements *about* that same theory largely disappeared. Similarly, the approach I have taken here embeds knowledge within reality in such a way that we do not need to "transcend" the process of ordinary knowing in order to contemplate knowledge itself. Our general understanding becomes able to understand its own reality.

Is there a crucial methodological difference that makes such a result possible? I believe there is, and that it exists in the distinction with which this work started—that between maxima and minima. Traditional approaches to scientific and philosophical questions have devolved into searches for minima: hypostatizations by which theorizers could claim they had combined the orders of reality and excluded error. Such monolithic unanalyzable concepts ordinarily form the foundations of theoretical systems. But regardless of how they are conceived, minima always drive a wedge between knowledge and its subject; they exist in one way and are known in another, entirely different way. The present approach, on the other hand, has been to seek ever-larger maxima in the contents of common sense. It has deliberately tried to integrate knowledge with its subject, by exploring reality as a whole.

An advantage of the maximalist approach is that it includes all other approaches as partial viewpoints. The traditional schools of science and philosophy fall within the organizations of human behavior, with nothing left out. The converse, however, is not the case—the complete maximalist viewpoint presented here cannot be included in any minimalist system of thought. The approach in terms of maxima seeks all of reality; as a result of its analysis we discover that reality cannot be filled by minima or any other entities we know, for it is larger than can be grasped by the present state of our evolving knowledge.

This insight emerges primarily because the present study is not a "search for truth," but an investigation of the *possibilities* of knowledge. The "search for truth," as traditionally carried out, is not only fruitless but counter-productive. It lands us in concepts of minima, which stultify further understanding. Only by starting from maxima and then developing them into a neutral viewpoint do we begin to grasp the patterns of reality in their entirety. It is then that we discover that reality offers more possibilities for knowledge than we will ever be able to attain; and with that discovery our understanding is freed to develop its full potential.

6.3 Extrapolations

> Our minds are finite, and yet even in these circumstances of finitude we are surrounded by possibilities that are infinite, and the purpose of human life is to grasp as much as we can out of that infinitude.
> WHITEHEAD

The arguments so far developed here may seem largely negative. Traditional theorizing has become encrusted with procedures that methodically stultify the growth of knowledge, and has become embedded in social organizations which subject it to detrimental controls. When these problems are avoided or neutralized, the possibilities for exploring reality are found to be far greater than any conception yet developed. These conclusions might be construed as a gloomy assessment of the architecture of knowledge to date.

Yet the important point is not that theorizers have done badly, but rather that they are capable of doing better. The method of ''comparative theorizing,'' wherein the primary organizations of human knowledge are freely and deliberately played off against one another in order to expand our understanding of each, constitutes one better way. It is negative in the sense that it rejects hypostatizations of minima and the concept of ''absolute truth''; but it is positive in the way it encourages a wide variety of speculative overlays among separate parts of reality. Much of its power lies in legitimizing what many theorizers would like to do anyway, but are presently constrained (socially) from doing because it seems ''undisciplined'' or ''improper.''

Fighting among theories is as wasteful as fighting among people. In the case of theories, the bullets are their notions of minima; when these are put under control, the combatants may eventually become able to understand one another. Instead of glorifying one particular organization of behavior and ridiculing all others, theorizers can recognize that all may be equally productive while being equally artificial. The object is not to settle on one and defend it to the death, but rather to use all of them freely, in their many combinations, so that our understanding of maxima grows.

199

Within the three orders of reality of present common sense, much remains to be discovered. Even physical reality, which has been the principal concern of life since its inception, yields new knowledge all the time. But more is mysterious about behavior, and ideals are the most unknown of all. It was only within this century, for instance, that the whole realm of ideals involved in symbolic logic was uncovered. Examples such as this add evidence to the conclusion that reality itself extends far more than our present grasp of it. Hence any relaxation of the constraints by which we artificially limit our explorations of reality should immediately yield new knowledge, even within the familiar physical, behavioral, and ideal orders.

But what may lie beyond present common sense? In discussing three orders of reality, I have several times remarked that there is no natural limit to their number. It simply appears that three is the number that have become manifested in human knowledge to date. Yet life so far has been an active, evolving process, adding new understandings of reality to its repertoire as fast as it could; there is no justification for assuming that the process has finally satisfied itself, with no new areas of reality to explore. A few indications of further orders of reality are suggested by present knowledge. In Section 3.3, I noted a correlation between the mathematical treatment of transfinite cardinal numbers and the currently known orders of reality. Three of these numbers—the power of enumerable collections, the power of a geometric continuum, and the power of the functional manifold—appear to denote the results of unlimited operations in behavior, physical reality, and ideals, respectively. These three are the only transfinite cardinals for which mathematicians have found "meanings" or "realizations." However, other such numbers of "higher order" are known to exist in abstraction, without having any heuristic "meaning." Perhaps when further orders of reality are uncovered, they will be found to offer a correlation with these additional forms of infinity.

It is therefore reasonable to assume that knowledge has a ways yet to go, that there are more orders of reality which life can eventually know beside physical reality, behavior, and ideals. On the other hand, it is probably useless at this stage to ask how many more, to speculate on the "ultimate dimensions" of knowledge. I cannot imagine even how to begin an argument that would lead to the conclusion that there are n possible orders of reality, of which we presently know three. There is an inherent impracticality in trying to enumerate discoveries that will be by their very nature wholly novel when first made.

Nevertheless there remains an area of useful speculations here. We can ask about the very next step, about a *fourth order of reality*. In fact, human experience today offers several scraps of evidence which point toward such a fourth order and suggest that we may slowly be developing an understanding of it. To pull these scraps together into a preliminary depiction, it is first necessary to identify (by extrapolation from past history) the indications which might be exhibited at the emergence of a new primary organization in human understanding. Then we can ask whether or not these indications are in fact present, and if so what they are able to tell us about the nature of the new reality.

In the last section I cited some characteristics that human beings presently find necessary for the recognition of any order of reality. These are that it be *objective*, i.e. that it have an existence prior to, independent of, and larger than our knowledge of it; that it be *relevant* to ourselves in the sense of being usable and comprehensible; and that it be *logically unique*, so that we can compare it with other reality by framing definitions of error around it. These general categorizations of reality as a whole are directly traceable to the present state of human knowledge: objectivity, relevance, and logical un-iqueness are categories drawn from physical reality, behavior, and ideals respectively. In a sense, such a characterization of reality itself simply requires it (and by extrapolation, any fourth order we find in it) to be "the same sort of thing" as the more familiar objects of knowledge. Thus the first requirement for our understanding to develop a fourth primary organization would be for the objects it knows to display these characteristics.

A second characteristic which can be anticipated in any understanding of a new order of reality is that it will develop in areas of maximum human "surplus energy." Life, as I noted earlier, is frugal with energy, and does not waste it on evolving wholly new understandings unless other, current demands have been fairly well met. Thus we can expect that those individu-als who begin to develop an entirely new primary organization in their behavior will not only have already succeeded in feeding, housing, and protecting themselves; they will also have fairly completely rung all the possible changes on secondary and tertiary organizations in their lives, before allocating energy to striking off into relative *terra incognita*. Such behavior will be practical only among those who have a substantial surplus of available energy (in the sense used here of the total potentialities for human action) over the demands for energy made upon them.

A final characteristic likely to be found in any new primary organization of behavior is that its validity will be rejected by the current architecture of knowledge. It is only beyond the fringes of what human beings presently call reality that any wholly new reality can be found. The "conservatism" of life is such that any material which can possibly be assimilated into present understandings ultimately will be, by one construal or another; so that only the truly independent, novel, and intractable can remain. For that reason, however, this material will be such that in our commonsense knowledge we not only cannot understand it, we are strongly inclined to deny that it refers to existence at all. We will feel that our ideas of it must be inherently erroneous. Thus a fourth order of reality is likely to be grasped first in the most confused, misunderstood, and disreputable arena of human consciousness.

These considerations suggest one place where we might look for an emerging fourth primary organization in human understanding: it is in that confused area of experience sometimes called "parapsychology," or studies of the "paranormal." Mysticism was mentioned earlier (Section 4.2) as a manifestation of the tertiary pairing of intellection and orthodoxy; most parapsychology has hitherto been relegated to mysticism (when not rejected as fakery), and handled in knowledge by cross-categorizing behavior with ideals. But when we examine the subject carefully we find much that is left over. This residue is not purely behavioral, because it seems to display an objective, external order all its own; nor is it purely ideal either, because it mocks at the logical concepts of negation and identity that lie at the core of such reality. On the basis of existing commonsense knowledge, it is tempting to assign all material in this general area to varieties of mysticism, the felt union of behavior with ideals. But in view of the possibility that it represents evidence of the emergence of a new primary organization, we should re-examine it.

The proponents of parapsychology (as well as the practitioners of the even more inchoate fields of "spiritualism" and "psychic phenomena"), although seldom agreeing on details, commonly claim for their subject all the characteristics previously cited as the most basic properties of an order of reality. Firstly, the entities and events they describe are for them not only objective, but often *more* objective than the three traditional orders of reality. William James's classic *Varieties of Religious Experience*, an early guidebook to this field, identifies a faculty of human experience that generates

> *a sense of reality, a feeling of objective presence, a perception* of what we may call 'something there,' more deep and more general than any of the particular senses by which current psychology supposes existent realities to be originally revealed.[39]

The literature on this subject written by those who profess it is filled with references to "visions of absolute reality" and "the union with pure existence" that qualify as assertions of objectivity fully as much as the less passionate statements of empirical scientists.

Secondly, insights generated in this area are clearly relevant to human behavior. They are fully usable and comprehensible in the lives of those who have them, however incommunicable they may be. Again, James speaks of "a state of insight into truths unplumbed by the discursive intellect" and concludes that

> ...our normal waking consciousness, rational consciousness as we call it, is but one special type of consciousness, whilst all about it, parted from it by the filmiest of screens, there lie potential forms of consciousness entirely different... No account of the universe in its totality can be final which leaves these other forms of consciousness quite disregarded.[40]

As a purely practical matter, those who have (or claim to have) attained such consciousness in fact behave differently from other people. They are the "enlightened," the explorers of "the other side"; and they return, like travelers to an exotic world, not quite the same as when they left. It is not hard to believe that their behavior has acquired a new primary organization.

Thirdly, for those who know them the subjects envisioned in this area are logically unique and independent types of things. They satisfy the requirement that we be able to separate them from other reality and frame concepts of error across the separation. Whether populated by "paranormal processes" or "universal spirits," the reality they find operates by its own rules. It is commonly used to distinguish and criticize parts of physical reality, behavior, and ideals by comparison to itself. The last thing any proponent of this area of knowledge would accept is the idea that what he knows can be tucked away in an existing body of understanding; in fact (as writers such as Evelyn Underhill document at length) a common prerequisite for attaining such knowledge is to first purge oneself of as much traditional learning and worldly involvement as possible. This is the origin of many forms of asceticism, anchoritism, withdrawal, and meditation.

Thus the subject-matter of parapsychology displays the expected characteristics of a fourth order of reality. Moreover, the process by which this subject is entering into human understanding conforms to the other anticipations cited earlier: it first appears in areas of surplus human energy, and it is rejected by traditional patterns of knowledge. It is typically the case that those who pursue the subject do so from a background of leisure and surplus energy, like the Pythagoreans pursuing the dawn of mathematics. They are insulated from day-to-day demands, either because they have joined some form of institutionalized retreat or just because they have regulated their lives so as to reduce other commitments. Whatever energy they have is largely available for these new explorations. It is also typically the case that the understanding generated in this area is almost totally rejected by the canons of science and "disciplined" knowledge; nor does it fare much better in common sense. It is truly misunderstood and disreputable. It fits no traditional "ologies," gains no academic followers, and tends to make pariahs of its adherents. Traditional psychologists call it "hysteria," physicists call it "unscientific," anthropologists call it "primitive supernaturalism." None but its proponents call it knowledge.

These remarks do not constitute an endorsement of any specific doctrine or system of parapsychology. All that is suggested here is that it is a general area of human behavior which displays the earmarks of an emerging understanding of a fourth order of reality. When that understanding coalesces into a viable primary organization—when it becomes a necessary part of existence for some segment of life—it may bear little resemblance to the material presently found. Such an organization might even be adopted by living units other than man. Individual adoption of the primary organization of ideals created a radical difference between man and other forms of life, so there is no reason to assume that the adoption of a fourth primary organization by life might not engender a similarly wide distinction. Finally, the time scale for its full emergence may be measured in millenia. It is not a matter of just picking up a new theory; it requires building an utterly new kind of involvement with reality, as basic as the physical, behavioral, and ideal involvements we presently have.

Thus parapsychology and its allied pursuits fill the role we would anticipate for the emergence of a fourth primary organization in human understanding. It produces knowledge that is objective, relevant, and logically unique; it is explored only under conditions of surplus behavioral energy; and its pronouncements are almost totally rejected by the knowledge generated by other primary organizations. Yet we can analyze the status of parapsychology even one step further. In the context of the whole development of knowledge—from the first emergence of behavior in life—it appears that this is just the area where the next basic stage of understanding should be expected to form.

Section 3.1 described how behavior first emerged as a new (and physically inexplicable) pattern superimposed upon physical reality. As hypothetical extraterrestrial visitors observing the dawn of life on earth, we would have noted certain chains of events for which physical knowledge could offer no explanation except to say that they occurred. We would have been forced to understand behavior in order to comprehend these events. More importantly, the events themselves were producing living organisms which ultimately depended on an understanding of behavior in order to survive. In this way, behavior emerged as a second order of reality on earth.

Later on a new pattern, intelligence, began to be superimposed upon behavior. It appeared first at the level of species, and consisted of evolved life techniques which were encoded genetically and handed down from individual to individual. Again, as hypothetical extraterrestrials we would have been at a loss to explain instinctual life techniques strictly in terms of behavior; knowledge of ideals was needed. As speciation continued, intelligence began to be invested in individuals, with the same ideal-based patterns becoming more complex and more volatile. Eventually human beings evolved, exhibiting individual intelligence in a highly developed state.

At this stage, human beings began building complex secondary and tertiary organizations in their behavior upon the foundation of three primary organizations with which they were endowed by evolution. Their activities today are wholly dominated by the results of this work. But the creation of these new organizations has engendered new opportunities and new problems in human life. For a while it has been possible to exploit the possibilities and solve the problems just by shifting about among secondary and tertiary organizations. At some point, however, these tools must begin to lose their effectiveness: problems will arise that can no longer be resolved by applications of legalism, or communalism, or any of the other patterns derived from the three traditional primary organizations. Only a *new* primary organization will permit their solution.

Many people feel that such problems are already pressing upon us. For example, it is now technically possible for a few willful individuals to destroy all life on earth. As situations such as this become more acute, life as an adaptive process may be expected to seek out a new order of reality, manifesting its new understanding as a pattern *superimposed upon intelligence*. This is exactly what parapsychology purports to find.

If the hypothetical extraterrestrial observers were to revisit earth today and examine the operation of human individual intelligence, they would find most of it explicable in terms of secondary and tertiary organizations derived from the native human grasp of physical reality, behavior, and ideals. Yet here and there in human thought they would run across manifestations of parapsychological events. At first it would be tempting to fit these somehow into existing knowledge, just as science attempts to cover them today with a mixture of anthropology and abnormal psychology. But at some stage it would become necessary to fashion an entirely new understanding, a knowledge of these events in their own terms—just as in the "primordial broth" it eventually became necessary to understand behavior as an independent order of reality. In the "primordial broth," behavior unquestionably qualified as a new order of reality when organisms began to depend on it, when it became a

205

vital factor in their survival. By extrapolation, the point at which the events discussed here would unquestionably qualify as a new order of reality would be when intelligence came to depend on them. This has not yet happened; they can still be ignored, or disposed of within traditional common sense. But the trend appears to be running toward knowing parapsychological entities in their own terms. When such knowledge develops to the stage where human intelligence cannot function without it, we will be forced to recognize a fourth primary organization in our behavior.

Perhaps one reason why knowledge in this field has been weak so far is that the theorizing which generates it has drawn its categories largely from ideals and behavior. In the case of ideals, "metaphysical" libraries are filled with very difficult books that attempt to set up abstract systematizations for this as yet highly fragmentary subject matter. Mathematical ideas are often pirated from science, such as the notion of "psychic vibrations." Occult writings, which sometimes sound like mixed-up physics, hypostatize minima of very little practical use, while at the same time plagiarizing terminology in a way that irritates scientists.

Behavioral categorizations of the field are attempted by the more traditional books of paranormal events—the writings of St. Theresa and St. John of the Cross, "The Cloud of Unknowing," and so on. These tend to be highly personalized; and although one can sense in them the sincerity of their authors, the impressions they try to record are intrinsically hard to communicate. They are trying to tell us something, but we are never clear what it is.

The problem, I believe, is that most fledgling areas of knowledge first get off the ground when they are presented in terms of *physical* categories. This is because physical reality is the oldest and most familiar of the orders of reality, and hence makes an ideal setting for the absorption of difficult new understandings. For example, Pythagoras and Euclid successfully launched our formal knowledge of ideals by categorizing them as the forms of physical quantities and shapes, although religions had been categorizing ideals by behavior for a long time previously. As Plato demonstrated in the *Meno*, even a slave boy could be taught a geometric proof and would agree with you about it. The same is not the case with an ethical or moralistic argument, where ideals are treated behaviorally.

Thus our understanding of a fourth order of reality is most likely to progress when we theorize with physical categories. To this end, some headway has been made in demonstrating the existence of paranormal physical events, such as telepathy and clairvoyance. Inroads are being made into showing the reality of psychokinesis. Here parapsychological reality is placed in a physical setting, making it much easier to secure agreement on the results of its exploration. At a more general level, such studies as Jung's on "archetypes" have attempted to express parapsychological patterns in visual form, with some success. The narrations of "Carlos Castaneda," whether or not they are genuine, are certainly more assimilable than those, say, of St. John of the Cross, simply because they deal in more concrete images. It is by such means, then, that parapsychological knowledge is most likely to gain a foothold in human understanding—and ultimately lead to the emergence of this material as a fourth complete primary organization in human behavior.

When this happens will the process of acquiring knowledge end? Proponents of "spiritualism" sometime look forward to a "final age" when humanity, and in fact all existence, will become integrated into some kind of changeless unity. But I see no reason why this should happen, at least not in a way that would mark the end of life's process of exploring reality. Life has come a long way so far; but reality has always managed to spread before it a vista of new knowledge far greater than it could encompass at any time. Now we envision a totally novel kind of reality to be known. At the same time that we expand our total understanding by grasping it, we lend evidence to the proposition that reality is even larger than we had imagined.

We suffer nothing by believing that there is no end to this process, or at least no end that we can anticipate. On the contrary, we gain. By abandoning the vision of an ultimate, perfect, and final resting place for our explorations of reality, we turn our attention from sterility to creativity, from artificially limited ideas to an evolving architecture of knowledge.

References

1. T. S. Kuhn, *The Structure of Scientific Revolutions* (2nd Edition), University of Chicago Press 1970.
2. P. W. Bridgman, *The Logic of Modern Physics*, New York 1927.
3. S. Toulmin and J. Goodfield, *The Architecture of Matter*, Harper and Row 1966, p. 55.
4. Kuhn, op. cit. (1), p. 77.
5. Kuhn, op. cit. (1), p. 158.
6. R. F. Fortune, *Sorcerers of Dobu*, Dutton 1963, pp. 95, 97.
7. E. B. Tylor, *Primitive Culture*, London 1920, vol. II, p. 108.
8. L. Lévy-Bruhl, *How Natives Think* (tr. by L. A. Clare), New York 1966, pp. 30-31.
9. B. Malinowski, "Magic, Science and Religion" in J. Needham, *Science, Religion and Reality*, New York 1955, p. 84.
10. St. Augustine, *Enchiridion*, III.9, tr. in Runes, *Treasury of Philosophy*, Philosophical Library 1955.
11. I. Kant, *Critique of Pure Reason* (tr. by F. M. Müller), Anchor 1966, p. 62.
12. Toulmin and Goodfield, op. cit. (3), p. 124.
13. J. Dewey, *Human Nature and Conduct*, New York 1922, Part I.
14. J. Dewey, *Essays in Experimental Logic*, New York 1916, pp. 18-19.
15. E. A. Burtt, *The Metaphysical Foundations of Modern Science* (Rev. Ed.), Anchor 1954, pp. 223-24.
16. P. Frank, *Foundations of Physics*, University of Chicago 1946, p. 6.
17. P. W. Bridgman, op. cit. (2).
18. P. A. M. Dirac, "The Evolution of the Physicist's Picture of Nature," *Scientific American* vol. 208 no. 5 (May 1963), p. 53.
19. R. Descartes, *Meditations Concerning First Philosophy*, II.
20. H. Gardner, *The Quest for Mind*, Vintage Books 1974, p. 6.
21. M. Merleau-Ponty, *The Structure of Behavior* (tr. by A. L. Fisher), Beacon 1963, p. 131.

22. A. Einstein, *Out of My Later Years*, Philosophical Library 1950, p. 78.
23. E. Laszlo, *Introduction to Systems Philosophy*, Gordon and Breach 1972, p. 24.
24. P. A. Weiss, "The Living System: Determinism Stratified" in Koestler and Smythies, *Beyond Reductionism*, Macmillan 1970, p. 13.
25. S. C. Pepper, *The Sources of Value*, University of California Press 1958, pp. 57-58.
26. P. MacLean, *A Triune Concept of the Brain and Behavior*, University of Toronto Press 1973.
27. C. Sagan, *The Dragons of Eden*, Random House 1977.
28. E. Schrödinger, *What is Life?*, Cambridge 1967, p. 76.
29. S. L. Glashow, "Quarks with Color and Flavor," *Scientific American* vol. 233 no. 4 (Oct. 1975), p. 38.
30. Kuhn, op. cit. (1), p. 171.
31. L. A. Steen, "Foundations of Mathematics: Unsolvable Problems," *Science* vol. 189 no. 4198 (18 Jul 1975), pp. 209-210.
32. M. Mead, *Sex and Temperament in Three Primitive Societies*, New York 1963, p. 32.
33. J. Piaget, *The Moral Judgment of the Child* (tr. by M. Gabain), Free Press 1965, p. 28.
34. P. Laplace, *Systeme du Monde*, Book III.
35. S. C. Pepper, *World Hypotheses*, University of California Press 1961, p. 152.
36. E. Underhill, *Mysticism*, Meridian 1955, pp. 36-37.
37. Kuhn, op. cit. (1), pp. 157-58.
38. K. Gödel, *On Formally Undecidable Propositions*, Basic Books 1962.
39. W. James, *Varieties of Religious Experience*, Modern Library 1936, p. 58.
40. W. James, op. cit. (39), pp. 378-79.

Index

Deduction 131, 143
Deism 125, 127
Democracy 130
Democritus 31
Descartes, René 73
Dewey, John 58, 62, 126
Dirac, P. A. M. 68
Dobu 45-46, 63, 65-66, 115

Eastern philosophy 147, 150
Economics 129, 141
Eddington, Arthur 99
Education 125, 139, 173
Egocentric predicament 191-92
Einstein, Albert 6, 18-19, 44-45, 69, 76, 99, 104-5
Electrons 6, 34
Elements, ancient 17-18, 30
Elements, modern 52-53
Empedokles 17, 30
Empiricism 122, 133
Encyclopedists, French 6
Energy, behavioral 154, 188, 201
Energy, physical 33, 68, 84-85, 97, 104-5, 154, 187
Engineering 76-77
Entropy 84, 97-99, 106, 187
Error 55, 59-61, 80, 184, 186, 191-92, 196
Ether 35
Ethics 128, 139-40, 149
Euclid 18, 26, 206
Evolution 82, 88-89, 94-96
Exclusivity in theorizing 110, 112, 182, 188
Experience 58

Family life 138, 172-73
Faraday, Michael 75
Fermat, Pierre de 20
Fermentation 84, 185-86
Field theorizing 75-76, 185
Forces 6, 31-34
Formism 131-32
Framework theorizing 141, 143, 149
Frank, Philipp 68
Freedom 151-52, 159, 161, 163, 165
Freud 6, 177
Functional manifold 108

Gardner, Howard 73-74
Generalization 1-4
Geometry 17-19, 26
Glashow, S. L. 109
Gödel, Kurt 197
Gravitation 33, 38-39, 104, 132
Greek language 14-16, 21-22

Hegel 128, 147
Heraclitus 30
Hilbert, David 20
Humanism 164
Hume, David 33, 122-23, 139
Husserl, Edmund 25, 127

Idealism 128, 147
Ideals 20-21, 25-27, 30-31, 53, 88-89, 134, 158, 182, 186, 192
Illusions 59, 80
Imprinting 89, 95
Incantation 46
Incest taboos 176-177
Individualism 147-48, 151-52, 165
Induction 60, 131, 143
Inertia 33, 104
Infinity 107-8, 200
Initiation ceremonies 125-26
Instincts 89-91, 94-95, 186
Intellection 117-18, 125-27, 139-40, 147-48, 158-61, 173
Intelligence 93-95, 186-87, 205

James, William 126, 202-3
John of the Cross, St. 206-7
Jung, C. G. 206-7

Kant 1-2, 50-51, 107
Kepler, Johann 33
Kingship 123, 125, 159
Kuhn, Thomas 3, 44, 110, 169

Language 22, 64, 111, 148
Laplace, Pierre 130, 151
Laszlo, Ervin 77
Latency 173, 176
Lavoisier, Antoine 71
Laws, natural 31, 33-34, 98, 130, 132, 141, 161
Laws, social 129, 141

212

Legalism 117-18, 123, 129-30, 133, 135-36, 140-44, 147-48, 161-63, 174, 189
Leukippos 31
Lévy-Bruhl, Lucien 47
Lévy-Strauss, Claude 74-75
Lexicography 64
Light 34-35, 44-45, 104-6
Limbic system 96
Locke, John 55-56, 122
Logic 8, 64-65, 111, 126

MacLean, Paul 95-96
Malinowski, Bronislaw 47
Mariotte, Edme 71
Marx, Karl 128
Mass 33, 105
Materialism 26, 151-52
Mathematics 19-20, 68-69, 130, 134, 143, 162-63
Maxima 5, 8, 10-14, 37, 81, 181-82, 197-98
Maxwell, Clerk 6, 43, 75
Mead, Margaret 122
Mendeleev, Dimitri 6
Merleau-Ponty, Maurice 74
Michelson-Morley experiment 45, 49-50
Militarism 145-46
Miller, Stanley L. 83
Minima 5, 8-12, 28-29, 34-36, 40-41, 66-67, 70-72, 77-80, 91, 142-43, 181-85, 197-99
Minkowski, Hermann 19
Monasticism 126
Mysticism 140, 202

Neocortex 96
Newton 6, 33, 43-44, 67, 71, 105
Non-Euclidean geometry 19

Objectivism 196-97
Obligations 142-43
Oedipus complex 176
Oparin, A. I. 83-84
Operational definitions 68-70
Operationalism 14
Orders of reality 13, 16-17, 21, 27-28, 60, 65, 79, 107, 116, 171, 182-83, 200-202

Organicism 128
Organizations 116, 188
Orthodoxy 117-18, 127-29, 133-34, 139-40, 144-47, 160-62, 173-74
Ostwald, Wilhelm 98

Parallelisms, theoretical 37-38, 40, 184-85
Parapsychology 202-7
Particles 6, 8-9, 31-35, 40, 70-71, 76, 99-102, 185
Pasteur, Louis 83
Peano, G. 19, 126
Pepper, Stephen C. 93-94, 132
Perception 57, 59, 62, 80, 122, 138-39
Permutations 99-100
Phenomenology 25
Photons 35
Photosynthesis 84
Physical reality 14-15, 21-23, 29-34, 55-56, 133, 182, 192-93
Physics 5-11, 29, 34-36, 40, 45, 71, 114, 133, 143, 183-84
Piaget, Jean 78, 124
Plato 14-18, 20, 25-26, 30, 48-49, 62, 131-32, 206
Platonic solids 17-18
Poincaré, Henri 67-68
Positivism 14
Potentials 75-76
Pragmatism 126-27
Prejudices 177
Primary organizations 116-18, 134-35, 149, 172, 188, 191
Property 129-30, 141
Psychic phenomena 202
Ptolemy 33
Pythagoreans 25, 30-31, 66, 112, 161, 203, 206

Qualities, primary 55-56
Qualities, secondary 56
Quantity 107, 187
Quantum theory 34
Quarks 35, 40, 72, 109

Reality 180, 191-97
Reality models 193-95
Reductio ad absurdum 112

213